Deleuze *on Literature*

Deleuze *on Literature*

RONALD BOGUE

Routledge
New York and London

Published in 2003 by
Routledge
29 West 35th Street
New York, NY 10001
routledge-ny.com

Published in Great Britain by
Routledge
11 New Fetter Lane
London EC4P 4EE
routledge.co.uk

10 9 8 7 6 5 4 3 2 1
Cataloging-in-Publication Data is available from the Library of Congress

ISBN 0–415–96605–1 (hb)
ISBN 0–415–96606–X (pb)

For my wife, Svea

Contents

Abbreviations

All translations from Deleuze, Guattari and Deleuze-Guattari are my own. For works that have appeared in English translation, citations include page numbers of the original French edition followed by the page numbers of the corresponding passages in the English translation.

AO   Deleuze and Guattari. *L'Anti-Oedipe: Capitalisme et schizophrénie I.* Paris: Minuit, 1972. *Anti-Oedipus.* Trans. Robert Hurley, Mark Seem and Helen R. Lane. Minneapolis: University of Minnesota Press, 1977.

B   Deleuze. *Le Bergsonisme.* Paris: Presses Universitaires de France, 1966. *Bergsonism.* Trans. Hugh Tomlinson and Barbara Habberjam. New York: Zone Books, 1991.

CC   Deleuze. *Critique et clinique.* Paris: Minuit, 1993. *Essays Critical and Clinical.* Trans. Daniel W. Smith and Michael A. Greco. Minneapolis: University of Minnesota Press, 1997.

D   Deleuze and Claire Parnet. *Dialogues.* Paris: Flammarion, 1977. *Dialogues.* Trans. Hugh Tomlinson and Barbara Habberjam. New York: Columbia University Press, 1987.

DR   *Différence et répétition*. Paris: Presses Universitaires de France, 1968. *Difference and Repetition*. Trans. Paul Patton. New York: Columbia University Press, 1994.

E   Deleuze. *L'Épuisé* (published with Samuel Beckett's *Quad*). Paris: Minuit, 1992. "The Exhausted," Trans. Anthony Uhlmann in *Essays Critical and Clinical*. Trans. Daniel W. Smith and Michael A. Greco. Minneapolis: University of Minnesota Press, 1997, pp. 152–74.

F   Deleuze. *Foucault*. Paris: Minuit, 1986. *Foucault*. Trans. Seán Hand. Minneapolis: University of Minnesota Press, 1988.

FB   Deleuze. *Francis Bacon: Logique de la sensation*. Vol 1. Paris: Editions de la différence, 1981.

K   Deleuze and Guattari. *Kafka: Pour une littérature mineure*. Paris: Minuit, 1975. *Kafka: Toward a Minor Literature*. Trans. Dana Polan. Minneapolis: University of Minnesota Press, 1986.

LS   Deleuze. *Logique du sens*. Paris: Minuit, 1969. *The Logic of Sense*. Trans. Mark Lester, with Charles Stivale. Ed. Constantin V. Boundas. New York: Columbia University Press, 1990.

MM   Deleuze. "Mystique et masochisme." *La quinzaine littéraire* 25 (April 1-15, 1967): 12-13.

MP   Deleuze and Guattari. *Mille plateaux: Capitalisme et schizophrénie, II*. Paris: Minuit, 1980. *A Thousand Plateaus*. Trans. Brian Massumi. Minneapolis: University of Minnesota Press, 1987.

N   Deleuze. *Nietzsche*. Paris: Presses Universitaires de France, 1965.

NP   Deleuze. *Nietzsche et la philosophie*. Paris: Presses Universitaires de France, 1962. *Nietzsche and Philosophy*. Trans. Hugh Tomlinson. Minneapolis: University of Minnesota Press, 1983.

PO   Deleuze and Guattari, *Politique et psychanalyse*. Alençon: des mots perdus, 1977.

PP   Deleuze. *Pourparlers*. Paris: Minuit, 1990. *Negotiations*. Trans. Martin Joughin. New York: Columbia University Press, 1995.

PS   Deleuze. *Proust et les signes*. 3rd edition. Paris: Presses Universitaires de France, 1976. *Proust and Signs*. Trans. Richard Howard. New York: G. Braziller, 1972.

QP   Deleuze and Guattari. *Qu'est-ce que la philosophie?* Paris: Minuit, 1991. *What Is Philosophy?* Trans. Hugh Tomlinson and Graham Burchell. New York: Columbia University Press, 1994.

S   Deleuze. *Spinoza: Philosophie pratique*. 2nd edition. Paris: Minuit, 1981. *Spinoza: Practical Philosophy*. Trans. Robert Hurley. San Francisco: City Lights, 1988.

SM   Deleuze. *Présentation de Sacher-Masoch: le froid et le cruel*. Paris: Minuit, 1967. *Masochism: An Interpretation of Coldness and Cruelty*. Trans. Jean McNeil. New York: G. Braziller, 1971.

SP   Deleuze and Carmelo Bene. *Superpositions*. Paris: Minuit, 1979. "One Less Manifesto," trans. Alan Orenstein. In *The Deleuze Reader*. Ed. Constantin V. Boundas. New York: Columbia University Press, 1993, pp. 204–22.

Introduction

At the time of his death on November 4, 1995, Gilles Deleuze was recognized widely as one of the most important figures in late-twentieth-century French philosophy. Throughout his career, Deleuze showed an abiding interest in several of the arts, but perhaps in none more consistently than literature. Besides writing books on Proust (1964, revised and expanded in 1970 and 1976), the nineteenth-century novelist Leopold Sacher-Masoch, for whom masochism was named (1967), and Kafka (1975), as well as a final collection of essays on literature, titled *Essays Critical and Clinical* [CC] (1993), Deleuze made constant reference to novels, poems, plays and essays in virtually all of his works. Among the philosophers he most valued was Nietzsche, whom many would characterize as a decidedly literary figure, and other writer-philosophers and philosopher-writers made frequent appearance in his books—Kierkegaard, Blanchot, Michaux, Artaud, Klossowski, Beckett, Mallarmé, and Borges, among others. Deleuze's 1969 examination of the paradoxes of meaning, *The Logic of Sense* (LS), was as much a reading of Lewis Carroll as a treatment of Stoic philosophy, and scattered throughout the pages of the massive *A Thousand Plateaus* (MP) (1980) were references to over seventy-five writers.

Yet despite the ubiquity of literary concerns and citations in his works, nowhere does Deleuze directly offer a systematic "theory" of literature, nor is one easily extrapolated from his various literary studies. Much of Deleuze's writing on literature is a thinking-alongside literary works, an engagement of philosophical issues generated from and developed through encounters with literary texts. Hence, to a certain extent his thought about literature cannot be fully appreciated apart from a consideration of the works that instigate it. He engages a host of issues related to language, meaning, writing and literature, but in such different contexts and toward such diverse ends that it is sometimes difficult to see how one analysis might be related to another. Nonetheless, a single line of conceptual development traverses all of Deleuze's writings on literature, one generated by the driving concerns of his philosophy. He is no systematic philosopher, in the traditional sense of the term, but there is cohesion in his thought and a wideranging interrelation of motifs across the various disciplines and domains of his speculation. My effort in this book is to examine Deleuze's central texts on literature, language and writing, determine his understanding of the nature and function of the literary within the general domain of social practices and suggest the broad trajectory of his thought that passes through his diverse engagements with literary works over the course of his career.

The writer for Deleuze is a Nietzschean physician of culture, both a symptomatologist who reads culture's signs of sickness and health, and a therapist whose remedies promote new possibilities for life. In the first chapter, I examine the figure of the cultural physician as Deleuze develops it in his early *Nietzsche and Philosophy* (NP), and then consider two pairs of writers whom Deleuze treats as cultural physicians—Sade and Masoch in *Masochism: An Interpretation of Coldness and Cruelty*, and Carroll and Artaud in *The Logic of Sense*. Nietzsche's cultural physician above all engages in an assessment of values, which entails both a diagnosis of the forces and attitudes that shape the world, and a creative deployment of forces in new configurations. The cultural physician is not simply an interpreter of signs, but also an artist who joyfully eradicates cultural pathogens and invents new values that promote and enhance life. Sade and Masoch are often viewed as specimens of the perversions associated with their names, but Deleuze argues that each is a great symptomatologist of social structures of power and desire. Each fashions a double of the universe that functions as a form of cultural critique and that opens new possibilities for life. But the worlds each constructs are incommensurable, Deleuze claims, and not to be understood in terms of the false syndrome of sadomasochism. Sade's universe is one of rational delirium, ironic demonstration and reiterated mechanical movement, whereas Masoch's is one of imaginary phantasy, humorous education and frozen suspension. As symptomatologists, Sade and Masoch disclose and critique different groupings of signs, and as artists they turn the elements of perversions into the constituents of new worlds. In a parallel fashion, Carroll and Artaud, like Sade and Masoch, are often treated as specimens of psychological disorders, and in some instances, of the same disorder— schizophrenia. Through an analysis of Artaud's very free translation of "Jabberwocky," Deleuze shows that Carroll and Artaud inhabit quite different universes and that each is a symptomatologist and topologist of rare insight. Carroll's nonsense reveals a world of surfaces and events, reminiscent of the domain of Stoic incorporeals, whereas Artaud's word-screams and sonic shards open up a realm of roiling depths and interpenetrating bodies. Carroll's perverse nonsense has nothing to do with Artaud's schizophrenic verbal shrapnel, nor are the two to be assimilated within what Deleuze calls the "grotesque trinity of the child, the poet, and the madman" (LS 101; 83). Carroll may resemble a childlike pervert, and Artaud a raving madman, but as writers they are cultural physicians whose differential diagnoses unfold divergent realities and alternative modes of life.

Deleuze refers to Proust's *A la recherche du temps perdu* as "a general semiology, a symptomatology of worlds" (PP 195; 142-43), and in chapter 2 I turn to Deleuze's extended analysis of that semiology and symptomatology in his *Proust and Signs* (PS) (1964; augmented second edition, 1970). In this work, Deleuze develops two readings of Proust, the first in terms of the interpretation of signs (the original 1964 edition), the second in terms of the production of signs (the long section added in the second edition). The Proustian sign is a hieroglyph, an enigma that enfolds a hidden content that must be unfolded through interpretation. Proust's *Recherche* documents Marcel's apprenticeship in signs, whereby the young man moves from the vapid signs of the world, through the deceptive signs of love and the sensual signs of involuntary memory, to the profound signs of art. Once Marcel grasps that the signs of art express essences, the other signs are transformed, and he discovers his vocation as an artist. Yet the truth of artistic signs, Deleuze shows, is not that of an objective reality nor one of subjective associations, but the truth of a self-differentiating difference that unfolds itself and thereby creates a universe. The artist, the surrounding world and the work of art are all part of an apersonal unfolding of signs, and the finished artwork is a Joycean "chaosmos," a chaos-become-cosmos. Marcel's interpretation of signs thus leads inevitably to the artistic production of signs, and in the second part of *Proust and Signs* Deleuze shows how the *Recherche* itself may be seen as a productive generator of signs, a veritable sign machine. The modern artwork does not mean so much as it functions, says Deleuze, and in this sense it is a machine. Proust's interpretation of signs is part of the unfolding of a chaosmos, one that includes its author within it, and that issues from a specific point of view, but that finally transcends the author and makes of him a mere component of the chaosmos-machine's functioning. Proust is a great interpreter of signs and symptomatologist of cultural ills, but as cultural physician he is ultimately the constructor and construction of a giant literary machine.

Chapter 3 focuses on the notion of the literary machine as it is developed in *Kafka: Toward a Minor Literature* (K), which Deleuze wrote with Félix Guattari in 1975. In *Anti-Oedipus* (AO) (1972), Deleuze and Guattari articulate a general theory of nature as a "machining" of flows, and it is from this extremely broad conception of the machine that they approach the work of Kafka. Kafka's diaries, letters, short stories and unfinished novels, they claim, are all parts of a writing machine, whose purpose is simply to avoid closure and keep flows moving. Deleuze and Guattari make no distinction between Kafka's life and art, arguing that his diaries and letters communicate directly with his fiction, and that in his stories and novels he engages forces that are part of the real world. Kafka's correspondence documents his futile efforts to sustain the flow of letters while avoiding entrapment within marriage, and his short stories are filled with dead ends and failed attempts to escape familial and social confinement. But in the novels, Kafka finds a means of perpetuating movement and keeping the writing machine operating, and it is for this reason that the novels are never completed. *The Trial* especially reveals the open-ended functioning of the literary machine, as K. moves from one agent of the Law to another. The Law itself is a massive machine, with the novel's diverse characters, institutions and sites all serving as interconnected and interacting parts of the machine. The Law has no ultimate purpose other than its own functioning, and K.'s pursuit of the Law leads only to a series of inconclusive encounters and indefinite postponements. This narrative of the Law is no mere fiction for Deleuze and Guattari, for they argue that in *The Trial* Kafka discloses the "diabolical powers of the future"—those of Nazism, Stalinism and bureaucratic capitalism—by engaging tendencies that are immanent within the Austro-Hungarian Empire. Those tendencies are virtual rather than actual, but they are nonetheless real, for which reason *The Trial* is not simply a representation of the social machine of the Law but itself an experimentation on the real.

The Trial, then, is at once a machine and an instrument of social critique. Thus, like Sade, Masoch and Proust, Kafka is a cultural physician, in that he diagnoses the diabolical powers of the future and prescribes lines of flight from those powers. And like Proust, he is the constructor of a literary machine, which is itself part of a larger complex of social and material machines. As cultural physician and inventor of machines he practices a form of writing that is simultaneously political and experimental, producing what Deleuze and Guattari call "minor literature," which is the subject of chapter 4. Deleuze and Guattari take the term from Kafka's diary entry outlining the traits of a "minor literature" such as that of the Czechs of his native Prague, but Deleuze and Guattari argue that Kafka's concept is less one of a literature written by a linguistic or cultural minority per se, than one of a literature issuing from a minor *usage* of language, that is, from a manipulation of linguistic variables that sets them in disequilibrium. For Deleuze and Guattari, language is a form of action, and linguistic regularities are merely partial components of power structures that enforce regular patterns of practice. When writers subvert phonetic, syntactic and semantic conventions, they activate lines of continuous variation that are immanent within language and thereby disrupt the regular functioning of fixed power relations. Deleuze and Guattari see Kafka as a writer who "minorizes" the major configurations of power that play through words, exploiting the instabilities and anomalies of his linguistic situation and inventing new semantic usages of the speech-acts that circulate in his milieu. Far from being a private voice of despair, they claim, Kafka is a political writer who engages a collective function of language in an effort to invent a people and a line of flight away from the diabolical powers of the future.

In his essay "One Less Manifesto," Deleuze expands on the concept of minor literature while providing an extended discussion of the theater and its relation to the "minor." The essay accompanies the text of Carmelo Bene's drama *Richard III* in a volume titled *Superpositions* (SP) (Italian edition 1978, French edition 1979), and in chapter 5 I offer a reading of this book, attempting through Bene's example and Deleuze's commentary to outline the characteristics of a "minor theater." Bene's play is an experimental appropriation and transformation of Shakespeare's *Richard III*, and both he and Deleuze approach the figure of Richard III as a "man of war" engaged in a "becoming-woman." Deleuze derives the concept of the warrior's becoming-woman from Kleist's *Penthesilea*, and in Bene's play and Deleuze's essay the Kleistian model is used to interpret the actions of Shakespeare's great villain. The lines of Bene's play are excerpted from Shakespeare, though only Richard III and Shakespeare's female characters appear on the stage. The action, however, is decidedly unshakespearean, its purpose being to strip Shakespeare's history play of its conventional markers of power and expose the links between Richard's treachery and the women around him. Bene's play functions as a critique of the power relations represented in Shakespeare's original, but it also undermines the forms of the conventional theater, and Deleuze sees in this combination of critique and experimentation the essence of a minor usage of the stage. A minor theater sets in variation all the elements of a performance—speech, gestures, costumes, props, sets, lighting, and so on—and combines them in a metamorphic, contrapuntal composition, though not as a mere exercise in the subversion of conventions, but as a means of inventing new modes of living and a people to come.

Literature invents new possibilities for life, and in his last book, *Essays Critical and Clinical* (1993), Deleuze suggests various ways in which writers achieve this purpose. Chapter 6 concentrates on two such means: the production of "lines of flight" and the creation of "visions and auditions." Deleuze speaks frequently of writing, and of life as a whole, in terms of "lines," and it is within this broad context that the full import of his concept of the "line of flight" becomes evident. The line of flight ultimately is the trajectory of a process of becoming-other, the course of a line that always "passes between." The line of flight is both inside and outside language, and its presence is manifest in a constant tendency of language to move beyond itself. Great writers (that is, practitioners of a minor usage of language) discover a foreign tongue within their own language. They make language itself stutter, and in so doing, they instigate a linguistic process of becoming-other. But they also fashion "visions and auditions," sights and sounds that "language alone makes possible" (CC 9; lv) yet that are themselves nonlinguistic elements. Visions and auditions form the outside surface of language and constitute "a painting and a music proper to writing, like effects of colors and sonorities that rise above the words" (CC 9; lv). In his late studies of T. E. Lawrence's *Seven Pillars of Wisdom* and Beckett's television plays, Deleuze elaborates on the concept of visions and auditions, suggesting finally that literature's vocation is always to push language to its outside, and in the process to open words to the world.

This book is one of three I have written on Deleuze and the arts, the other two being *Deleuze on Cinema* and *Deleuze on Music, Painting, and the Arts*. Each volume is meant to stand on its own, but all three form part of a single project. My primary purpose in this book is to treat Deleuze's thought on literature, but it is difficult to separate his views on that art from his understanding of the arts in general or from his philosophy as a whole. Deleuze has much to say to students and practitioners of all the arts, and many of the concepts he develops in his literary analyses should be of interest to those outside the field as well. I have therefore endeavored to make my remarks accessible to specialists and nonspecialists alike, in the hope that readers of various backgrounds will be encouraged by this book to explore Deleuze's writings on music, painting and cinema as well as his many studies of literature.

Over the last several years, a number of excellent works on Deleuze have appeared both in French and in English. I have profited greatly from many of them, but I have not engaged in extended discussion of any of these works, citing only those texts that help illuminate a particular point in Deleuze's arguments. I have found especially useful the groundbreaking essays of Bensmaïa, Boundas and Smith, as well as the books of Alliez, Ansell Pearson, Buchanan, Buydens, Colebrook, Colombat, Goodchild, Hardt, Holland, Kennedy, Lambert, Massumi, May, Olkowski, Patton, Rajchman, Rodowick, Stivale and Zourabichvili. Anyone interested in grappling with the difficulties of Deleuze's texts will find these works well worth reading.

One final methodological note: All who write on Deleuze face a peculiar dilemma that affords no easy remedy. Four of Deleuze's most important books were cowritten with Félix Guattari in a collaborative process unique in the history of philosophy. Guattari is a major theorist in his own right, and his many books deserve careful study and discussion. There is no doubt that his contributions to the collaborative projects are substantial, in terms of both content and style. Deleuze-Guattari texts are unmistakable in their humor, energy and audacity, and unlike anything that Deleuze or Guattari created individually. Yet it is impossible to separate Deleuze from Guattari in these works, so thorough is the integration of their styles and thought. When they return to individual projects after a given joint venture, each treats the earlier collaborative work as his own, freely elaborating on that work's concepts and developing them in new directions. I have therefore seen no alternative but to treat Deleuze's works and the Deleuze-Guattari volumes both as constituents of Deleuze's *oeuvre*. Were I to write on Guattari, I would likewise assimilate his books and the Deleuze-Guattari texts within a single Guattari corpus. Nonetheless, although I do not address the subject, in no way should the importance of Guattari's contribution to the development of Deleuze's thought be minimized.

This project has extended for over a decade, and there are many who have assisted me directly and indirectly.[1] I wish to thank the University of Georgia Research Foundation and the University of Georgia Center for Humanities and Arts for providing release time for research and writing. Ian Buchanan, Constantin V. Boundas, Paul Patton and Charles J. Stivale offered welcome encouragement at various junctures of the process. I am especially grateful to Jerry Herron and my colleague Mihai Spariosu for their continued friendship and support and to Florin Berindeanu for his enthusiastic comments on the manuscript as it slowly took shape. Students in my Deleuze seminars have also taught me much, especially Michael Baltasi, Ravinder Kaur Banerjee, Andrew Brown, Balance Chow, Hyung-chul Chung, Letitia Guran, Paulo Oneto, Aaron Parrett, Wei Qin, Astra Taylor and Maria Chung-min Tu. But I owe the most to my family, for their enduring patience, faith and support from start to finish.

---

1. An abridged version of chapter 2 appeared as "Difference and Repetition in Deleuze's Proustian Sign and Time Machine," in *Concentric* 27.1 (January 2001) © 2001 by The Department of English, National Taiwan Normal University. I am grateful to the editors for permission to reprint the essay.

Chapter One

SICKNESS, SIGNS, AND SENSE

When asked in a 1988 interview about plans to write a work devoted to literature, Deleuze said that he "dreamed of a group of studies under the general title, 'Critique et Clinique'" (PP 195; 142).[1] In 1993 such a work finally appeared—Deleuze's last book, *Critique et Clinique* (*Essays Critical and Clinical*), a collection of eighteen essays—eight published between 1970 and 1993 and ten new studies—many focused on literature, with a few concentrating on topics in philosophy, psychoanalysis and film. Yet throughout most of his writings, Deleuze had dealt frequently with literature, and the theme of the "critical" and the "clinical" was one he had enunciated as early as 1967 in the *Présentation de Sacher-Masoch: le froid et le cruel* (translated as *Masochism: An Interpretation of Coldness and Cruelty*). There Deleuze expressed the hope that in his examination of Sade and Masoch "perhaps *la critique* (in the literary sense) and *la clinique* (in the medical sense) might be made to enter into new relations, in which the one teaches the other, and vice versa" (SM 11; 14). This link between literature and medicine was itself one Deleuze had already touched on in *Nietzsche and Philosophy* (1962), where interpretation was treated as a form of symptomatology and semeiology. In this chapter, we will consider briefly first the notion of *critique* and its relation to medicine in Deleuze's Nietzsche, then the mutual reinforcement of *critique* and *clinique* in his book on Masoch, and finally the connection between signs, symptoms and sense in *The Logic of Sense*.² Throughout, our concern will be to ask how Deleuze differentiates literature from other forms of writing and to determine the specific functions Deleuze ascribes to literary works of art.

INTERPRETATION AND EVALUATION

Deleuze sees Nietzsche as completing the critical project inaugurated by Kant, "the first philosopher to understand critique as having to be total and positive as critique" (NP 102; 89). According to this reading, in his critical philosophy Kant questions the claims of truth and morality, but he leaves unexamined the values that underlie them. "He conceived of critique as a force which must be brought to bear on all pretensions to knowledge and truth, but not on knowledge itself, nor on truth itself. As a force which must be brought to bear on all the pretensions of morality, but not on morality itself" (NP 102; 89). Nietzsche takes critique to its end and conducts a revaluation of all values, including those of the true and the good. Deleuze differentiates in Nietzsche's critique two basic activities: an interpretation of sense [*sens*, sense or meaning] and an evaluation of value. Both activities entail an assessment of forces, interpretation involving the quality of forces in a relation, evaluation the quality of the will to power manifest in a given relation of forces.

The sense of an object derives from "the force that appropriates the thing, that exploits it, that seizes hold of it or expresses itself in it" (NP 3; 3). Every force is an appropriation of a portion of reality, and the history of a thing is a history of the succession of forces that have taken possession of it. "A single object, a single phenomenon changes sense according to the force that appropriates it" (NP 4; 3). Forces are always multiple, and hence interpretation is inherently plural. Forces also mask themselves under the guise of forces that have previously appropriated the same objects, for which reason "the art of interpretation must also be an art of piercing masks" (NP 6; 5). Hence, "a phenomenon is not an appearance or even an apparition, but a sign, a symptom which finds its sense in an actual force. Philosophy as a whole is a symptomatology and a semeiology. The sciences as a whole are a symptomatological and semeiological system" (NP 3; 3). In *The Genealogy of Morals*, for example, Nietzsche shows that the slave's interpretation of an object as "good" is qualitatively different from the master's sense of the object. The slave's "good" assumes the mask of the master's "good," but the two senses of the word derive from different configurations of forces. The slave's "good" issues from a reactive relation of forces, whereas the master's "good" expresses an active relation of forces. The slave resents the master's superiority and conceives of the good as the negation of the master's evil power. The master, by contrast, understands the good simply as an affirmation of his or her own being. The slave's interpretation of an object, like the master's, is a symptom of a certain mentality, a sign of a certain relation of forces, and the art of interpretation (i.e., the interpretation of the slave's and master's interpretations) consists of a careful discrimination of the forces that give sense to an object, whether they be active or reactive, noble or base.

Interpretation, however, only gains its full significance when coupled with the activity of evaluation, which involves the will to power. Deleuze argues that for Nietzsche the world consists of dynamic quantities of forces in relation to one another. Forces have specific quantities, but a quantity of force is misconstrued if taken in isolation from other forces. All forces are in relation with other forces, and no two related forces have the same quantity; one force is always greater than the other, and from that differential relation of quantities of forces issues the quality of each force. In terms of their quantities, forces are either dominant or dominated; in terms of their qualities, forces are either active or reactive (NP 60; 53). But forces would never enter into relation with one another if there were no dynamic element within forces that engendered relations. That element Nietzsche calls "will to power." The will to power "thus is added to force, but as the differential and genetic element, as the internal element of its production" (NP 57–58; 51). As differential element, the will to power produces a relation of differences of quantities of forces; as genetic element, it produces a relation of qualities of forces. If *dominant and dominated* designate quantities of force, and *active and reactive* the qualities of force, "*affirmative and negative* designate the primordial qualities of the will to power" (NP 60; 53–54). To interpret is "to determine the force which gives a sense to the thing," and to evaluate is "to determine the will to power that gives the thing a value" (NP 61; 54). Hence, to interpret is to assess the active or reactive quality of a force, and to evaluate is to assess the affirmative or negative quality of the will to power expressed in a given relation of forces.

Such talk of force, power and domination may suggest a crudely mechanistic world of "might makes right" and "survival of the fittest," but Deleuze draws important distinctions that counter such a reading. First, will to power in its affirmative guise is not a will to power *over* another.[3] Such a view of power is typical of the slave, who resents the master and wants to gain revenge by reversing the relation of power between master and slave. Active forces dominate other forces, but to dominate "means to impose forms, to create forms in exploiting circumstances" (NP 48; 42). The affirmative will to power is metamorphic, self-transforming. "The power [*puissance*] of transformation, the Dionysian power [*pouvoir*], is the first definition of activity" (NP 48; 42). Second, will to power is a power both of affecting and of *being affected*. A body is a set of forces in relation with other forces. The potency or capability of a body, its *puissance*, is determined by the forces it affects but also by the various ways in which it can be affected. A body's power of being affected is not necessarily a form of passivity, "but *affectivity*, sensibility, sensation" (NP 70; 62). Hence, will to power "manifests itself as the sensibility of force" (NP 71; 62–63). Third, the affirmative will to power is not simply a power of action, but also a power of *acting one's reactions* (NP 127; 111). All bodies are comprised of a multiplicity of forces and thus necessarily of a combination of active and reactive forces. Each body in turn is related to multiple forces, both active and reactive. What differentiates the affirmative from the negative will to power, then, is not the absence or presence of reactive forces within a body, but the way in which reactive forces play out their relations. Masters occasionally encounter superior forces, but they do not dwell on them. They respond and move on. They act their reactions. Slaves, by contrast, can never have done with superior forces. They possess a pathological memory that cannot forget, a diseased organ that makes impossible the discharge of reactions. In them, a negative will to power infects all relations of forces and instills a general becoming-reactive of forces, whereby forces are turned against themselves and kept from fulfilling their capabilities.

Ultimately, what Deleuze finds in the affirmative will to power is an artistic sensibility—a will to form and create, to enhance affectivity, to induce and undergo metamorphosis and transformation. The philosophy of the will to power "has two principles that inform its joyous message: to will = to create, will = joy" (NP 96; 84). Only slaves conceive of mastery as subjugation of others, as insensitivity to others and as invulnerability and isolation from superior forces. Masters affirm their being through a creative donation of value, through a heightened power of affecting and being affected by others, and through an ability to act their actions and reactions. The problem as Nietzsche sees it, however, is that the history of humankind is one of a universal becoming-reactive of forces. Everywhere the negative will to power triumphs, everywhere slaves prevail, not through superior numbers or greater quantities of force, but through the sickness of bad conscience, which causes masters to turn upon themselves, to limit their forces and prevent forces from actualizing their powers. The negative will to power comes to infect all humans with reactivity and *ressentiment*, with a ubiquitous hatred of life. The disease of negativity is the universal disease, and for this reason the philosopher of affirmation must be a physician, both a diagnostician who interprets properly the signs of the disease, and a healer who prescribes a cure.[4] As healer the physician creates new possibilities for life, functioning in this regard as an artist affirming metamorphosis and transformation and a legislator fashioning new values. Hence the "Nietzschean trinity of the 'philosopher of the future'" (NP 86; 75): the philosopher-physician, the philosopher-artist and the philosopher-legislator.

Critique involves the interpretation of sense and the evaluation of values, but neither interpretation nor evaluation is primarily a receptive activity. One generally thinks of the interpreter as a reader and the evaluator as a critic, but Nietzsche's interpreter/evaluator is always a physician/artist/legislator, at once an assessor and a creator. As Deleuze points out, Nietzsche generally views art from the vantage of the artist rather than the audience (NP 116–17; 102–3), just as he approaches philology from the perspective of the inventors of words rather than their mere users (NP 84–85; 74–75). So, too, critique is essentially active rather than receptive, a process of interpretation and evaluation that transforms and creates. It is also affirmative, but one should stress that critique is not therefore all-accepting and all-embracing. To say "yes" to everything is to say "yes" to all the sickness and poison of the negative will to power. The symbol of acceptance is the beast of burden, Zarathustra's ass who says "Yea-Yuh" to every weight placed on his back.[5] Critique is creation, but it is also joyous destruction of all that is negative and opposed to life. The Dionysian "yes" of affirmative critique "knows how to say no: it is pure affirmation, it has conquered nihilism and divested negation of all its autonomous power. . . . To affirm is to create, not to bear, to endure, to assume" (NP 213; 185–86).

Deleuze regards Nietzsche's thought as a critical philosophy of interpretation and evaluation. The philosopher of the future is at once physician, artist and legislator, but above all, an artist who affirms life through creation. Art, then, serves as a model for understanding Nietzsche's conception of philosophy, but what specific role art might fulfill as distinct from that of philosophy Deleuze does not say in *Nietzsche and Philosophy*. We might note, however, that Deleuze does briefly suggest an intimate connection between literature and philosophy in Nietzsche's practice as a writer and thinker. Nietzsche "integrates within philosophy two means of expression, the aphorism and the poem. These forms imply a new conception of philosophy, a new image of the thinker and of thought" (N 17). The aphorism is a fragment, and as such "the form of pluralist thought" (NP 35; 31). Its object is "the sense of a being, an action, a thing" (NP 35; 31). The aphorism alone "is capable of articulating sense, the aphorism is interpretation and the art of interpretation" (NP 36; 31). Similarly, the poem is "evaluation and the art of evaluating: it articulates *values*" (NP 36; 31). The sense of the aphorism derives from the differential element that determines relations of forces, whether active or reactive, and the value of the poem issues from the same differential element, that of an affirmative or negative will to power. Yet this differential element, though always present, is "also always implicit or hidden in the poem or the aphorism" (NP 36; 31) and hence in need of further interpretation and evaluation. The aphorism is an interpretation, then, but one that requires a second interpretation, just as the poem is an evaluation requiring a second evaluation. It is in disclosing the differential element of the will to power, which is always present but hidden in the aphorism and the poem, that "philosophy, in its essential relation with the poem and the aphorism, constitutes complete interpretation and evaluation, that is, the art of thinking, the faculty of superior thought or 'faculty of rumination'" (NP 36; 31).[6] Literature, it would seem, provides Nietzsche with first-level interpretations and evaluations, which he then submits to philosophical, second-level interpretation and evaluation. But whether Nietzsche is a philosophical aphorist/poet practicing a hybrid form of philosophy and literature, or a philosopher adapting literary aphorisms and poems for his own philosophical ends, is not clear.[7]

Throughout *Nietzsche and Philosophy*, Deleuze's focus is on critique in the philosophical sense, which he divides into the complementary activities of the interpretation of sense and the evaluation of values. The philosopher of the future is at once artist and physician, and in this regard an individual whose critique of sense and values subsumes within it the broad functions of art and medicine—those of creation and healing. In his *Masochism*, Deleuze brings art and medicine together in a more specific fashion, considering the novels of Leopold Ritter von Sacher-Masoch (1836-1895)[8] as both literary works about and clinical studies in masochism. Deleuze frames his discussion in terms of "*critique* (in the literary sense) and *clinique* (in the medical sense)" (SM 11; 14), but literary *critique* is less his concern than is literary *creation*, which he treats as a mode of thought. Masoch's name has come to be linked to the psychological phenomenon of masochism, just as Sade's to sadism, and Deleuze finds implicit in this association of writers and perversions an unexamined assumption that their works are merely unconscious symptoms of psychological disorders. Deleuze contends, however, that Masoch and Sade are great clinicians, as well as great writers. Perhaps they "suffer" from the conditions they analyze, but "whether 'patients' or clinicians, Sade and Masoch are also great anthropologists, in the manner of those who know how to engage in their work an entire conception of man, culture and nature—and great artists, in the manner of those who know how to extract new forms and create new ways of feeling and thinking, an entirely new language" (SM 16; 16). The objects of Masoch's and Sade's analyses are not, then, simply peculiar and isolated pathologies. As Deleuze explains in *The Logic of Sense*, "artists are clinicians, not of their individual case nor even of a case in general, but clinicians of civilization. In this regard we cannot follow those who think that Sade has nothing essential to say about sadism, or Masoch about masochism" (LS 276-77). Masoch and Sade, in short, are Nietzschean artist-physicians, symptomatologists of civilization and inventors of new ways of feeling and thinking.[9]

Symptomatology is the branch of medicine concerned with the interpretation of signs (hence its traditional name *semeiology*). It is also the foundation of *la clinique* or the art of diagnosis through the direct observation of patients.[10] The great clinicians are symptomatologists who regroup signs, undoing previous concatenations of symptoms and establishing new associations of hitherto unrelated symptoms in "a profoundly original clinical picture [*tableau*]" (SM 15; 15). In "Mystique et masochisme" (MM) (1967), a brief interview on his *Masochism*, Deleuze observes that, unlike "etiology, or research into causes" and "therapeutics, or research into and application of a treatment," which are integral components of medicine, symptomatology occupies a "sort of neutral point, a limit-point, premedical or submedical, belonging as much to art as to medicine." It is situated "almost on the exterior of medicine, at a neutral point, a zero point, where artists and philosophers and physicians and patients can meet one another" (MM 12–13). Great clinicians are artists, and artists may be great clinicians. Sade is one such artist-clinician, and Masoch is "a great clinician" who perhaps "goes even further than Sade himself" (SM 36; 40).

Both symptomatologists and writers perform linguistic and semiotic acts in the naming of signs, but it is in the domain of psychological phenomena that medicine and literature seem especially germane to one another. Deleuze notes that "there is, in effect, a basis common to literary creation and the constitution of symptoms: the phantasy [*le phantasme*]" (MM 13).[11] Yet there is a crucial difference between a literary work and an illness, which arises from "the kind of *work* that is performed on the phantasy. In the two cases the source—the phantasy—is the same, but starting from there the work is very different, without common measure: the artistic work and the pathological work" (MM 13). In the instances of Sade and Masoch, their artistic work is specific to a particular kind of literary project. Echoing Freud's observations on writing, daydreaming and fantasy,[12] Deleuze remarks that "for most writers the phantasy is the source of their work." But for Sade, Masoch and a few others (Deleuze cites Robbe-Grillet and Klossowski as examples), "the phantasy has become also the object itself and the last word of the work, as if the entire work reflected its proper origin" (MM 13).

The central problem Deleuze addresses in his study of Masoch is that of the subsumption of Sade and Masoch within a single pathology—that of sadomasochism. Masoch is generally regarded as the mirror image of Sade, and while many critics have come to study Sade's works and take his thoughts seriously, Masoch remains today largely unread and unappreciated, despite the popularity and prestige he once enjoyed in the 1860s and 1870s. Deleuze contends, however, that Masoch is Sade's equal as a writer and symptomatologist and that sadism and masochism are fundamentally different phenomena. Sadomasochism is not a disease but a *syndrome*, a false grouping of signs of diverse provenance that have only a name in common.[13] As soon as one actually reads Masoch, "one senses that his universe has nothing to do with Sade's universe" (SM 11; 13). Deleuze's object is to distinguish between these two universes and disclose the logic that organizes their separate domains of signs.

Throughout his work, Sade seeks a rational delirium of pure negation. Following Klossowski's analysis, Deleuze distinguishes two natures in Sade: a secondary nature of destruction and creation, a confused mixture of birth, metamorphosis and death; and a primary nature of pure negation, an "original delirium, a primordial chaos made solely of furious and lacerating molecules" (SM 25; 27). That primary nature is never given in reality; it is an Idea, delirious to be sure, but "a delirium proper to reason" (SM 25; 27). Sade's goal is to create a world of primary nature, in which a cruel order is imposed with the implacable rationality of a violent logical demonstration. The mother as procreator is associated with secondary nature, the father with primary nature—hence the central phantasy of the "father, destroyer of his own family, impelling the daughter to torture and murder the mother" (SM 52-53; 59). A certain "masochism" exists when the father figure submits himself to his own violent principle, but it is a masochism proper to the Sadean universe, an ultimate implementation of the mechanism of pure negation. A cruel apathy prevails as all sentiment, associated with secondary nature, is eradicated. A form of eros remains, but it is that of a libidinized impersonal Idea of pure negation.

Deleuze finds two natures in Masoch as well, but incommensurable with those in Sade. Masoch's secondary nature is structured by two poles, represented by the female figures of "the hetaera or Aphrodite, generator of disorder" (SM 42; 47), and the sadistic torturer. In this world, men and women are forever at war. The hetaera practices an unconstrained sensuality, creating havoc through her liaisons with multiple partners, while the sadistic woman dominates man through eroticized violence. In secondary nature, "violence and trickery, hatred and destruction, disorder and sensuality are everywhere at work" (SM 49; 54). Masoch's primary nature is revealed in a third female figure, the oral mother, who is "cold, maternal, severe" (SM 45; 51). The masochist's dream is of a nature free of the heat of sensuality, filled with a cool, suprasensual sentimentality and a strict, cathartic order that purifies and makes possible the miraculous parthenogenesis of a new man. If the father dominates in Sade, the mother rules in Masoch. In the masochistic phantasy, it is the image of the father that the mother beats, humiliates and destroys when she disciplines the son, thereby enabling a reconciliation of man and woman in the triumphant moment when the son is reborn as a transformed being and united with the mother. Unlike Sadean apathy, which proceeds from a delirious rational negation, Masoch's coldness reflects the imagination's disavowal (*dénégation*) of reality.[14] Disavowal is a simultaneous denial and acceptance of the real, an imaginative "suspension" of reality paradigmatically exhibited in fetishism (central to masochism, but not to sadism). In Freud's analysis, the fetish as substitute for the maternal phallus allows the subject at once to admit and deny female castration. Deleuze sees disavowal as a function of the faculty of imagination, and in Masoch's phantasy of a primary nature he finds a suspension of the disorderly violence of secondary nature, an idealizing neutralization of the real that allows for the unfolding of a new world.

Masoch's most original contribution as symptomatologist, in Deleuze's view, is his insistence on the importance of the contract in masochistic phantasies. The masochist trains his punisher, persuades and educates her (whereas the sadist never educates but only demonstrates), and formalizes the mistress-slave relationship in a written contract, which serves as a defense against anything in the external world that might disturb the phantasy. The masochist's contract seems to honor the law, but successive revisions of the contract often exaggerate the mistress's tyrannical powers and render the law ludicrous. Further, the law that normally inflicts pain and forbids pleasure in this instance makes punishment the provocation and guarantee of pleasure. Unlike the sadist, who ironically rises above law and imposes a cruel institution of universal negation, the masochist humorously obeys contracts that subvert the notion of law and thereby renders void the regimes of secondary nature. Finally, the contract establishes a zone of ritual practices and in this way affords the masochist passage from the personal realm of phantasy into the universal domain of myth (specifically, that of the cold, sentimental and severe mother of primary nature). "From contract to myth, through the intermediary of law: law comes out of the contract, but throws us into rites. . . . What the *masochist* establishes contractually, at a specific moment and for a specific time, is also that which is contained for all time, ritually, in the symbolic order of *masochism*" (SM 89; 102).

In "Mystique et masochisme," we will recall, Deleuze locates the difference between literature and *la clinique* in the work that is performed on the phantasy. What, then, is the work specific to literature? Deleuze does not address this question directly in *Masochism*, but hints of a response are scattered throughout the text. In a brief memoir, reprinted as an appendix to *Masochism*, Masoch tells of a female type that has always haunted him. From this "figure," says Masoch, a "problem" arises that generates all the subsequent images of his literary creations. Deleuze comments that "in defining the art of the novel, Masoch said that one must go from the 'figure' to the 'problem': one must start from the obsessive phantasy in order to rise to the problem, to the theoretical structure where the problem is posed" (SM 47–48; 53). In other words, the artist begins with a personal phantasy, an obsessional "figure" that might well form part of a neurosis, perversion or other psychological fixation, but then converts the "figure" into a properly artistic "problem" by determining its structure and engaging that structure as the material for artistic creation. In Masoch's fictional elaboration of the "figure," the phantasy "finds that which it needs, a theoretical, ideological structure, which gives it the value of a general conception of human nature and the world" (SM 47–48; 53). Deleuze insists that Masoch, like Sade, creates a separate "universe" (SM 11; 13), a separate "world" or "*Umwelt*" (SM 37; 42). The sadist and masochist each "perform a sufficient and complete drama, with different characters, with nothing that allows them to communicate with one another, neither from within nor without" (SM 40; 45). In Sade and Masoch, literature seeks to name not the world "but a double of the world, capable of gathering within it the world's violence and excess" (SM 33; 37). Psychoanalysts approach Sade and Masoch in terms of a common sadomasochistic *content*, either a libidinal brute "matter" of pleasure/pain or a moral dimension of guilt and expiation, but what they ignore are the distinctive *forms* of sadism and masochism, and it is from their forms, their theoretical and ideological structures, that the coherence of their divergent worlds arises. "Masochism finally is neither material nor moral, but formal, entirely formal" (SM 66; 74). The forms specific to masochism include those of disavowal, suspense and the fetish, as well as those of the contract and the ritual, but also the form of a particular "form of time" (SM 63; 71), a complex time of waiting [*attente*] in which two temporal streams coexist, one promising an awaited pleasure, the other holding forth an expected punishment, both maintained in a perpetual state of suspension.

Hence, "disavowal, suspense, waiting, fetishism and the phantasy form the properly masochistic constellation" (SM 63; 72), but most important is the phantasy.[15] Disavowal makes the real pass into phantasy, suspense puts the ideal in phantasy, waiting is "the unity of the real and the ideal, the form or temporality of the phantasy" (SM 63; 71), and the fetish is the quintessential object of phantasy. "Masochism is the art of the phantasy" (SM 59; 66) in other regards as well. First, the phantasy in general "plays on two series, on two limits, two 'borders'; between the two is established a resonance which constitutes the true life of the phantasy" (SM 59; 66). In Masoch, the borders are the polar figures of the haetera and the sadistic torturer, and in between is the phantasmatic oral mother, "cold, maternal, severe." Second, the phantasy is the basic element of dreams and daydreams. Whereas the sadist attempts to project a violent phantasmatic Idea into the real, the masochist tries to "neutralize the real and suspend the ideal within the pure interior of the phantasy" (SM 65; 72). In this respect, the sadist believes that he is not dreaming, even when he is; the masochist, that he is dreaming, even when he is not. Finally, the phantasy is an imaginary *scene*, and in Masoch's novels the real tends to be transformed into a theater, a series of atmospheric tableaus. Whereas in Sade erotic scenes are repeated with violent and mechanical reiteration, in Masoch phantasy figures are identified with motionless art objects—statues, portraits, photographs—components of scenes that are repeated in a stuttering sequence of frozen images. Sade seeks the violence of continuous movement and hence abjures the stasis of the art object, whereas Masoch aspires to a world of suspense and waiting, and thus aestheticizes the real as a series of *tableaux vivants*.

If pornography is "literature reduced to a few commands [*mots d'ordre*] (do this, do that . . .), followed by obscene descriptions" (SM 17; 17), then Sade and Masoch are "pornologists" rather than "pornographers," argues Deleuze, for they invent new functions for commands and descriptions. In Sade, commands function as violent demonstrations of a delirious reason and descriptions as accelerating reiterations of an apathetic obscenity; in Masoch, commands function as persuasive teachings of an idealizing imagination and descriptions as repeated tableaux of an atmospheric erotics. Like all writers, Sade and Masoch begin with phantasy, but unlike many, they take phantasy as the object of their work, Masoch especially making his art the art of the phantasy. Each manages to take a personal obsession and convert it into material for artistic invention. Each creates a double of the world, a complexly structured set of forms that counter the real, either through negation or disavowal. By way of such counterworlds, each diagnoses civilization's illnesses by clarifying and emphasizing their structures, and each opens new possibilities for life by ironically or humorously warping and transforming those structures. Like pornographers, they engage the domain of violence and eros, yet as pornologists they attempt to "put language in relation with its proper limit, with a sort of 'non-language' (violence which does not speak, eroticism about which one does not speak)" (SM 22; 22). They do so through "a doubling internal to language" (SM 22; 22), through the invention of new uses of commands and descriptions. Thus, Deleuze asserts, Sade and Masoch not only fashion a double of the world, but also "form in language a sort of double of language, capable of acting directly on the senses" (SM 33; 37).[16]

What finally is the relationship between *la critique* and *la clinique*? Symptomatology is a zero point "where artists and philosophers and physicians and patients can meet one another" (MM 13). Unlike patients, whose disorders speak through them in an indirect and unanalyzed fashion, writers such as Sade and Masoch articulate a world in such a way that its forms and structures display their coherence. Like philosophers, they engage in a mode of thought, but it is thought in the form of commands and descriptions, scenes, dramas, rites and actions, doubles of the world and language. Sade and Masoch share with psychoanalysts an interest in perversions, but it is fiction that should guide psychoanalysis, not the reverse. Masochism is essentially formal, "and the worlds of perversion in general demand that psychoanalysis be truly a formal psychoanalysis, almost deductive, one that first considers the formalism of processes as so many novelistic elements" (SM 66; 74). Hence, literary thought should lead medical thought in the realm of symptomatology, the forms of a world articulated in a work of literature allowing the differentiation of true symptoms from false syndromes. And if Sade and Masoch are themselves patients, their malady is a condition of civilization, and their critical analysis of that condition a means of envisioning other possibilities for life. They disclose a double of the world, one that perhaps may be deemed a sickness, but one also that ironically or humorously disrupts the real and clears the way for something new.

SENSE AND SURFACES

In "Of the Schizophrenic and the Little Girl," the thirteenth section of *The Logic of Sense* (1969), Deleuze returns to the concepts of *critique* and *clinique*, examining the relationship between the child, the mad person [*le fou*] and the writers Lewis Carroll and Antonin Artaud. Deleuze's point of entry is Artaud's quasi-translation with commentary of "Jabberwocky," a poem, says Artaud, "I have never liked" (cited in LS 113; 92). Carroll's nonsense verse is often classified as children's literature, and many of Artaud's texts read like incoherent psychotic emissions, but the difference between the two versions of "Jabberwocky" is not to be found in the opposition of the young Alice and the schizophrenic. Deleuze warns that poetry, nursery rhymes and mad ramblings must not be confused, even if all three occasionally make use of similar techniques, such as portmanteau words. "A great poet may write in a direct relation with the child he has been and the children he loves; a madman may bring with him the most immense poetic *oeuvre*, in a direct relation with the poet he has been and does not cease to be. Yet in no way does this justify the grotesque trinity of the child, the poet and the madman" (LS 101; 82–83). Carroll and Artaud address different questions in their Jabberwockys, and those differ from the issues at stake in children's rhymes and madmen's inventions. "The problem is that of *la clinique*, that is, of the sliding from one organization to another, or of the formation of a progressive and creative disorganization. The problem is also that of *la critique*, that is, of the determination of differential levels where nonsense changes its figure, the portmanteau word its nature, language as a whole its dimension" (LS 102; 83). The clinical problem revealed in the opposition of Carroll and Artaud is one of *surfaces* and *depths*, Deleuze argues, the critical problem, one of linguistic elements characteristic of those two dimensions. Carroll's surfaces and Artaud's depths have much to teach us about infantile neurosis and schizophrenic dissociation, but only if *la clinique* is guided by *la critique*, psychoanalytic theory by literary invention.

In *The Logic of Sense*, Deleuze develops a theory of sense, or meaning, through the improbable juxtaposition of the works of Lewis Carroll and the thought of the Stoics.[17] In the nonsense and paradoxes of *Alice in Wonderland*, *Through the Looking-Glass* and other works, Deleuze shows that Carroll rediscovers the enigmatic surface of meaning that the Stoics articulate in their theory of incorporeals.[18] For the Stoics, only bodies have real being (though "bodies" is construed in the broadest terms to include even such entities as the soul). Bodies are conceived of as growing, self-forming entities, along the lines of organic beings such as plants and animals. They are causes of themselves, and though they act on one another, they do not enter into relations of cause and effect. Rather, they are causes among one another, for ultimately all bodies are part of the single body of the universe, or God. Bodies interpenetrate and intermingle, as when someone drinks wine or a knife cuts through flesh, but the actions and passions of bodies remain exclusively causes of one another, not causes and effects. The knife does not cause the effect of a gash in the flesh; rather, the knife and flesh intermingle in the self-causing development of the cosmic body of God.

And yet there are such things as effects, though they do not belong to the world of bodies. They are surface phenomena that have no real being, but simply "insist," "persist" or "subsist." They are incorporeals (*asomata*). The Stoics start from the commonsense observation that when a dog walks across a road, the walking adds nothing to the body of the dog. But they go further, regarding the "greening" of the tree as equally insubstantial, a mere surface effect produced by the self-causing development of the body of the tree. Everywhere, bodies produce effects, surface emanations that play over bodies like fogs or auras. Such incorporeal effects are events, with their own temporality. Only the present has real being, and bodies exist in a perpetual present. The duration of a body may be conceived of as an extended present, the totality of time being included in the Great Present of the body of God. This is the time Deleuze calls *Chronos*. Past and future, the dimensions of memory and anticipation, have no real existence, yet they persist or insist, and they are manifest in the time of the event, which Deleuze labels *Aion*. The time of Aion is that of the infinitive, the verb in its undifferentiated, amorphous temporality, one that extends over past and future without ever entering into an actual present moment. A time of pure becoming informs events, whereas bodies inhabit a time of pure present being.[19]

The quintessential event is the battle (LS 122–23; 100–101). Everywhere on the battlefield bodies encounter other bodies, piercing, cutting, tearing and penetrating one another, yet "the battle" is nowhere present at a given locus, always somewhere else. The battle emanates from the bodies, hovers over them like a fog. It is produced by the bodies as an effect, yet it preexists them as the condition of their possible encounters.

Events, then, are attributes of bodies, manners of being that are best thought of as verbs, whereas the real characteristics of bodies are qualities, adjectives that inhere in nouns. Yet though events and bodies each have their linguistic counterparts, language itself has a privileged relationship to events. "The event is coextensive with becoming, and becoming itself is coextensive with language" (LS 18; 8). The most important of the incorporeals recognized by the Stoics is the *lekton*, the "significate," "expressible" or "thing meant."[20] When a Greek speaks to a Barbarian, the words are incomprehensible, yet when another Greek hears those same words, they are understood. In both cases, the same body of sound is emitted by the speaker, but in the second instance something is added to the physical sounds, a surface effect of meaning. Such linguistic effects are *lekta*, "expressibles" that emanate from the surfaces of bodies and make possible the delineation of words and things. The words express a meaning, but that which is expressed is an attribute of things, an event. The *lekton* is simultaneously the surface of the sonic body of the word and the surface attribute of the thing. It is the surface between words and things, a single surface of meaning-events. The surface-border between words and things "does not mix them, nor does it unite them (it is no more a monism than a dualism), it is rather like the articulation of their difference: body/language" (LS 37; 24).

This surface Deleuze labels *sens*, sense or meaning, and throughout *The Logic of Sense* he demonstrates that the paradoxes of linguistic sense are one with the paradoxes of events and becoming. Words produce meaning as a secondary effect, yet in a way meaning precedes words as the element within which language takes place. "As Bergson says, one does not go from sounds to images and from images to sense [*sens*]: one situates oneself 'from the start' within sense. Sense is like the sphere in which I am already situated in order to carry out possible designations, and even think of their conditions" (LS 41; 28). Meaning in this regard is then both before and after language, its condition of possibility and its residual effect. Yet meaning is also never fully present, in that it may be expressed in a specific linguistic utterance, but that meaning can only be designated in a second utterance, whose meaning in turn must be designated in a third utterance, and so on. Hence, meaning generates an infinite regression of designations that cannot be exhausted or brought to a conclusion. Like the event, meaning inhabits both past and future without ever existing in the present. Meaning also includes within it nonsense, in that imaginary entities (griffins), impossible objects (square circles) and even sequences of nonce words ("'Twas brillig, and the slithy toves. . . ") all have sense, just not good sense. Indeed, Deleuze argues, good sense, *le bon sens*, is simply limited sense, sense in a single direction (*sens* in French also having the meaning of "direction," as in *sens unique*, "one-way street"). In nonsense, causal relations are frequently reversed, temporal sequences ignored, identities confused. The paradoxes of nonsense are those of the "becoming" Plato so distrusts (*Philebus* 24 a–d, *Parmenides* 154–55), of objects that simultaneously are hotter and colder, older and younger, bigger and smaller. Alice grows larger than she was, but the Alice she was (Alice A) is smaller than the Alice she becomes (Alice B). In that the Alice-becoming-larger (Alice A becoming Alice B) is the same Alice (but is she any longer the same Alice at either point A or B?), Alice is becoming both larger and smaller at the same time (or rather, within the same becoming, Aion, never at the same present moment, Chronos). In nonsense, quite simply, the world becomes in all directions in the same Aion.

Carroll's nonsense, far from being an absence of sense, is the multidirectional field of sense within which good sense takes place, and genuine non-sense, Deleuze argues, is the generative element from which that broad field of sense arises. In "The Hunting of the Snark," the word "Snark" may seem a mere portmanteau combination of "shark" and "snake," but its function is to generate two divergent series of elements.

> They sought it with thimbles, they sought it with care,
> They pursued it with forks and hope;
> They threatened its life with a railway-share;
> They charmed it with smiles and soap.

The Snark is the juncture of a series of bodies (thimbles, forks, soap) and a series of incorporeals (care, hope, life, railway-share, smiles). Its non-sense is the differential element from which sense (the two series) derives. If the two series are thought of geometrically as diverging lines comprised of multiple points, "Snark" is an "aleatory point" (LS 72; 56), seemingly in both lines at once, yet never at any single point at a given moment. The Snark as aleatory point is like the object Alice confronts in the shop tended by the Sheep (*Through the Looking-Glass*,175–76): It is never where she looks, but always on the shelf above or below. It is an empty space lacking its own place, an unfixable element from which determinate elements arise. The aleatory point and the two divergent series it inhabits constitute the minimal elements of any structure, according to Deleuze, and just as the domain of sense is generated through the play of the aleatory point of non-sense, so the domain of events issues from the play of aleatory points, for the aleatory point, finally, is simply a figure for difference—a self-differentiating (i.e., generative) differentiation (through divergent determinations) differing from itself (nowhere itself fixed, stable or possessed of a single identity).

The nonsense of Carroll's "Jabberwocky" is that of a surface play of *sens*, of portmanteau words disclosing divergent series of terms through the pursuit and conquest of the Jabberwock.

'Twas brillig, and the slithy toves
    Did gyre and gimble in the wabe:
All mimsy were the borogoves,
    And the mome raths outgrabe.

As Humpty Dumpty explains, *brillig* means "four o'clock in the afternoon—the time when you begin *broiling* things for dinner," *slithy* means "lithe and slimy"; and *toves* "are something like badgers—they're something like lizards—and they're something like corkscrews" (Carroll 187–88). Four p.m./broiling, lithe/slimy, badgers/lizards/corkscrews: multiple series generated through the aleatory point of the Jabberwock, meaning-events on a surface between words and things. But in Artaud's "translation" of Carroll's poem, Deleuze finds another sort of nonsense entirely:

Il était roparant, et les vliqueux tarands
    Allaient en gibroyant et en brimbulkdriquant

Jusque là où la rourghe est à rouarghe a rangmbde et rangmbde a
 rouarghambde:
Tous les falomitards étaient les chat-huants
Et les Ghoré Uk'hatis dans le Grabugeument. (Cited in LS 103;
 342)

It is possible, of course, to treat this text as would Humpty Dumpty, and indeed, Artaud himself suggests that *"rourghe"* and *"rouarghe"* bring together *ruée* [rush], *roue* [wheel], *route* [route], *règle* [rule], *route à régler* [literally: road to fix; figuratively: matter to be straightened out]. Yet to regard *"rourghe"* as a version of "slithy," says Deleuze, is to make a serious critical and clinical error. There may be zones of contact between Carroll and Artaud, instances in which Artaud's linguistic inventions remain on the surface of sense, but in a sequence such as *rourghe, rouargh, rangmbde, rouarghambde,* the surface of sense dissolves and collapses as words become sonic bodies interacting with other bodies in a physical domain of profligate and unregulated mixtures, interminglings and interpenetrations. Schizophrenics, Deleuze observes, often experience words as lacerating, persecuting objects that rip into the flesh. These are "passion-words," shards that mix with the schizophrenic body, which itself does not exist as a coherent organism but as a *body-sieve* of permeable holes, a *fragmented body* of heterogeneous scraps and pieces, a *dissociated body* with no barrier between inside and outside (LS 107; 87). Passion-words commingle in a terrifying realm of ceaseless cannibalistic dismemberment, dissolution, absorption and expulsion. However, there are also moments in which the schizophrenic body attains a perfect totality, not as an organism but as a body "without parts, which does everything through insufflation, inspiration, evaporation, fluid transmission (the superior body, the body without organs of Artaud)" (LS 108; 88). To this miraculous body correspond "action-words," sound-bodies that form indissociable blocks of sonic matter. Unlike the passively suffered passion-words, which atomize linguistic signs into splintered phonetic elements, the actively enjoyed action-words take on the *"exclusively tonic values"* of a *"language without articulation"* (LS 108-9; 88–89). The *cris-souffles* (cries-breaths) Artaud speaks of are such action-words, cry-words and breath-words that fuse consonants and vowels in inseparable sonic amalgams. Passion-words and action-words are void of sense, but their non-sense is that of bodies, not incorporeal surfaces. "They relate to two types of non-sense, passive and active: that of the word deprived of sense that is decomposed into phonetic elements, that of tonic elements that form an undecomposable word no less deprived of sense" (LS 110–11; 90). In Artaud's "Jabberwocky," the nonsense of surfaces gives way to the non-sense of passion-words and action-words, terrifying body fragments and the glorious body without organs, phonetic fragments and tonic fusions.

Some psychoanalysts have pointed to schizophrenic motifs in Carroll, such as Alice's metamorphosing body, her obsessions with food, confusions of identity, hallucinatory characters (the March Hare, the Mad Hatter, the Cheshire Cat, etc.), but in such a reading "one simultaneously botches both the clinical psychiatric aspect [*l'aspect clinique psychiatrique*] and the literary critical aspect [*l'aspect critique littéraire*]" (LS 113; 92). Psychoanalysis must first be "geographic," says Deleuze, for it must distinguish surfaces from depths. In differentiating Carroll from Artaud, we will recall, Deleuze initially frames the clinical problem as that of "the sliding [*le glissement*] from one organization to another, or of the formation of a progressive and creative disorganization" (LS 102; 83). Carroll induces in language a sliding from good sense into nonsense, but such that a surface between words and things is sustained. The organized regularities of good sense are undermined, but they are replaced by the organized forms of nonsense, which are structured by the play of aleatory points across divergent series. Artaud, by contrast, engages a progressive and creative disorganization of words, a dissolution of signs into phonetic fragments and tonic blocks, asyntactic, agrammatical sonic bodies that mingle with other bodies in a flux of coexistent shattering parts and melding accretions (bodies without organs). One can see, then, why the problem of *la critique* posed by Carroll and Artaud is that of "the determination of differential levels where nonsense changes its figure, the portmanteau word its nature, language as a whole its dimension" (LS 102; 83), for in Carroll's surfaces language maintains its organization and nonsense its own strangely structured sense, whereas in Artaud's depths language disappears into the fathomless seas of terrifying and miraculous bodies.

The "grotesque trinity of the child, the poet, and the madman" (LS 101; 83) suggests itself because the child, like Carroll, plays with the incorporeal surface effects of language (in nursery rhymes, nonsense phrases, etc.), whereas the madman, like Artaud, suffers and enjoys the movements of sonic flows within the corporeal depths. Writers, however, experiment with language in ways that differ from the practices of the child and the madman, for their inventions display an autonomy, impersonality and analytic lucidity that children and madmen lack. Carroll not only fashions entertaining nonsense but also discloses an entire "logic of sense" that synthesizes the findings of a tradition running from the Stoics through the Scholastics to Meinong and Husserl. Artaud not only dissolves language but also articulates its inarticulable passions and actions, converting cry-words and breath-words into a theater of cruelty. When in *The Logic of Sense* Deleuze discusses authors as "clinicians of civilization" (LS 277; 237), he contrasts the modes in which neurotics and novelists inhabit surfaces. Neurotics are possessed by a "family romance" [Freud's *Familienroman, roman familial* in French, literally "family novel"], whereas novelists extract from surfaces a "pure event," one that is depersonalized and then unfolded through the characters and actions of a given work of art.[21] A similar artistic autonomy and impersonality separate Carroll as poet/novelist from the child (and the grown-child neurotic). Likewise, Artaud as poet/dramatist does more than exude psychotic symptoms. Deleuze finds helpful guides to Artaud's artistic practices in the writings of the schizophrenic Louis Wolfson, but the "beauty, the density" of Wolfson's texts "remain clinical" and his talents "far from the genius of Artaud" (LS 104; 84). Wolfson's symptoms write *him* in a single, redundant story, whereas Artaud's *cris-souffles* take on multiple forms in diverse settings and scenes.[22]

The Logic of Sense is Deleuze's most extended discussion of language, but in certain regards the book occupies an anomalous position within his works. The opposition of surfaces and bodies, elaborated at such length and in such detail, disappears in *Anti-Oedipus* and subsequent books—indeed, one might say that surfaces and depths are combined eventually as *Anti-Oedipus'* desiring-machines and bodies without organs give way to *A Thousand Plateaus'* assemblages on planes of consistency.[23] In the second half of *The Logic of Sense*, Deleuze develops a complex psychoanalytic account of the genesis of the surface of language from the depths of the body, utilizing the full panoply of Freudian and Lacanian terminology, but in *Anti-Oedipus* he launches a frontal attack on psychoanalysis and thereafter virtually abandons the vocabulary of psychoanalysis. Sense is said to pertain exclusively to surfaces as opposed to bodies, and in the

Stoic cosmology incorporeal facts/events are opposed to corporeal forces, but in *Nietzsche and Philosophy*, as we saw, the sense of interpretation is determined by relations of force and the will to power. This same emphasis on force and power as determinants of all semiotic systems is prominent in much of Deleuze's work, especially in *Anti-Oedipus*, *A Thousand Plateaus* and *Foucault*. Finally, at several points in *The Logic of Sense*, Deleuze seems to promote a language-centered view of events, as when he asserts that the event "is coextensive with becoming, and becoming itself is coextensive with language" (LS 18; 8), that "the event belongs essentially to language, it is in an essential relation with language" (LS 34; 22), or that "events-effects do not exist outside the propositions that express them" (LS 36; 23). Yet the characteristics of events (summarized so well in the Fifteenth Series, "Of Singularities" [LS 122-32; 100–108]) are essentially those of "becomings" as outlined in *A Thousand Plateaus*, and it is evident there that becomings can exist outside language. In fact, it is the possibility of a separation between language and the event that allows Deleuze to develop a theory of the arts that grants each art its own autonomous mode of engaging the event.

Deleuze's interest in the relationship between *critique* in its literary sense and *clinique* in its medical sense comes at the height of his preoccupation with psychoanalytic theory. In *Masochism* he contrasts the symptomatologists Sade and Masoch, whose novels articulate the forms of the clinical entities known as sadism and masochism, and in *The Logic of Sense*, he opposes Carroll and Artaud as semeiologists of perverse surfaces and psychotic depths. As Deleuze turns away from psychoanalysis, he ceases to explore the specific connection between literature and clinical medicine, yet throughout his work he retains the broad conception of the writer as Nietzschean interpreter of signs and physician of civilization. In his study of Proust, Deleuze examines writing as the explication and production of signs, and in his work on Kafka, he treats the author of "minor literature" as a diagnostician of culture. As Deleuze remarks in a 1988 interview, Proust's "*Recherche* is a general semiology, a symptomatology of worlds. The work of Kafka is the diagnosis of all the diabolical powers that await us. Nietzsche said it, the artist and the philosopher are physicians of civilization" (PP 195; 142-43). In the next three chapters we will consider in some detail Proust's symptomatology of worlds and Kafka's diagnosis of diabolical powers, in both cases attempting to discern what specific function Deleuze attributes to literature.

Chapter Two

PROUST'S SIGN MACHINE

In his preface to the third edition of *Proust and Signs* (1976), Deleuze explains that the first part, published as *Marcel Proust and Signs* in 1964, concerns the "emission and interpretation of signs," whereas part two, added in a second edition in 1970 and divided into chapters in 1976, concerns "the production and multiplication of signs themselves, from the point of view of the composition of the *Recherche*." In both instances, the problem Deleuze addresses is that of the unity of Proust's *A la recherche du temps perdu*, this mammoth search for, inquiry into, and research on lost time (and the regained time ["*temps retrouvé*"] of the seventh volume). What is the singleness of a novel that has as its subject something that by its very nature cannot be grasped as a whole—i.e., time? What is the "unity *of* this multiple, *of* this multiplicity, as a whole *of* these fragments: a One and a Whole which would not be a principle, but on the contrary the 'effect' of the multiple and its disconnected parts" (PS 195; 144)? From the perspective of the emission and interpretation of signs, the *Recherche* is "the story of an apprenticeship" (PS 10; 4) in signs, but one that must be grasped from the point of view both of an ongoing process of discovery and of a final revelation of the truth of signs in the work of art. From the perspective of the multiplication and production of signs, the *Recherche* is a machine that produces "unity effects" as well as changes in the reader. Time is the narrator's object of investigation and the medium in which that investigation takes place, but time is also the active subject that produces signs and the unity effects of the *Recherche*, for "such is time, the dimension of the narrator, which has the power [*puissance*] to be the whole [*le tout*] *of* these parts without totalizing them, the unity *of* these parts without unifying them" (PS 203; 150).

THE EMISSION AND INTERPRETATION OF SIGNS

One of Deleuze's basic goals is to challenge the common notion that involuntary memory and subjective association hold the key to an interpretation of the *Recherche*. Marcel's madeleine is an important element of the novel, but it is only one kind of sign, and a careful reading of the seventh volume, *Le temps retrouvé*, makes it clear that the truths revealed through signs concern more than mere psychological states. Signs for Proust are enigmas, says Deleuze, hieroglyphs that resist ready decoding. Signs both reveal and conceal, and to the extent that they function as signs, they deny immediate comprehension and induce a process of indirect decipherment. The contents of signs are enfolded within them, rolled up, compressed, disguised, and to interpret signs is to unfold them, to *explicate* them (Latin *explicare*: to unfold, to unroll). In this regard, the madeleine is indeed paradigmatic of signs, for as Marcel remarks, the explication of this sign is like "the game wherein the Japanese amuse themselves by filling a porcelain bowl with water and steeping in it little pieces of paper which until then are without character or form, but the moment they become wet, stretch and twist and take on colour and distinctive shape, become flowers or houses or people, solid and recognisable" (Proust I 51).

The madeleine, however, represents only one of four kinds of signs. First, there are *worldly signs*, the signs of social convention, polite conversation, proper form, etiquette, custom, decorum, and so on. Worldly signs pose many enigmas: why is one individual admitted to a certain circle and another not, what delineates one coterie from another, what is meant by a certain oblique remark, furtive glance or sudden blush? Such signs finally refer to nothing else, but simply "hold the place" of an action or a thought. They are vapid and stereotypical, "but this vacuity confers upon them a ritual perfection, a formalism, that one cannot find elsewhere" (PS 13; 7). Second are the *signs of love*, those of the beloved who expresses an unknown world. "The loved one implicates, envelops, imprisons a world that must be deciphered, that is, interpreted" (PS 14; 7). Indeed, multiple worlds are enfolded within the beloved, and to love is to explicate and develop those hidden, mysterious landscapes that seem to emanate from the beloved's eyes. Necessarily, however, the lover is excluded from some of these enfolded worlds, and it is for this reason that jealousy and disappointment hold the truth of love. The beloved's remarks inevitably deceive, for they always enfold worlds the lover cannot know. "The lies of the beloved are the hieroglyphs of love. The interpretation of amorous signs is necessarily the interpretation of lies" (PS 16; 9). Third are *sensual signs*, like the madeleine, the uneven paving stones of Venice, the stiffly folded napkin at the *hôtel de Guermantes*. These are the well-known signs of involuntary memory, whereby an implicated world unfolds from a sudden, unexpected sensate experience. As Marcel remarks of the madeleine, "in a moment all the flowers in our garden and in M. Swann's park, and the water-lilies on the Vivonne and the good folk of the village and their little dwellings and the parish church and the whole of Combray and its surroundings, taking shape and solidity, sprang into being, towns and gardens alike, from my cup of tea" (Proust I 51). Such signs bring overwhelming joy and force thought into action, demanding interpretation and explication. They reveal more than a mere association of ideas or confluence of reminiscences, for they disclose essences—an essence of Combray, of Balbec, of Venice—that go beyond any sense experience or memory. Yet these signs remain material, and the essences incarnate in them are fleeting, rare and difficult to sustain. Only in the fourth kind of signs, the *signs of art*, are essences dematerialized and thereby rendered autonomous and self-sustaining. The signs of involuntary memory are important, yet not as ends in themselves, but as gateways to the signs of art, in which essences are revealed in their full and proper form.

Proust's "search for lost time" is a search for truth—the truth of signs—but truth is not to be found through good will and voluntary action. Signs impinge on thought, induce disequilibrium and disorientation. In reflecting on the sensation of the uneven paving stones, Marcel notes that it was "the fortuitous and inevitable fashion in which this and the other sensations had been encountered that proved the trueness of the past which they brought back to life" (Proust III 913). The ideas formulated by intelligence alone "have no more than a logical, possible truth, they are arbitrarily chosen. The book whose hiero-glyphs are patterns not traced by us is the only book that really belongs to us. Not that the ideas which we form for ourselves cannot be correct in logic; that they may well be, but we cannot know whether they are true" (Proust III 914). Truth, then, is both fortuitous and inevitable, and its exploration proceeds through chance encounters with signs that select the truth to be explored. To search for truth is to interpret signs, but the act of explicating the sign, of unfolding its hidden sense, is inseparable from the sign's own unfolding, its own self-development. In this sense, the search for truth is always temporal, "and the truth, always a truth of time" (PS 25; 17). Hence, Deleuze distinguishes four structures of time, each with its truth, which Marcel encounters in his apprenticeship in signs. "Time that passes" is one form of "lost time" (*temps perdu*), the time of alteration, aging, decay and destruction. Worldly signs betray this time in the obvious form of the physical decline of various social figures, but also in the changing modes and fashions that preoccupy polite society. The passage of time is also evi-dent in the signs of love and not simply because the beloved grows old. "If the signs of love and of jealousy bring with them their own alter-ation, it is for a simple reason: love never ceases to prepare for its own disappearance, to mime its own rupture" (PS 27; 18). And in sensual signs too the decay of time can be felt, as in Marcel's overwhelming anguish as he removes his boot and remembers his dead grandmother, in *Sodome et Gomorrhe* (Proust II 783). Only in the signs of art is the time that passes overcome. Lost time can also take the form of "the time one loses," the wasted time of worldly diversions, of failed loves and even of sensual indulgences in such trivialities as the taste of a madeleine. And yet attention to more serious matters does not necessarily lead to truth, for hard work and deep purpose belong to the will, and truth reveals itself through the contingent encounter with signs. The wasted time of worldly, amorous and sensual signs proves finally to be a necessary part of Marcel's apprenticeship, the mysterious means whereby an educa-tion in signs takes its course. "One never knows how someone learns: but however one learns, it is always through the intermediary of signs, in losing one's time, and not through the assimilation of objective con-tents" (PS 31; 21–22). A third form of time is "the time one regains" [*le temps qu'on retrouve*], and this is a time grasped only by the intelligence. Proust seemingly discounts the use of intelligence in the search for truth, but this is simply when intelligence operates on its own, seeking logical truths ungrounded in the necessity of an encounter with signs. When intelligence comes *after* an encounter with signs, it is the sole faculty capable of extracting the truth of the sign and hence the truth of time. "The impression is for the writer what experiment is for the scientist, with the difference that in the scientist the work of the intelligence precedes the experiment and in the writer it comes after the impression" (Proust III 914). Through retrospective analysis, the intelligence reveals that the empty signs of the world conform to general laws, the deceptive signs of love reiterate a repetitive theme and the ephemeral signs of involuntary memory disclose immaterial essences. In this sense, lost, wasted time becomes time one regains. But a fourth form of time exists in the work of art, "time regained" [*le temps retrouvé*], time in its pure form, whose truth transforms all worldly, amorous and sensuous signs. This pure time Marcel can only discover at the end of his search.

Marcel's apprenticeship involves four kinds of signs—worldly, amorous, sensual and artistic—and the course of his search is structured by four forms of time—the time that passes, the time one loses, the time one regains and regained time. It also finds its complex rhythms in necessary patterns of confusion and disappointment. Marcel inevitably misunderstands signs in two ways. First, he assumes that the object of the sign somehow holds its truth. He repeatedly sips his tea as if he could discover the secret of Combray in the bowl itself. He pronounces the name "Guermantes" over and over again, as if the syllables themselves held the prestige of Mme. de Guermantes. In his early encounters with the world, "he believes that those who emit signs are also those who understand and possess their code" (PS 38; 27). Such confusion is unavoidable, for perception naturally attributes the qualities of signs to the objects from which they originate. Desire, too, assumes that the object itself is desirable, and for that reason lovers seek to possess the beloved. And intelligence likewise has an inherent tendency toward objectivity in its belief that truth must be articulated and communicated. It is this prejudice that leads one to seek truth through conversation, friendship, work and philosophy—that is, through the good will and voluntary action of traditional discursive thought. But if a sign designates an object, it always signifies something else. Hence, Marcel is perpetually disappointed in the objects of his quest, in the entities designated by signs. For this reason, he frequently turns to a compensatory subjectivism, which constitutes the second error of his apprenticeship. If the secret of the sign is not in the object it designates, he thinks, perhaps it resides in a subjective association. But "everything is permissible in the exercise of associations" (PS 48; 35), anything may be linked to anything else. It may seem that involuntary memory teaches a lesson of subjective associationism, but if so, then the madeleine can show Marcel nothing about art, save that the power of the madeleine and the power of the Vinteuil sonata reside alike in arbitrary and ephemeral associations of a strictly personal and idiosyncratic nature. Such is not the case, however, for the secret of a sign lies in neither the designated object nor the interpreting subject, but in the essence enfolded in the sign.

What distinguishes the signs of art from other signs is that in art the sign is immaterial. True, the violin and piano emit the phrase of the Vinteuil sonata, but the artistic sign is an essence, an idea, not a material entity, despite its conveyance through a sonic medium.[1] In worldly, amorous and sensual signs, the meaning of the sign is found in something else, but "Art gives us veritable unity: the unity of an immaterial sign and a completely spiritual meaning" (PS 53; 40–41). Deleuze argues that for Proust, an essence is "a difference, the ultimate and absolute Difference" (PS 53; 41). Deleuze finds a first approximation of what this might mean in Marcel's remark that "style for the writer, no less than colour for the painter, is a question not of technique but of vision: it is the revelation, which by direct and conscious methods would be impossible, of the qualitative difference, the uniqueness of the fashion in which the world appears to each one of us, a difference which, if there were no art, would remain for ever the secret of every individual" (Proust III 931–32). Each individual expresses the world from a particular point of view, and "the point of view is difference itself, internal absolute difference" (PS 55; 42). Yet this does not amount to subjectivism, for the world that is expressed is not a function of the subject that expresses it. The subject does not produce the world and its internal absolute difference; the subject and the world emerge together through the unfolding of that difference. "It is not the subject that explicates the essence, it is rather the essence that implicates itself, envelops itself, rolls itself up in the subject" (PS 56; 43). Every subject is like a Leibnizian monad, which contains within itself the entire world, though in an obscure fashion. The world unfolds, explicates itself in monads, and the world is enfolded, implicated within each monad, the individual monad's expression of the world being limited by the illumination of its particular perspective. As Leibniz often remarks, the world is like a city and the monads its inhabitants, whose various views of the city are different views of the whole. But in Proust there is no "preestablished harmony" to ensure the unity of the world and its monads. Every subject expresses a different world, and only in art can these worlds be put in communication with one another. As Marcel remarks, "through art alone we are able to emerge from ourselves, to know what another person sees of a universe which is not the same as our own and of which, without art, the landscapes would remain as unknown to us as those that may exist in the moon. Thanks to art, instead of seeing one world only, our own, we see that world multiply itself and we have at our disposal as many worlds as there are original artists, worlds more different one from the other than those which revolve in infinite space" (Proust III 932).

When listening to the Vinteuil sonata's dialogue of piano and violin, Swann muses that "it was as at the beginning of the world, as if there were as yet only the two of them on the earth, or rather in this world closed to all the rest, so fashioned by the logic of its creator that in it there should never be any but themselves: the world of this sonata" (Proust I 382). Deleuze argues that for Proust every work of art is a beginning of the world, "a radical, absolute beginning" (PS 57; 44). In each work one finds what Marcel discerns in the faces of adolescent girls, "a play of unstable forces which recalls that perpetual re-creation of the primordial elements of nature which we contemplate when we stand before the sea" (Proust I 967). But in addition to a play of the unstable forces of primordial nature, a beginning of the world entails a beginning of time, and this is the time disclosed in the work of art—a qualitatively different form of time, the regained time, *le temps retrouvé*, of essences. Deleuze notes that some Neoplatonic philosophers designate an originary state of the world, before its unfolding in the act of creation, by the term *complicatio*, "the *complication* which envelops the multiple in the One and affirms the One of the multiple" (PS 58; 44). The *complicatio* is outside normal, chronological time, but it is not timeless; rather, it is "the complicated state of time itself" (PS 58; 45). The *complicatio* is time wrapped up within itself, a pure form of time, which subsequently unfolds itself in the various dimensions of actual temporal experience during the process of creation. The work of art is a radical, absolute beginning of the world, then, in the sense that the essence revealed in it effects "the perpetual re-creation of the primordial elements of nature," and in the sense that essence partakes of a *temps retrouvé*, a complicated time, or time as pure form, as condition of possibility of time.

How, then, are essences embodied in art?, asks Deleuze. Essence manifests itself in the physical materials of artworks, but "art is a veritable transmutation of matter" (PS 61; 46), and the means whereby art transmutes matter is style. In *Le temps retrouvé*, Marcel considers the way in which the heterogeneous sensations and associations of a particular moment combine present stimuli and past memories in a single experience. He reflects that the writer may describe in great detail the individual objects of a given scene, "but truth will be attained by him only when he takes two different objects, states the connection between them—a connection analogous in the world of art to the unique connection which in the world of science is provided by the law of causality—and encloses them in the necessary links of a well-wrought style; truth—and life too—can be attained by us only when, by comparing a quality common to two sensations, we succeed in extracting their common essence and in reuniting them to each other, liberated from the contingencies of time, within a metaphor" (Proust III 924–25). At its most fundamental level, then, style is metaphor, in that it forges the "necessary links" between different objects. But style is more than a mere play of words. The link between different objects is a common quality, which is the expression of an essence, "petrified in this luminous matter, plunged into this refracting milieu" (PS 61; 47). An essence is "the quality of an original world" (PS 61; 47), and through the "necessary links" of style an artist can "extract" from different objects "their common essence" and liberate them "from the contingencies of time." But Deleuze insists further that if style is metaphor, "metaphor is essentially metamorphosis" (PS 61; 47). If within matter art forges necessary links through common qualities, it also induces a transformation of matter. As in the paintings of Elstir, the sea becomes land and the land sea, the aqueous land forms and geological ocean waves functioning as pliable masses traversed by unfolding forces. Style, "in order to spiritualize matter and render it adequate to essence, reproduces the unstable opposition, the original complication, the struggle and exchange of primordial elements that constitute essence itself" (PS 62; 47).

If essence is a beginning of the world, it also is an ongoing power of creation. Essence is both an originary difference and an individualizing force, which "itself individualizes and determines the matters in which it incarnates itself, like the objects it encloses in the links of style" (PS 62; 48). Essence is a difference that repeats itself, a continuing process of self-differentiation and self-individuation that plays through the world that unfolds in the work of art. Difference and repetition, rather than opposing one another, "are the two powers [*puissances*] of essence, inseparable and correlative" (PS 63; 48). Difference, as quality of a world, "only affirms itself through a sort of auto-repetition that traverses various milieus and unites diverse objects; repetition constitutes the degrees of an original difference, but diversity also constitutes the levels of a no less fundamental repetition" (PS 63; 48). Essence, then, is a beginning of the world, a play of primordial elements and unstable forces in a complicated time, but also a beginning that continually repeats itself in an ongoing re-beginning of the world it causes to unfold. In the artwork, matter is transmuted, dematerialized and rendered adequate to essence. As a result, the signs of art are transparent; their meaning is the essence that plays through them. Style, as the artistic force that encloses signs in necessary links and transmutes matter, is one with essence, the power of difference and repetition that unfolds a world. "Identity of a sign, as style, and a meaning as essence: such is the characteristic of the work of art" (PS 64; 49). Buffon says that "le style, c'est l'homme même," but style is not simply the invention of the artist-subject. Style is the self-differentiating difference that unfolds itself in a world that includes the subject as point of view, that necessarily passes through the subject, but that far from originating in the subject, merely constitutes the subject as component of that world. In this sense, "style is not the man; style is essence itself" (PS 62; 48).

THE REINTERPRETATION OF SIGNS

If Marcel's apprenticeship in signs leads him from the material signs of the world, love and the senses to the immaterial signs of art, his full understanding of art in turn makes possible a new understanding of sensual, amorous and worldly signs. This is especially the case with the signs of involuntary memory, which only receive an adequate analysis in the last volume of the *Recherche*. Initially, it seems that involuntary memory is simply a matter of an unconscious association of ideas, a resemblance between a present and a past sensation. But the overwhelming joy Marcel experiences is more than the result of an encounter with a childhood reminiscence. First, it is a revelation of a different form of time, _"the being in itself of the past"_ (PS 72; 56). Deleuze argues that in this regard, Proust is Bergsonian.[2] Bergson notes that the present would never pass if it were a simple point in time. In order that the present move toward a future, there must be a continuity between any present moment and the moment immediately preceding it, a coexistence of present and past within an ongoing movement. From this, Bergson concludes that at every moment of the present there is a coexisting past moment, but he asserts further that the past moment is part of a single past that includes all past moments as a continuous, coexisting whole. The past is like a cone, whose base extends infinitely back in time and whose tip is its point of coexistence with the present. Yet if the past coexists with the present, the two exist in qualitatively different ways. The past has a virtual existence, whereas the present has an actual existence. Both are real, but the virtual past has never been actual. Hence, when one remembers, one does not bring into the present the trace of a moment that was once present and has now fallen into the past. Instead, one makes a qualitative leap into the field of the virtual past, where all past events coexist with one another in a single temporal dimension. This Bergsonian virtual past, Deleuze claims, is very much like the past Marcel explores through involuntary memory. "A moment of the past, did I say? Was it not perhaps very much more: something that, common both to the past and to the present, is much more essential than either of them?" (Proust III 905). In the simple present, the senses languish. "But let a noise or a scent, once heard or once smelt, be heard or smelt again in the present and at the same time in the past, real without being actual, ideal without being abstract, and immediately the permanent and habitually concealed essence of things is liberated" (Proust III 905-6). Involuntary memory, like the Bergsonian past, is "real without being actual, ideal without being abstract," an experience of a temporal dimension that exists "in the present and at the same time in the past." Through involuntary memory, a minute "has been freed from the order of time" (Proust III 906); access has been granted to "a fragment of time in the pure state" (Proust III 905).

But there is more to Proustian involuntary memory than the disclosure of a virtual past. There is also a revelation of essences as enfolded and unfolding differences. Rather than simply fashioning a resemblance between two sensations, involuntary memory reveals "a strict *identity*: the identity of a quality common to two sensations, or a sensation common to two moments, the present and the past" (PS 74; 58). When Marcel savors the madeleine, its taste is a quality common to two different moments. But he experiences more than a simple association of Combray and the taste of the madeleine. In the voluntary exercise of memory, the taste and the reminiscences of Combray are contiguous to one another, but external. Through involuntary memory, however, the context in which the madeleine was tasted in the past becomes internal to the present experience. Involuntary memory "internalizes the context, it renders the former context inseparable from the present sensation" (PS 75; 58). Combray surges forth within the present taste of the madeleine. In this sense, within the identity of a common quality—the taste of the madeleine—a difference is internalized, the past Combray as present. But that Combray is itself a difference, not the Combray as experienced in the past, but an essence of Combray, as it could never be experienced: "not in reality, but in its truth; not in its external and contingent relations, but in its internalized difference, in its essence" (PS 76; 59). Involuntary memory, then, is the analog of art, in that a necessary link between two different things is forged through a common quality, which internalizes their difference. The common quality proves to be an essence unfolding a world and "a fragment of time in the pure state." Yet the signs of involuntary memory differ from those of art in several ways. The matter in which they are embodied is more opaque, less pliable, than in art. They are tied to locales—Combray, Balbec, Venice—and specific sensory objects, and they are evanescent and difficult to sustain. The time they disclose points toward the complicated, originary time of art, but the time of involuntary memory is not the "regained time" of art. It "arises abruptly in a time already deployed, developed. At the heart of the time that passes, it rediscovers a center of envelopment, but this is only the image of original time" (PS 78; 61). Finally, whereas in works of art the selection and relation of different elements "are entirely determined by an essence that incarnates itself in a ductile or transparent medium," in involuntary memory relations depend on a contingent association.

"Thus essence itself is no longer master of its own incarnation, of its own selection, but is selected according to givens that remain external to it" (PS 80; 63).

The truth of signs is "fortuitous and inevitable" (Proust III 913), involuntary rather than freely chosen, necessary rather than contingent. In art, there is an adequation of sign and meaning; essence unfolds according to its inner necessity, and the world it discloses is not one the artist selects, but one that unfolds the artist as part of that inevitable world. And in this adequation of sign and meaning, essence singularizes, in that it produces a singular point of view, "individual and even individualizing" (PS 77; 60). Though sensual signs to a large extent are "fortuitous and inevitable," they are more contingent and general than the signs of art. The essences revealed by sensual signs depend on external circumstances for their selection, and the worlds they disclose are common worlds between two moments, slightly more general than the singular worlds of art.

In amorous and worldly signs, essences take on forms that are increasingly contingent and general, at their limit tending toward a "law." Essence discloses itself in amorous signs as a theme, a general motif that plays through the moments of love and arranges them in series. Marcel's loves of Gilberte, Mme. de Guermantes, Albertine, constitute "a series in which each term contains its small difference" (PS 85; 67). Each love also contains a series of subdivisions within it, Marcel loving a multiple succession of Albertines, his affections following a series of differential stages. And transsubjective series link various love relations as well, Swann's love of Odette forming part of the series that includes Marcel, Gilberte, Mme. de Guermantes and Albertine, in addition to the complex series involving Marcel and his mother. But the general law of love, its broadest serial truth, is revealed in the sequestration of the sexes, the partitioning of the worlds of Sodom and Gomorrah. The signs of love enfold the secrets of hidden worlds, and the secret of Albertine's lesbianism unveils for Marcel a proliferating series of homoerotic relations in the world of Gomorrah. In like manner, Charlus's meeting with Jupin discloses the parallel series of the world of Sodom. Yet within each individual, there is also a sequestration of the sexes, a primal hermaphrodism that universalizes the law of Sodom and Gomorrah. Every individual contains both sexes, like a hermaphroditic plant or snail, whose fertilization can only take place through an exter-

nal, contingent element. Even in heterosexual love, the woman functions as male for the man, the man serves as female for the woman.

A general theme, then, passes through a sequence of loves, a cascade of moments within the same love, and a transsubjective network
of reverberating loves; but at a global level, that theme echoes through
the reiterated series of homosexual loves that separate the sexes both
within society and within each individual. An essence reveals itself, but
in a confused, contingent form, and one that can be comprehended
only when the lover is no longer in love. The pain of jealousy compels
the lover to interpret amorous signs, but the joy of understanding only
arrives when the love has died. Essence remains an unconscious theme
within love, and "the selection of the essence which incarnates itself in
amorous signs depends on extrinsic conditions and subjective contingencies much more so than in sensual signs" (PS 93; 73). It is indeed the
Theme, or Idea, that "determines the series of our subjective states, but
also the chance events of our subjective relations that determine the
selection of the Idea" (PS 93; 73).

In worldly signs, essence finds its most general and contingent
embodiment, not in series, but in "the generality of the group" (PS 100;
79). At the end of the *Recherche*, the narrator remarks that in his por-
trayal of social manners, critics thought they saw a meticulous, micro-
scopic examination of details, "when on the contrary it was a telescope
that I had used to observe things which were indeed very small to the
naked eye, but only because they were situated at a great distance, and
which were each one of them in itself a world. Those passages in which
I was trying to arrive at general laws were described as so much pedan-
tic investigation of detail" (Proust III 1098–1099). A multiplicity of
events, be they political, historical, cultural or familial, occupies the
time of polite society, but ultimately the signs of the world are empty.
They simply hold the place of thoughts and actions, stand in for sentiments and ideas. They are finally signs of stupidity. "The stupidest people, in their gestures, their remarks, the sentiments which they
involuntarily express, manifest laws which they do not themselves perceive but which the artist surprises in them" (Proust III 938). A ritual
formalism prevails, and essence shows a certain comic power as it
loosely and broadly manifests itself in the world. Individuals repeat one
another's thoughts, and their clichéd opinions suggest group mentali-
ties, hidden affinities that the artist/analyst can extract. "There is a feel-

ing for generality which, in the future writer, itself picks out what is general and can for that reason one day enter into a work of art. And this has made him listen to people only when, stupid or absurd though they may have been, they have turned themselves, by repeating like parrots what other people of similar character are in the habit of saying, into birds of augury, mouthpieces of a psychological law" (Proust III 937).

Worldly signs initiate Marcel's apprenticeship, but their significance is only evident at the end of his search. Signs require a double reading, a first in terms of a progressive understanding, a second in terms of a retrospective comprehension. The unity of the *Recherche* Deleuze finds in Marcel's apprenticeship in signs. As he unfolds the signs of vapid, worldly exchange, the signs of deceptive, jealous love, the arresting signs of involuntary memory and the immaterial signs of art, he gradually comes to see signs as implicated essences. In his quest for the truth of signs, he discovers as well different forms of time, the time of decay, the time one wastes, the "fragment of time in a pure state" liberated in a sensate experience, the complicated, originary time of art. He passes through various disappointments and illusions, mistakenly locating the truth of signs in the objects they designate or the subjects who perceive them. But once the signs of art are comprehended, other signs are transformed. All signs implicate, enfold essences, though those essences are expressed in different signs at varying degrees of generality and contingency, in matter of diverse levels of malleability and resistance. In the work of art, an individualizing, singular difference repeats itself in a transmuted matter, disclosing an autonomous world and point of view. In the sensual sign, a common quality internalizes an essential local difference and a virtual past. In the signs of love, a general theme repeats itself in an individual's sequence of passions, in the subdivisions within a particular relationship, in transsubjective networks of affections and in the parallel series of the sequestrated sexes. And in worldly signs, essence reveals itself in the general laws of ritual form and broad group affinities.

In one sense, the unity Deleuze delineates is a thematic unity, the "thought" or "content" of the *Recherche*. In another, however, the unity of the apprenticeship in signs characterizes the *Recherche* in its "form" and its formation. The interpretation of signs is an unfolding and explicating of enfolded, implicated difference; but the interpretation of signs simply follows the course of the sign's own movement. "For the sign develops, unrolls itself at the same time that it is interpreted" (PS 110; 89). Marcel's explication of the signs of his apprenticeship is the unfolding of the signs of the *Recherche*, signs of art that disclose a singular world and point of view. An essence differentiates itself through a transmuted matter, transforming worldly, amorous and sensual signs into the signs of art, enclosing them in the necessary links of style. The world of essences disclosed to Marcel at the end of the novel *is* the *Recherche* that has unfolded in his search for the truth of signs. It is a truth *in* time, the course of a gradual revelation, a truth *about* time, in its multiple guises, and a truth *of* time, an artwork unfolding in its own complicated, originary time. "Thanks to art, instead of seeing one world only, our own, we see that world multiply itself and we have at our disposal as many worlds as there are original artists" (Proust III 932). One such world is the *Recherche*.

THE MULTIPLICATION AND PRODUCTION OF SIGNS

In 1970, Deleuze adds a second section to his study of Proust, turning his attention, he says, from the emission and interpretation of signs to the multiplication and production of signs. In part one he shows that the unity of the *Recherche* does not reside in involuntary memory but in the story of Marcel's apprenticeship in signs. Yet there is much that might be misunderstood in this statement. Is the *Recherche* simply a *Bildungsroman*, whose coherence stems from its narrative trajectory? Not if we mean that the novel's shape derives from a necessary or logical sequence of lessons. Deleuze systematizes the kinds of signs, the forms of time and the types of illusions that Marcel encounters, but Marcel's movement toward understanding proceeds by fits and starts, haphazard turns, regressions and reiterations, sporadic leaps and loops. And his retroactive reinterpretation of signs in the light of the revelation of art, besides forcing a rereading of the *Recherche*, offers no single map of the territory traversed but multiple possible reroutings. Is the *Recherche* then unified by a semiotic system? Not if we keep in mind that signs are hieroglyphs that enfold differences, that signs impinge on thought in a fortuitous yet inevitable fashion and that signs disclose not a common world of universal communication but singular worlds of art. And finally, is the *Recherche* in fact unified? An essence may be an individuating difference that repeats itself, and the world it unfolds may be singular, but is essence or that world One? What might it mean to speak of the *unity* of the signs of the *Recherche*, given the nature of signs as Deleuze describes them?

Proust's thought is an *antilogos*, Deleuze argues. The *logos*, the thought of the dominant Western philosophical tradition, always presumes a Whole that contains the Parts and a truth that precedes its decipherment. "To observe each thing as a whole, then to conceive of it in terms of its law as the part of a whole, the whole itself present through its Idea in each of its parts: is this not the universal logos, this taste for totalization?" (PS 127; 93–94). In the logos, intelligence always comes first, and no matter what path thought takes to the truth, thought only discovers what was there from the beginning. In Proust, by contrast, intelligence comes after, and there is no preexisting truth that thought rediscovers. There is, however, a degree of Platonism in Proust, Deleuze notes, but the differences between the two figures are instructive. Both are concerned with memory and essences, and both acknowledge the involuntary origin of genuine thought. In Book VII of the *Republic*, Socrates observes that thought is only provoked or awakened through contradictory perceptions, degrees of hardness and softness, or bigness and smallness, whereby one might say of the same thing that it is both hard and soft, big and small.[3] Yet this troubling fusion of qualities is identified as a state of the object, which imitates the Idea to a lesser or greater extent. The endpoint of rememoration is the Idea, a stable Essence that separates the contradictory qualities, and that endpoint is already presupposed at the onset of thought's encounter with the contradictory perception. In Proust, by contrast, the contradictory sensation is internal, not in objects or the world. Memory intervenes "because the quality is inseparable from a subjective chain of association, which we are not free to experiment with the first time we undergo it" (PS 132; 97). But the essence discovered is not subjective. It is not something viewed, "but a sort of superior *point of view*. An irreducible point of view, which signifies at once the birth of the world and the original character of a world" (PS 133; 98). The point of view is not that of an individual subject, but a principle of individuation. "Herein precisely lies the originality of Proustian reminiscence: it goes from a state of the soul, and of its associative chains, to a creative or transcendent point of view—and not, like Plato, from a state of the world to viewed objectivities" (PS 134; 98).

If Proustian reminiscence arrives at essence, it is not an essence as preexisting order. In Proust, the question of objectivity and unity raised by Plato receives what Deleuze identifies as a "modern" formulation, one that he sees as essential to modern literature. For the modern writer, there is no order in the states of the world, nor in the essences or Ideas that the world might be said to imitate. The world is fragmented and chaotic, and only in the work of art can a certain coherence be attained. "Precisely because reminiscence goes from subjective associations to an originary point of view, objectivity can no longer exist except in the work of art: it no longer exists in significant contents as states of the world, nor in ideal significations as stable essences, but solely in the formal signifying structure of the work, that is, in style" (PS 134; 98–99). In Proustian reminiscence, a chain of associations impinges on the subject. The chain of associations is pursued until it breaks, and then there is a leap outside the subject, and an individualizing point of view is established from which issues retrospectively an unfolding world that includes the subject and the chain of associations.

A part, or a fragment, Deleuze notes, can be of value because it refers to a whole, "or, on the contrary, because there is no other part which corresponds to it, no totality into which it can enter, no unity from which it has been wrested and to which it can be returned" (PS 136; 100). A work about Time cannot relate fragments to a whole, since time is untotalizable. Indeed, Deleuze asserts that time is best defined in terms of fragments and parts: "Perhaps this is what time is: the ultimate existence of parts of different sizes and forms which do not allow themselves to be adapted, which do not develop at the same rhythm, and which the flow of style does not carry along at the same speed" (PS 137; 101). If a unity exists in the work of art, it comes from the formal structure of the work, without external reference, and the element that produces the work's unity is itself a part. In *Le temps retrouvé*, Marcel finds enlightenment about involuntary memory in a line from Chateaubriand's *Mémoires d'Outre-tombe*: "A sweet and subtle scent of heliotrope was exhaled by a little patch of beans that were in flower; it was brought to us not by a breeze from our own country but by a wild Newfoundland wind [*par un vent sauvage de Terre-Neuve*], unrelated to the exiled plant, without sympathy of shared memory or pleasure" (Proust III 959). That which puts the subject and the heliotrope in contact with one another is without relation to the plant—a wind from a

New World. It is an anomalous part that connects other parts, without pertaining to a whole. In this consists Proust's modern conception of reminiscence: *"an anomalous associative chain is only unified by a creative point of view, which itself plays the role of anomalous part in the ensemble"* (PS 138; 102). The creative point of view, Deleuze indicates, is like a seed crystal ("like a fragment that determines a crystallization" [PS 138; 102]). There are certain chemical solutions that remain in a liquid state until an individual crystal is added to the solution. In some cases, the solution can form different crystals depending on the nature of the seed crystal introduced. Once the initial crystal is added, a process of crystallization begins, and a cascade of individuations transforms a metastable, amorphous medium into a stable crystalline solid.[4] What Bergotte admires in Vermeer's *View of Delft* is not its unity, but the "little patch of yellow wall, with a sloping roof" (Proust III 185); Swann and Odette value the "little bit" of the phrase from the Vinteuil sonata (Proust I 238); Marcel focuses on the detail of the dragons carved on the capital of the Balbec cathedral. If there is a unity in these artworks, it comes not from a preconceived plan or an organic necessity, but from the anomalous parts, which like seed crystals induce a process of transformation and reconfiguration.

Rather than focus on the Whole, Deleuze insists that an analysis of the *Recherche* begin with its parts: "the disparity, the incommensurability, the disintegration of the parts of the *Recherche*, with their ruptures, hiatuses, lacunae, intermittences that guarantee its ultimate diversity" (PS 140; 103). Two basic figures characterize the relationships between the work's parts: boxes and closed vessels, the first concerning the relation *contents-container*, the second the relation *parts-whole*. Signs are like unopened boxes with hidden contents, their secrets encased, enveloped, enfolded within. This is the figure of implication and explication that Deleuze explores at length in the first part of his study. But what he stresses in the second half is the lack of common measure between contents and container and the fragmentation that affects both contents and container in the process of interpretation. The boxes to be opened include things, beings and names—the madeleine, Albertine, the word *Balbec*, for example. The box of the madeleine is actually not the madeleine itself, but its sensual quality, its flavor, and its content is not the chain of associations surrounding Combray, but the essence of Combray as it has never been lived. Though the content unfolds from the container, the emergence of Combray as essence entails a break in the associative chain and the spontaneous appearance of a pure point of view, outside that of the empirical subject. The memory of Combray is so distant that its supposed revival is actually a new creation, from which a resurrected self arises. Combray as essence is thus incommensurable with the box from which it issues forth. The box of Albertine contains the landscape of Balbec, while at the same time the Balbec landscape encases Albertine. But again, "the chain of associations only exists in relation to a force that will break it" (PS 145; 107), for the narrator, the self that opens the box, finds himself captured by the world he unfolds, placed in the landscape and emptied of self. A superior, non-personal point of view arises from the rupture in the associative chain, as the world that includes Albertine, the landscape and the dispossessed Marcel unfolds. The box of *Balbec* contains the mystery of the place, but when Marcel projects that content on the real city, as inevitably he must, the link between the syllables and their hidden secret is broken.[5] In all three instances, the content is incommensurable with the container: "*a lost content*, which one regains in the splendor of an essence that resuscitates a former self, *an emptied content*, which brings with it the death of the self, *a separated content*, which throws us into an inevitable disappointment" (PS 147; 108). In each case the content explodes the container, but in each also the content shatters as it unfolds. Even in the great work of art, such as the Vinteuil septet, the content sustains a conflict of parts: "A phrase of a plaintive kind rose in answer to it, but so profound, so vague, so internal, almost so organic and visceral, that one could not tell at each of its re-entries whether it was a theme or an attack of neuralgia. Presently these two motifs were wrestling together in a close embrace [*les deux motifs luttèrent ensemble dans un corps à corps*] in which at times one of them would disappear entirely, and then only a fragment of the other could be glimpsed" (Proust III 262).

The second figure Deleuze delineates is that of the *vase clos*, the French term for a chemical retort, or sealed glass vessel. Marcel remarks that the "Méséglise way" and the "Guermantes way" existed "far apart from one another and unaware of each other's existence, in the airtight compartments of separate afternoons [*inconnaissables l'un à l'autre, dans les vases clos et sans communication, entre eux d'après-midi différents*]" (Proust I 147). In *Le temps retrouvé*, Marcel observes of the multiple associations inseparable from a given sensation that "the simplest act or gesture remains immured as within a thousand sealed vessels [*comme dans mille vases clos*], each one of them filled with things of a colour, a scent, a temperature that are absolutely different one from another, vessels, moreover, which being disposed over the whole range of our years, during which we have never ceased to change if only in our dreams and our thoughts, are situated at the most various moral altitudes and give us the sensation of extraordinarily diverse atmospheres" (Proust III 903). The sealed vessel "*marks the opposition of a part with a vicinity without communication [un voisinage sans communication]*" (PS 149; 110), each vessel like the Méséglise way or the Guermantes way, a distinct element contiguous to another element, enclosed hermetically and separate from the other, and yet determined in its situation through a relation of non-communication. Though self-enclosed, however, the sealed vessel does not itself constitute a whole. Each vessel is capable of splitting into other vessels, each world into subworlds, each Albertine into micro-Albertines, each self into multiple selves. Hence, the identity of a given sealed vessel is "only statistical" (PS 152; 112), determined by the percentage of aggregate elements dominant in a particular mixture. Yet, though each vessel exists in a "vicinity without communication," nonetheless movement between vessels is possible through *transversals*, "those star-shaped cross-roads in a forest where roads converge that have come, in the forest as in our lives, from the most diverse quarters" (Proust III 1082–3). The Méséglise and Guermantes ways were separate worlds for Marcel, "and then between these two high roads a network of transversals was set up" (Proust III 1083). But transversals do not totalize or unify; rather, they open passages that affirm difference. As Marcel says of a railway trip, "the specific attraction of a journey lies not in our being able to alight at places on the way and to stop altogether as soon as we grow tired, but in its making the difference between departure and arrival not as imperceptible but as intense as possible" (Proust I 693). The journey, then, is the transversal of places, a passage that renders maximum intensity to the difference between multiple locations.

To interpret signs that are boxes is to open them and unfold their contents, but to interpret sealed vessel signs is to choose from among those vessels connected through transversals, "to elect, to choose a non-communicating part, a closed vessel, with the self which is found therein" (PS 154; 113). The purest form of this choice occurs when one awakens from sleep. Sleep is the transversal that connects multiple moments, that makes multiple worlds and selves spin in a circle around the sleeper. Upon awakening, the sleeper chooses a self and world. "One is no longer a person. How then, searching for one's thoughts, one's personality, as one searches for a lost object, does one recover one's own self rather than any other? Why, when one begins again to think, is it not a personality other than the previous one that becomes incarnate in one. One fails to see what dictates the choice, or why, among the millions of human beings one might be, is it on the being one was the day before that unerringly one lays one's hand" (Proust II 86). And who chooses? Not the self that is chosen. Rather, an apersonal choice, a pure act of interpretation, takes place. "Then from those profound slumbers we awake in a dawn, not knowing who we are, being nobody, newly born, ready for anything, the brain emptied of that past which was life until then. . . . Then, from the black storm through which we seem to have passed (but we do not even say *we*), we emerge prostrate, without a thought, a *we* that is void of content" (Proust II 1014). The "we that is void of content" is the interpreter, the selection that selects a closed vessel and the self within, but also the selection that confirms a transversal that connects closed vessels without unifying them. "The 'subject' of the *Recherche* finally is no self, but this *we* without content that distributes Swann, the narrator, Charlus, distributes them or chooses them without totalizing them" (PS 156; 114).

Boxes are figures of the incommensurability of containers and contents, yet such that the contents reside within the containers; closed vessels are figures of noncommunication, yet such that vessels are in the vicinity of one another. A force of incommensurability holds containers and contents together, a force of noncommunication connects vessels in a vicinity. And both those forces are the forces of time, "this system of non-spatial distances, this distance proper to the contiguous itself, to the content itself, *distances without intervals*" (PS 156; 115). Lost time introduces distances between the contiguous, as when one forgets and can no longer bring once-related things together. Regained time brings distant things in contiguity with one another, as when one resurrects a long-lost memory and revives it in the present. But in both cases, a contiguous distance is maintained, a distance without interval, and this is precisely what a transversal is—a passage without interval that affirms a difference. Time, then, as the system of distances without interval, is the true interpreter and the great transversal: "time, the ultimate interpreter, the ultimate act of interpretation, has the strange power of simultaneously affirming pieces which do not form a whole in space, any more than they form a whole through succession in time. Time is exactly the transversal of all possible spaces, including the spaces of time" (PS 157; 115).

MACHINES

In the explication of the contents of a box-sign, a break in an associative chain takes place, and an apersonal point of view emerges, from which a self and world unfold. In the choice of a closed vessel, a "we without content" selects and reveals a network of transversals. Both the apersonal point of view and the "we without content" produce something, a truth that pertains to signs but does not preexist their interpretation. To interpret is neither to discover something that is already there, nor to create something *ex nihilo*; rather, it is to produce an effect, to make something happen. In this regard, the modern work of art "is essentially productive, productive of certain truths" (PS 176; 129). In that it is essentially productive, says Deleuze, the modern work of art is a machine, something that does not mean so much as it *works*, as it does something. "To the *logos*, organ and organon whose meaning must be discovered in the whole to which it belongs, is opposed the anti-logos, machine and machinery whose meaning (whatever you want) depends solely on its functioning, and its functioning on its detached pieces. The modern work of art has no problem of meaning, only a problem of usage" (PS 176; 129).

The *Recherche* is a machine, a producer of truths, and the production of truths takes place through the interpretation of signs. To interpret is to produce thought within thought, to put thought into motion through the disorienting impingement of a sign. "Imagination, the reflective faculty [*la pensée*] may be admirable machines in themselves but they may also be inert. Suffering sets them in motion" (Proust III 946). The sign produces thought, instigates interpretation, but interpretation in turn produces apersonal points of view from which truths emerge. In the *Recherche*, those truths are truths of time. Deleuze identifies four kinds of time in the first part of his study, two types of *temps perdu*—the time that passes and the time one loses—and two types of *temps retrouvé*—the time one regains and regained time. In part two, however, he asserts that the movement of the text forces us to isolate three orders of time: the lost time most clearly evident in the proliferating series and general laws of amorous and worldly signs, the regained time of essences as disclosed in artworks and involuntary memories; and the time of "*universal* alteration, death and the idea of death, the production of catastrophe (signs of aging, illness, death)" (PS 179; 132).

To each of these orders of time and their orders of truth corresponds a machine. The first machine produces the truths of lost time, the truths of general series and laws, but it does so only through the fragmentation of objects, through the production of heterogeneous boxes and closed vessels, "a production of *partial objects* as they have been defined previously, fragments without totality, disintegrated parts, vessels without communication, sequestered scenes" (PS 180; 133). The first machine, then, produces partial objects and the related truths of series and groups. The second machine produces resonances, most notably in involuntary memory, when two moments are put in resonance with one another, but also in art, as in the Vinteuil sonata when the violin and piano echo one another, or in the Vinteuil septet when the instruments engage in their "*corps-à-corps*." The second machine, however, does not depend on the first, thereby merely setting the first machine's partial objects in vibratory communication. Each machine forms its own fragments and its own order of truth and time. The first produces series and laws along with partial objects, whereas the second machine produces "the singular Essence, the Point of View superior to the two moments that resonate" (PS 183; 134), as well as the pieces that interact and the full time with which they are imbued. The third machine produces the truths of universal decay and the idea of death through a forced movement that makes time itself palpable. At the end of the *Recherche*, Marcel finds the greatest challenge to his artistic project in the ubiquitous catastrophe of inevitable decline and death, an order of time that seems totally unproductive and capable of obliterating everything produced by the other two machines. What Marcel finally discovers, however, is the *idea* of death and a third experience of time. In contemplating the aged men and women he had known decades earlier, Marcel senses a sudden dilation of time as the past figures he had remembered are pushed back "into a past that was more than remote, that was almost unimaginable," a past that makes him "think of the vast periods which must have elapsed before such a revolution could be accomplished in the geology of a face" (Proust III

982–83). The past and present undergo a forced movement of mutual repulsion, and in the great space of this dilated time, a confusion sets in whereby one can no longer tell the living from the dead. "In these regions of advanced age death was everywhere at work and had at the same time become more indefinite" (Proust III 1025), the uncertainty of who is still living and who already dead making of the living and dead alike simply one species of beings in a perpetual process of dying. Yet the inhabitants of this time also grow to enormous proportions as they occupy this dilated time, "for simultaneously, like giants plunged into the years, they touch epochs that are immensely far apart, separated by the slow accretion of many, many days" (Proust II 1107). And time, "which by Habit is made invisible," is suddenly allowed "to become visible" (Proust III 964). Universal decay, then, does not prove to be the totally unproductive catastrophe it at first appeared to be, for the third machine does produce something—an idea of death, a sensible revelation of time as a forced movement of maximal dilation.

Proust's great achievement, Deleuze argues, is not simply to have discovered these three machines, with their diverse orders of truth and time, but to have internalized their effect and operation within the work of art. This is especially the case with the second machine, for many writers besides Proust have focused their attention on sensual ecstasies and transcendent moments of revelation. Yet in Proust the second machine functions not simply as a means of isolating transformative sensual experiences, but as a properly literary machine. In the closing pages of the *Recherche*, involuntary memories arrive at an accelerating pace, the uneven paving stones, the clink of a serving spoon and the feel of a stiff napkin punctuating Marcel's reflections, as if the second machine had at last reached its optimal level of operation. Not simply a means of linking the writer with extraliterary experiences, the proliferating involuntary memories are disclosed as effects within the work of literature. "*It is the work of art that produces in itself and on itself its own effects, and fills itself with them, feeds itself on them*: it feeds itself on the truths that it engenders" (PS 185; 136). If this were not the case, there would be no need for art, for there would be nothing that the work of art could add to such ecstatic experiences as involuntary memories. But what art furnishes is an autonomous and self-determined production of resonances, a generative process that depends on no external circumstances or involuntary impositions for its continuation. "But in the end, one sees what art can

add to nature: it produces resonances themselves, because *style* makes
any two objects resonate and disengages from them a 'precious image,'
substituting for the determined conditions of a natural unconscious product the free
conditions of an artistic production" (PS 186; 137).

Proust's literary machines not only feed on themselves, thereby creating internal effects, but also act on the world outside, producing
effects in readers. The book Marcel plans to write would make of its
readers "readers of their own selves, my book being merely a sort of
magnifying glass like those which the optician at Combray used to
offer his customers—it would be my book, but with its help I would fur-
nish them with the means of reading what lay inside themselves. So
that I should not ask them to praise me or to censure me, but simply to
tell me whether 'it really is like that,' I should ask them whether the
words that they read within themselves are the same as those which I
have written" (Proust III 1089). The great painter or great writer "proceeds on the lines of the oculist," Marcel observes at another point,
such that the world around us "appears to us entirely different from
the old world, but perfectly clear" (Proust III 338). Renoir once was difficult to interpret, but now one can see the world as a Renoir painting.
"Women pass in the street, different from those we formerly saw,
because they are Renoirs, those Renoirs we persistently refused to see as
women. The carriages, too, are Renoirs, and the water, and the sky. . . .
Such is the new and perishable universe which has just been created"
(Proust II 338-39). Thus, the *Recherche* is a machine that produces
effects both on itself and on its readers, generating the materials of its
own construction and those of another world, a Proustian universe
"entirely different from the old world, but perfectly clear."

Three machines function in the *Recherche*, a partial object machine,
a resonance machine and a forced movement machine, the three
together producing internal, self-generative effects and external effects
on readers. But what holds the machines together, what gives this
assemblage of machines its unity? The essential point, says Deleuze, "is
that the parts of the *Recherche* remain broken, fragmented, *without any-*
thing being lacking" (PS 193; 142-43). If we look to the Essence of the
Recherche for its unity, we find only an additional part, for the essence,
the "individuating point of view superior to the individuals themselves,
appears *alongside* the chains, incarnated in a closed part, *adjacent* to that
which it dominates, *contiguous* to that which it makes visible" (PS 194;

143). Further, the essence of a work of art is a difference that repeats itself, a point of view that in individuating itself fractures into multiple points of view. Nor is the unity of the *Recherche* to be found in its style, for style is "the explication of signs, at different speeds of development, following associative chains proper to each of them, attaining for each of them the point of rupture of the essence as Point of view" (PS 199; 147). Style is the process of the unfolding of signs, and it generates effects through the three machines, producing partial objects, resonances and forced movements, but style is not itself a totalizing force. The *Recherche* does have a unity, but a unity of its particular assemblage of fragments, a "One and Whole which would function as effect, effect of machines, rather than act as principles" (PS 195–96; 144). Marcel remarks in *La prisonnière* that the great works of the nineteenth century are "always incomplete" (Proust III 157), yet they somehow possess a kind of retrospective unity. Balzac's *Comédie humaine* was constructed in pieces, with no controlling plan and no organic necessity, yet at the end of the process Balzac looked on his books and decided "that they would be better brought together in a cycle in which the same characters would reappear, and touched up his work with a swift brushstroke, the last and the most sublime. An ulterior unity, but not a factitious one. . . . Not factitious, perhaps indeed all the more real for being ulterior, for being born of a moment of enthusiasm when it is discovered to exist among fragments which need only to be joined together; a unity that was unaware of itself, hence vital and not logical, that did not prohibit variety, dampen invention. It emerges (but applied this time to the work as a whole) like such and such a fragment composed separately" (Proust III 158). The unity effect is an aftereffect, a last stroke of the brush that induces a retrospective unification, as a seed crystal induces a process of crystallization that transforms a metastable chemical solution into a particular configuration of stable forms. The last stroke is like an individuating essence, and like style (for in the work of art there is a full adequation of essence and style), an added part that institutes an aftereffect of a unity of the multiplicity. But what makes possible such an effect is an interconnection of the parts, a means of communication between noncommunicating closed vessels and boxes with incommensurable contents. Deleuze argues that in the modern artwork, since the world exists as a fragmented chaos, the "very special mode of unity irreducible to any 'unification'" can arise only from "the formal structure of the

work of art, insofar as it does not refer to anything else" (PS 201; 149).
But that formal structure consists of a network of transversals, distances without interval that affirm the differences they connect.[6]
Transversals connect the Méséglise and Guermantes ways, yet without
fusing them; they connect the two sexes, yet with each hermaphroditic
individual maintaining his or her sequestrated sexes; they connect fragmenting series, resonating sensual and artistic moments, and dilating
expanses of decay, yet without dissolving their distinctions and divi-
sions. "The new linguistic convention, the formal structure of the work,
is thus transversality, which traverses every sentence, which goes from
one sentence to another in the entire work, and which even unites the
book of Proust to those he loved, Nerval, Chateaubriand, Balzac . . . For
if a work of art communicates with a public, and even gives rise to a
public, if it communicates with other works by other artists, and gives
rise to those to come, it is always in this dimension of transversality,
where unity and totality are established for themselves, without unifying or totalizing objects or subjects" (PS 202; 149–50).

The difference between parts one and two of Deleuze's study of Proust,
between the "emission and interpretation of signs" and the "multiplication and production of signs," is finally one of degree and emphasis
rather than substance. The emphasis in the first part is on what one
might regard as a reader's activity, that of receiving and processing
signs, whereas part two would seem to stress the writer's activity of generating and configuring signs. Yet the interpretation of signs proves to
be an unfolding of signs, and that unfolding simply follows the sign's
own explication of itself. The interpreter's explication of a sign is insti-
gated by the sign's impingement on the interpreter, and the final interpretation of signs through the work of art involves the establishment
of an apersonal point of view from which unfolds a world that includes
the interpreter as a constituent component. One can say, then, that the
sign produces the onset of interpretation, produces each moment of
the process of interpretation and produces the interpreter as element of
an explicating world. It would seem inevitable, therefore, that an
apprenticeship in signs would lead not simply to the revelation of art as
the truth of signs, but also to the vocation of the interpreter as artist, as
active and autonomous producer of signs. Yet if Deleuze speaks of the
production of signs throughout *Proust et les signes*, he adds a crucial con-

cept in part two that helps dispel possible misunderstandings—the concept of the machine. Interpretation generally implies meaning, and though Deleuze stresses in part one that interpretation is not decoding but unfolding, there is always the danger that explication will be seen as an uncovering of the deep, hidden meaning of the sign. With the notion of the machine, however, Deleuze makes it clear that signs have no deep significance but only a function, and that function has no purpose other than to operate and produce effects. In the *Recherche*, there are indeed truths of signs and their orders of time, but these are produced by machines—the partial object machine, the resonance machine and the forced movement machine. The "meaning" of a sign may reside in the apersonal point of view from which it issues, but that "meaning" finally is simply a difference that repeats itself, a force of individuation and differentiation—again, a machine.

If there is a purpose to the production of signs, it would seem to lie in the work of art, in that for the modern artist, the world is a fragmented chaos, and the only wholeness and unity available is that which may be constructed in art. But Deleuze is not advocating any salvation through art, nor is he embracing a conventional aestheticism or formalism. The work of art does not stand over against the world as an independent creation. It is produced through an engagement with the unfolding signs of the world, and it functions in the world as an effect-producing machine, a machine that turns readers into "readers of themselves," that brings into existence a universe "entirely different from the old world, but perfectly clear." The work of art has a unity, perhaps, but it is a unity *of* a given multiplicity. Unity is an effect produced by an added part—a final brushstroke, an apersonal point of view, a seed crystal—an element that retroactively induces a whole as result rather than cause. The formal principle of that whole is transversality, the distance without interval that interconnects incommensurable and non-communicating parts and intensifies their differences rather than suppressing them. The order of art, then, is no retreat from the world, but a response in kind, the production of a world of transversally connected fragments that unfold from a self-repeating difference. The modern work of art is a Joycean "chaosmos," a chaos-become-cosmos, but a particular cosmos constructed according to the formal principles of chaos, the singular, individual cosmos of the artist, but one produced through the same explication of multiplicity that operates throughout the chaotic world.

Chapter Three

KAFKA'S LAW MACHINE

In part two of *Proust and Signs,* Deleuze asserts that the *Recherche* is a machine, thereby stressing the work's function as a force of production. The *Recherche* produces truths, neither discovering preexisting truths nor creating them *ex nihilo,* but bringing them forth through an experimentation on the real; and it produces effects, both within the work itself and in readers. In *Kafka: Toward a Minor Literature* (1975), Deleuze and Guattari develop further the notion of the machine, treating the entirety of Kafka's work as a "literary machine, a writing machine or expression machine" (K 52; 29). In *Kafka,* however, the focus is less on the problem of the transversal unity of multiplicity than on the question of the literary machine's effect within the real. Kafka is a practitioner of "minor literature," Deleuze and Guattari claim, a literature immediately social and political, affected by a high level of linguistic deterritorialization and expressive of a collective assemblage of enunciation. Kafka's literary machine is a minor machine, one whose components include his diaries, letters, short stories and novels, and whose function discloses "diabolic powers to come or revolutionary forces to be constructed" (K 33; 18). It is also a desiring machine, whose proliferating series, connectors and blocks transmit flows and intensities, induce movements and open lines of flight. In this chapter we will examine the concept of the machine—desiring machines, celibate machines, law machines, writing machines. In the next chapter, we will turn to the concept of minor literature.

DESIRING MACHINES AND DESIRING PRODUCTION

In his 1970 addendum to *Proust and Signs*, Deleuze remarks that the *Recherche*, like other modern artworks, does not mean so much as it functions: "The modern work of art has no problem of meaning [*sens*], it has only a problem of usage" (PS 176; 129). The analyst's job is not to uncover the hidden significance of the work but to describe its constituent parts and their operation. In this regard, the work of art is a machine, something, it would seem, with no depth or soul, only a device that either works or doesn't. The concept of the machine is not Deleuze's central concern in *Proust and Signs*, however, and only in *Anti-Oedipus* (1972) does the concept receive extended treatment. Here, it is not just the artwork that is identified as a machine, but everything in the world. "Everywhere there are machines, not at all metaphorically: machines of machines, with their couplings, their connections. An organ-machine is plugged into a source-machine: one emits a flux, the other cuts it" (AO 7; 1). These machines are "desiring machines," components of a universal process of "desiring production," by which term Deleuze and Guattari mean a ubiquitous activity suffused with affect.[1] In a rather playful response to the Freudian division of the psyche into id, ego and superego, Deleuze and Guattari identify the three basic components of desiring production as desiring machines, the body without organs and the nomadic subject, each of which is associated with a specific phase of desiring production—the production of production (desiring machines), the production of inscription (the body without organs) and the production of consumption/consummation (the nomadic subject). A simple model of desiring machines is that of an infant feeding at the mother's breast. A mouth-machine is coupled to a breast-machine, a flow of milk passing from the breast-machine to the mouth-machine. The infant's mouth-machine is in turn coupled to the various machines of the alimentary canal (an esophagus-machine, a stomach-machine, an intestinal-machine, a urethra-machine, an anus-machine), the flow of nutrients gradually being converted into various energy circuits of collateral desiring-machines (circulatory, neural, hormonal, etc.) within the infant's body, emerging eventually as flows of excretions. The flow of milk from the breast-machine itself issues from an alimentary circuit that extends to the multiple nutrients that enter into the mother's mouth-machine. Desiring machines, then, are coupled to one another in chains or circuits through which flows pass, each circuit extending into other circuits that spread in ever-widening networks of activity (e.g., the multiple circuits inherent in the production of the mother's nutrients, or the microbial circuits involved in the decomposition of the infant's excretions).

The infant's mouth-machine, however, is not simply an eating-machine. It is also a breathing-machine, a spitting-machine, a crying-machine, and so forth. In this sense, every desiring machine has "a sort of code that is engineered [*machiné*], stockpiled in it" (AO 46; 38), a switching mechanism that determines the specific circuit within which it functions at a given time. Further, no circuit of desiring machines exists in isolation from other circuits, the infant's alimentary circuit, for example, being connected to ocular circuits (the infant's eye-machine focused on a livingroom lamp, say), olfactory circuits (the nose-machine coupled to flows of kitchen odors), tactile circuits (epidermal machines in touch with heat, fabrics, flesh, mists, air currents). If one were to inscribe all these circuits as so many lines on a single surface, the grid-like surface would constitute a body without organs, a single map of coexisting circuits (in our example, alimentary, ocular, olfactory and tactile circuits) and alternating, disjunctive circuits (alimentary, breathing, crying circuits). The body without organs, it should be noted, is not to be confused with a unified psychic body image. First, its circuits extend indefinitely beyond any empirical body contour. If we speak loosely of the "infant's" body without organs, for instance, we must include within that body without organs the mother's breast, the living room lamp, the kitchen odors, the microbes converting food into nutrients and waste, and so on. Second, it does not constitute a unity in any conventional sense of the term. It includes within it conjunctions *and* disjunctions, heterogeneous circuits that in some instances coexist and cofunction, and in others succeed, supplant or counteract one another. Desiring production "is pure multiplicity, that is, affirmation irreducible to unity," and if we encounter a "whole" in the body without organs, it is a "totality alongside the parts, it is a whole *of* the parts, but which does not totalize them, a unity *of* the parts, but which does not unify them, and which is added to them as a new part constructed apart" (AO 50; 42).[2] Third, it is not a mere fantasy or mental image. Rather, it is a virtual entity, real without being actual. In one sense, it is produced by the desiring machines as an aftereffect, yet in another, it is the condition of possibility that precedes the functioning of the desiring machines, the grid of potential circuits that any given chain of desiring machines might actualize at a specific time.

From the interaction of the desiring machines and the body without organs arise what we might label two compound machines, the "paranoiac machine" and the "miraculating machine." The body without organs is not so much without organs as it is without regular, fixed organization. It is an antiorganism, a mode of disjunctive synthesis, a machine of antiproduction that constantly breaks down, stutters, freezes and collapses, thereby disconnecting and disrupting circuits of desiring machines, and yet at the same time a machine that puts various desiring machines in relation with one another in multiple, transversally connected circuits. The paranoiac machine is produced when the desiring machines repel the body without organs as an impending totality, as a persecutory order that they ward off as they break into discontinuous pieces. The miraculating machine appears when the desiring machines attract the body without organs, as if they were emanations of its marvelous surface.[3] Since the body without organs produces both disjunction and synthesis, both decomposition and composition, the paranoiac machine and the miraculating machine coexist as infinitely oscillating states of desiring production that are constantly fed back into one another.

The third component of desiring production is the nomadic subject, "a strange subject, without fixed identity, wandering over the body without organs, always alongside the desiring machines, defined by the portion it takes of what is produced, gathering everywhere the reward of a becoming or an avatar, born of the states it consumes and reborn with each new state" (AO 23; 16). If the body without organs is seen as a surface gridded by circuits of desiring machines, the nomadic subject is an errant point flashing here and there along the various paths inscribed on the surface, an adjunct machine of *consommation* (in French, both economic consumption and libidinal consummation).[4] The nomadic subject is created through the formation of a third compound machine—a "celibate machine," "a new alliance between the desiring machines and the body without organs that gives birth to a new humanity or a glorious organism" (AO 24; 17). What the celibate machine produces are "intensive quantities in a pure state, to the point of being almost unbearable—a celibate misery and glory endured to the highest point, like a cry suspended between life and death, a feeling of intense passage, states of pure and raw intensity stripped of their shape and their form" (AO 25; 18). The body without organs constitutes a zero-degree of intensity, the desiring machines marking various levels of affective intensity in their functioning. In the paranoiac machine, the desiring machines and the body without organs repel one another, and in the miraculating machine they attract one another, but in both cases the desiring machines determine positive levels of intensity. In the oscillation between repulsion and attraction, differences in levels of intensity arise, passages from one state of intensity to another, and at each such passage a nomadic subject emerges, and with it a new relation between desiring machines and the body without organs, a new functioning that "reconciles" the repulsion and attraction of the paranoiac and miraculating machines in the formation of a celibate machine.[5] "In short, the opposition of the forces of attraction and repulsion produces an open series of intensive elements, all positive, which never express the final equilibrium of a system, but an unlimited number of stationary metastable states through which a subject passes" (AO 26; 19).

WHAT IS A MACHINE?

We will return to the notion of the celibate machine, but first we must explore a bit further the concept of the machine itself. After delineating the three basic components of desiring production, Deleuze and Guattari ask, "in what sense are desiring machines truly machines, independent of any metaphor?" (AO 43; 36). A machine, they assert, "is defined as a *system of cuts* [*système de coupures*]" (AO 43; 36), and three different kinds of cuts pertain to the three components of desiring production: the portioning-cut [*coupure-prélèvement*] of desiring machines, the detachment-cut [*coupure-détachement*] from which issues the body without organs and the remainder-cut [*coupure-reste*] that produces the nomadic subject.[6] Every machine is first of all "in relation with a continuous material flow (*hylè*) into which it slices" (AO 43; 36). The infant's mouth-machine, for example, cuts into the flow of milk, its anus-machine cuts into the flow of excretion. Yet though we speak of machine and flow as separate entities, they actually constitute a single process. From the vantage of the infant's mouth-machine, the mother's breast-machine is a source of flow, just as the mouth-machine is a source of flow for the stomach-machine. "In short, every machine is a cut in the flow in relation to that to which it is connected, but it is also itself a flow or a production of flow in relation to the [next] machine connected to it" (AO 44; 36). Hence, Deleuze and Guattari speak of systems of "cut-flows," or "schiz-flows," circuits of matter-flow punctuated by various relays and processing stations along the flow. That matter-flow is *hylè* [Greek: matter], an ideal "continuous infinite flow" (AO 44; 36), which is clearly not restricted to a flow of positivistic brute matter, but that includes as well flows of energy (as in some ecological models), information (as defined in certain forms of information theory and systems theory) and signs (as characterized in various semiotic models, especially those of a Peircean orientation). Each flow is ideal in that it must be conceived of as "pure continuity" (AO 44; 36), a single, constant flow without beginning or end, and in that its continuity is not opposed to the action of cutting, for the cut "implies or defines that which it cuts as ideal continuity" (AO 44; 36). What this means is that the cut performs a connective synthesis, thereby bringing elements into relationship with one another through a common flow, one element emitting a flow, a second cutting that flow, but in so doing, emitting a flow that a third cuts, and so on, the sequence of flow-cuts constituting an ideal, open-ended linkage of elements that is strictly additive in nature (a + b + c + x + . . . , "and then, and then, and then . . . " [AO 44; 36]). This first cut of the machine, then, the portioning-cut [*coupure-prélèvement*], performs the paradoxical function of connecting by cutting, of establishing a continuity through a break, a schiz-flow of multiple elements operating within a single, unlimited process.

The second cut, the detachment-cut [*coupure-détachement*], creates a disjunctive synthesis, a relation of the type "a *or* b *or* c *or* x *or* . . . ," but such that the disjunctions are inclusive rather than exclusive, no alternative excluding another, each element affirmed as it is differentiated. These inclusive disjunctions together comprise the grid of the body without organs. As we will recall, every machine has varied functions and participates in multiple networks of activity; hence, each machine contains "a sort of code that is engineered [*machiné*], stockpiled in it" (AO 46; 38). The mouth-machine cuts various flows—food, liquid, air— and each of these cuts may be associated in diverse ways with other internal and external processes. If at a given moment the mouth-machine cuts a food flow, a complex chain of functions may be registered and encoded within the mouth-machine's food-cut. In our previous example of the feeding infant, the gleam of the lamp, the kitchen odors, the ruffle of fabric, and so on, might form part of an associative chain encoded in the operation of the infant's mouth-machine. The associative chain of the lamp circuit, the odor circuit, various tactile circuits and the alimentary circuit together comprise a kind of "block" of functions, and with each of the disjunctions that determines the specific operation of the mouth-machine—whether eating-machine, breathing-machine, drinking-machine—a block of associated circuits is activated, and that block is detached from other possible networks of circuits. In this sense, detachment-cuts "concern heterogeneous chains, and proceed by detachable segments, mobile stocks, like blocks or flying bricks" (AO 47; 39–40). Machines, then, make connective cuts in material flows, while simultaneously performing disjunctive cuts that detach chains or blocks of associated functions, but in such a fashion that the various blocks are inclusively disjoined, the inscription of the various detached blocks together gridding the surface of the body without organs.

The third cut, the remainder cut [*coupure-reste*], creates a residue, something left over. What it produces is "a subject alongside the machine, a piece adjacent to the machine" (AO 48; 40). That subject, we have seen, is without fixed identity, a nomadic flicker of intensity traversing the grid of the body without organs. It is a part produced alongside the machines, but it is itself also "a part . . . divided into parts [*une part . . . partagée*]," marked by "the parts corresponding to the detachments of the chain and to the partitionings [*prélèvements*] of the flows carried out by the machine" (AO 49; 40–41). Yet, if the subject is "a part made of parts, each of which in a moment fills up the body without organs" (AO 49; 41), one may say as well that the subject brings the parts together, conjoining them without unifying them. In this sense, the third cut performs a conjunctive synthesis, producing a summary moment in which the heterogeneous elements of connective flows and disjunctive chains coalesce in an additional part that "consumes the states through which it passes, and is born of those states" (AO 49; 41).

The machine, then, is a system of cuts, each of which performs a paradoxical synthesis. The portioning-cut both breaks a flow and connects other machines in an additive sequence, thereby producing a schiz-flow of divided yet connected elements. The detachment-cut creates disjunctions between chains, but inclusive disjunctions that allow a mode of coexistence of alternative circuits. And the remainder-cut produces a residual subject that splinters into parts yet conjoins those parts in a summary moment of consumption/consummation. All three syntheses, finally, are means of conceiving of _multiplicities_, heterogeneous entities that function together without being reducible to a totality or unity. The connective synthesis creates a nonunified flow of related desiring machines, the disjunctive synthesis fashions a nontotalizing grid of detached associative chains; and the conjunctive synthesis produces a nontotalizing adjunct part that brings together the parts that function in its formation.

Two questions remain: If desiring machines are machines, what then are the body without organs and the nomadic subject? And in what way does the exposition of a "system of cuts" demonstrate, as Deleuze and Guattari claim, that desiring machines are machines in a real rather than a metaphorical sense? The first question is in part terminological. Early in _Anti-Oedipus_, Deleuze and Guattari identify the three components of desiring production as desiring machines, the body without organs and the nomadic subject, but later in the book they refer to the three components as partial-objects,[7] the body without organs and the nomadic subject, speaking of all three as "desiring machines."[8] The simple answer to the first question, therefore, is that the body without organs and the nomadic subject are also machines. This terminological slippage is justified to some degree by the nature of the three components. Partial-objects (also referred to as "organs-partial objects" and "partial-organs") produce the body without organs as aftereffect and produce the nomadic subject as adjunct part. There is a real distinction between the partial-objects and the body without organs, yet in their mutual cofunctioning they operate as a single entity:

> At bottom, the partial-organs and the body without organs are a single and same thing, a single and same multiplicity which must be thought as such by schizo-analysis. _The partial objects are the direct powers of the body without organs, and the body without organs is_

the brute matter of partial objects. The body without organs is matter which always fills up space to such and such a degree of intensity, and the partial objects are these degrees, these intensive parts that produce the real in space from the starting point of matter as intensity '0'. (AO 390; 326–27)[9]

In the moment of repulsion between partial-objects and the body without organs, the latter "marks the external limit of the pure multiplicity that [the partial-objects] themselves form," and in the moment of attraction "the organs-partial objects cling to it, and on it enter into new syntheses of inclusive disjunction and nomadic conjunction" (AO 389; 326). The partial-objects are "like the working parts," and the body without organs is "like the immobile motor" (AO 390; 327), the two operating as a single machine. And the nomadic subject is simply the consumption and self-enjoyment (or auto-affection) of the states through which this single machine passes during its operation. In a sense, then, one can speak indifferently of the partial-objects alone, and of all three components of desiring production, as "desiring machines," in that the partial-objects as working parts always imply the existence of the immobile motor and the states through which the machine passes while functioning.

The second question concerns Deleuze and Guattari's assertion that desiring machines are not merely metaphorical but real machines. By defining the machine as a "system of cuts" within flows, Deleuze and Guattari provide a language that dissolves common sense distinctions between entities and suggests a world of multiple currents of flux and becoming interrelated solely through a universal process of cutting. Everywhere flows, everywhere machines. But most important is that the system of cuts is a system of syntheses. In the final chapter of *Anti-Oedipus*, after insisting at length that partial-objects are dispersed, nonunified and without fixed relation, Deleuze and Guattari ask, what makes possible the nontotalizing cofunctioning of heterogeneous parts, what allows heterogeneous parts "to form machines and assemblages of machines" (AO 388; 324)? The answer, they say, is to be found "in the passive character of the syntheses, or, what amounts to the same thing, in the indirect character of the interactions considered" (AO 388; 324). The syntheses are passive in that they are nonconscious and automatic, uncontrolled by any preexisting order or directing intelligence.[10] They are indirect in that they do not involve the mutual codetermination of parts according to a unified whole. A partial object cuts a given flow, and then itself emits a flow, but with no determination of the next partial object that cuts its flow. The formation of a sequence of partial objects in a flow operates indirectly, each stage an open-ended, undirected addition of a part to a part. With the overlapping of flows, inclusive disjunctions indirectly relate flows to one another across a grid of associative chains. Once flows overlap, a permutation of partial objects is possible, a passage from one state to another across the grid of associative chains proceeding by undetermined, indirect pathways. "All these indirect passive syntheses, by binarity [the connective synthesis], overlapping [the disjunctive synthesis], and permutation [the conjunctive synthesis], are a single and same machinery of desire" (AO 388–89; 325).

What this suggests, finally, is that machines are "synthesizers," producers of indirect passive syntheses. Machines are heterogeneous, dispersed parts that form connective, disjunctive and conjunctive relations through indirect processes, such that the parts function, interact, work, operate—yet all the while remaining parts. "Machine" is the name for that which puts parts in nontotalizing relation with one another, as well as the name for that which is put in relation. Machines in this sense "machine" themselves, form themselves as machines in the process of their operation. "The desiring machine is not a metaphor; it is that which cuts and is cut according to these three modes" (AO 49; 41). The cosmos consists of nothing but flows and cuts, schiz-flows connecting, overlapping and permutating, machines machining themselves into further machines. Machines are real rather than metaphorical since there is nothing in the real other than machines. And the essence of the machine is in its action, in its "machining" that produces the dynamic relationships between the parts of multiplicities.

THE CELIBATE MACHINE

When the movements of repulsion and attraction between partial-objects and the body without organs are "reconciled" in the production of a nomadic subject, a "celibate machine" is created, a third compound machine that succeeds the formation of the paranoiac machine and the miraculating machine. Deleuze and Guattari borrow the term from Michel Carrouges's *Les Machines célibataires*, a study of fantastic machines and machinelike devices in several nineteenth- and early twentieth-century works of literature, including Poe's "Pit and the Pendulum" (1843), Lautréamont's *Les Chants de Maldoror* (1869), Villiers de l'Isle-Adam's *L'Eve future* (1886), Jules Verne's *Le Château des Carpathes* (1892), Alfred Jarry's *Le Surmâle* (1902), Raymond Roussel's *Locus Solus* (1914) and Kafka's "In the Penal Colony" (1914; pub. 1919). Little of what Carrouges says bears directly on Deleuze and Guattari's concept of the nomadic subject, but his treatment of Kafka's penal colony torture machine is useful in elucidating Deleuze and Guattari's approach to Kafka's works as literary machines, as well as their understanding of machines in general.

Carrouges first conceived his project after noting startling resemblances between Kafka's torture machine and the strange mechanisms of Marcel Duchamp's great art work *La Mariée mis à nu par ses célibataires, même (Le Grand Verre)* [The Bride Stripped Bare by her Bachelors, Even (The Large Glass)] (1912-1923). He then discovered analogous mechanical relations in machines portrayed in several other literary and artistic creations, which led him to posit the existence of a modern myth he labeled "the myth of the celibate machine," in which is inscribed "the quadruple tragedy of our times: the Gordian knot of the interferences of machinism, of terror, of eroticism, and of religion or anti-religion" (Carrouges 24). These four themes he did not find patently evident in every work, but through a juxtaposition of the machines of Kafka and Duchamp, he was able to discern their presence in both those works and thereafter across a wide range of other examples.

Carrouges begins with a sketch of the torture machine from "In the Penal Colony." The "remarkable apparatus" has three parts, explains the officer in the story, each of which "has acquired a kind of popular nickname. The lower one is called the 'Bed' [*das Bett*], the upper one the 'Designer' [*der Zeichner*], and this one here in the middle that moves up and down is called the 'Harrow' [*die Egge*]" (Complete Stories 142). The prisoner to be executed is stripped naked and made to lie face down on the Bed, which is lined with cotton wool. The Harrow has toothlike needles embedded in glass that inscribe on the victim's body the commandment the victim has disobeyed (in the initial instance, "HONOR THY SUPERIORS!"). Both the Bed and the Harrow quiver in minute vibrations as the commandment is inscribed, their complex movements coordinated by the Designer, a dark wooden chest two meters above the

Bed, which is filled with cogwheels that translate the intricate designs of the Colony's former Commandant into the patterns of wounds in the victim's flesh. The execution takes place over twelve hours. At first the victim experiences only pain, but after six hours he begins to decipher his inscription through his wounds. "But how quiet he grows at just about the sixth hour! Enlightenment comes to the most dull-witted. It begins around the eyes. From there it radiates. A moment that might tempt one to get under the Harrow oneself" (Complete Stories 150).

Carrouges observes that the execution apparatus combines man and machine in a single construction, a terrifying law descending from a designing mechanism above to a body below. Copious religious allusions suggest that the machine once provided a cruel but efficacious revelation of divine commands, but that with the death of the former Commandant, only unenlightening pain is the share of the mechanism's victim (as is the case of the officer, who submits voluntarily to the machine's operation, but who dies with no sign on his face "of the promised redemption" [Complete Stories 166]). Hence Carrouges finds in Kafka's story "the tragedy of the death of God" (Carrouges 48), but combined with a myth of technological terror. In addition, Carrouges notes a latent voyeuristic sexuality in the machine's piercing motions across the victim's naked body and the Harrow's glass frame that allows observation of the torture.

In Duchamp's *The Bride Stripped Bare by her Bachelors, Even (The Large Glass)*, Carrouges discovers the same themes of machinism, terror, religion and sexuality, as well as multiple parallels between the components of Duchamp's machine and Kafka's. *The Large Glass* is perhaps one of the most complex artworks ever created, not simply because of its many constituent parts, but also because of its multiple visual allusions to other works and the profusion of documents Duchamp assembled as adjunct elements of the piece.[11] Duchamp provides names for the various objects in *The Large Glass* and details their functional relations in a dizzying proliferation of pataphysical commentaries and explanations. The composition consists of two large panels, the Bride's Domain above and the Bachelor Machine [*Machine Célibataire*] (or Bachelor Apparatus [*L'Appareil célibataire*], or simply Bachelor [*Célibataire*]) below. From her domain, the Bride communicates her commands to the Bachelors in a triple cipher through the three Draft Pistons (three squares in a horizontal row surrounded by a cloud called

The Milky Way, situated at the top of the work). As in Kafka's machine, an inscription from on high is transmitted to bodies below, and in the needlelike lower appendage of the Bride, Carrouges discerns an echo of the Harrow of the penal machine. The motif of death is found in Duchamp's references to the Bride as the Skeleton and as the *pendu femelle* (female hanged person) and to the Bachelors as the Cemetery of Uniforms and Liveries. A technological eroticism pervades the operation of the Bachelor Machine panel: The Bachelors (also called the Nine Malic Molds or Eros's Matrix), a set of nine figures on the upper left side of the Bachelor panel, emit a gas through the Capillary Tubes, which carry the gas to the arced sequence of seven cones known as the Sieves; there, the gas is frozen and converted into Spangles; the Spangles condense into a liquid suspension and then fall down the spiral Toboggan (bottom right of the Bachelor panel); Splashes are then directed from the base of the Toboggan to the Oculist Witnesses (top right), where they are communicated to the Bride panel. A corresponding mechanical eroticism is evident in the Bride panel, the Bride's Wasp/Sex Cylinder controlling the Spark of the Desire Magneto and secreting Love Gasoline that then feeds her Motor with Quite Feeble Cylinders.[12]

For Carrouges, the machines of Kafka and Duchamp convey the modern myth of a mechanical culture of violence and death, devoid of the sacred and dominated by a sterile, voyeuristic eroticism. Kafka's penal machine foregrounds the themes of religion and terror, Duchamp's *Large Glass* the theme of mechanical eroticism, and it is in the conjunction of the two that one meets the fully formed "celibate machine." Deleuze and Guattari do not embrace Carrouges's interpretation of celibate machines as the myth of a fourfold modern tragedy, but they find illuminating Carrouges's category and the examples he assembles within it. For them, celibate machines are desiring machines, and though Deleuze and Guattari do not say as much, it is evident that their sense of the term and their reading of Kafka's machines are shaped by the juxtaposition of Duchamp's *Large Glass* and Kafka's penal apparatus. In some ways, *The Large Glass* is a better example of desiring production than those Deleuze and Guattari highlight in *Anti-Oedipus*. It is a machine that operates explicitly through circuits of flows: The Bachelors's gas is frozen, cut into spangles, converted into a fog, condensed into a liquid and conveyed in a stream, while the Bride secretes love gasoline that fuels her Motor with Quite Feeble Cylinders. It combines the characteristics of a Rube Goldberg machine and the pocket-stone-mouth machine of Beckett's *Molloy*, which represent the two extremes of purposive inefficiency and purposeless efficiency that one meets in the assemblages of nature.[13] The intricate apparatus of *The Large Glass* rivals in complexity and improbability any of Rube Goldberg's contraptions, and its relentless execution of its mysterious purpose seems every bit as efficient and opaque in intention as Molloy's circuit of sucking stones. Duchamp's assemblage of heterogeneous components exemplifies aptly desiring production's juxtaposition of disparate entities in unconventional patterns. Pistons, Milky Way cloud, desire-magneto, pulse needle, motor with quite feeble cylinders, capillary tubes, butterfly pump, chocolate grinder, sieves, scissors, water mill, water wheel, chariot, toboggan, mobile weights, oculist charts, isolating plates, grilled cooler, the Bride's clothes—all come together in an unlikely collage of quotidian and technological objects. And integrated within these circuits are the Bride and the Bachelors, human beings yet themselves mechanisms (the Bride) or abstract industrial forms (the Bachelors as "nine malic molds"). Above all, *The Large Glass* is an eroticized machine, but one in which libido is evenly distributed throughout its circuits and curiously detached from any mere human sexual relations.

When describing the celibate machine in *Anti-Oedipus*, Deleuze and Guattari speak as if it were an amalgam of *The Large Glass* and the penal colony execution machine.[14] Such an integration of the two machines affects both in important ways. Viewing the penal apparatus as a Duchamp machine heightens the humor, irony and absurdity of Kafka's construction. Regarding *The Large Glass* from the vantage of Kafka forces a recognition of the serious social and political ramifications of Duchamp's apparently random collage of disparate elements. And seeing both as celibate machines clarifies the nature of desire in desiring production. It is important to note a basic ambiguity inherent in the word *célibataire* that does not exist in the English "bachelor" or German "Junggeselle." A *célibataire* can be simply an unmarried male, or he can be a man who is chaste or celibate. Duchamp's *machine célibataire* is at once the erotic machine of a bride being stripped bare by her unmarried suitors and the chaste machine of a paradoxically sexless libido. When Deleuze and Guattari adopt the term *machine célibataire*, they stress the anticonjugal and antifamilial nature of desire, which ignores distinctions of legitimate and illegitimate sexual relations. In *Kafka*, they argue that Gregor's attraction toward his sister in *The Metamorphosis* is an instance of schizo-incest, a form of desire that cannot be accommodated within the norms of marriage or even within the structure of an Oedipal attachment to the mother.[15] They see the series of sisters, maids and prostitutes in Kafka's works all as agents of anticonjugal, antifamilial desire, and in the same light they regard Kafka's homosexual doubles, brothers, bureaucrats and lone artists. But they finally argue that Kafka's artistic machine is *"une machine célibataire"* (K 128; 70), and that it is the *célibataire* whose desire goes beyond the connections opened up by Kafka's anticonjugal women or homosexual men. "The *célibataire* is a state of desire that is more vast and more intense than incestuous desire or homosexual desire" (K 129; 70), for such desire is ultimately apersonal, indifferently human and/or nonhuman.[16] Duchamp's *Large Glass* is most *célibataire* when desire communicates through capillary tubes, sieves, toboggans and oculist charts, when the conventional human relation between the bride and her suitors is in the process of dissolution. The penal colony torture machine is *célibataire* in that desire pervades the circuits of apparatus, victim and witnesses, with no conjugal or familial coordinates orienting its movement. Desire here is pure intensity, an ecstatic torture that makes no differentiation between enjoyment and pain. As *machine célibataire*, the torture apparatus produces "a pleasure one can qualify as autoerotic or rather automatic" (AO 25; 18), not simply because the isolated victim and machine form a discrete unit, but because desire is distributed throughout the unit, the victim-machine circuits undergoing an auto-affection or self-enjoyment that is self-engendering and hence automatic. And yet, though "without family and without conjugality," the *célibataire* is "all the more social, social-dangerous, social-traitor, a collectivity in himself." "The highest desire," the desire of the *célibataire*, "desires at the same time solitude and to be connected to all the machines of desire. A machine that is all the more social and collective for being solitary, *célibataire*" (K 130; 71). Kafka's penal machine tortures a solitary victim, but it is a machine of law—of commandments, crimes, verdicts, punishment, guilt and redemption—and as such, it is a social machine that extends immediately into the world. In a similar fashion, Duchamp's bride and nine *célibataires* remain separated from each other, solitary and celibate in their desire, yet their circuits branch out into a host of social, artistic, industrial, scientific and technological domains. Deleuze and Guattari characterize the celibate machine as the successor to the paranoiac and miraculating machines, but in a certain sense it is the culmination of desiring production, the desiring machine in which partial objects, body without organs and nomadic subject all function in apersonal, ahuman circuits that permeate nature and the sociopolitical real.

THE WRITING MACHINE

In *Anti-Oedipus*, the Penal Colony torture machine serves Deleuze and Guattari as a useful example of a desiring machine; since it is a machine in the ordinary sense of the word, its eroticism pertains to a solitary victim in interaction with a nonhuman mechanism, and yet its function is decidedly social and political. In *Kafka*, however, the torture apparatus is but one of the machines Deleuze and Guattari examine, and they argue that it is not Kafka's most successful machine, at least from the point of view of the production and continuation of celibate desire. It is too abstract, too much an isolated entity, closed in upon itself. It exists on an island, its connections to institutions other than the penal colony unspecified. As a result its elements are too easily assimilated within an Oedipal structure of father and son, former Commandant and officer/victim, as well as the parallel religious structure of Old Testament God and impotent Messiah. At the conclusion of the story, the machine breaks into pieces, the officer dies and the explorer escapes the island. With the exception of the explorer's flight, all movement has come to a close.

The function of machines is to "machine"—to form syntheses, to produce flows through binary connections, inclusive disjunctions and nomadic conjunctions. The problem for Kafka is to create a writing machine that synthesizes flows of desiring production, that forms multiple connections, disjunctions and conjunctions, and thereby produces and sustains movement.[17] In *Anti-Oedipus*, Deleuze and Guattari describe the movement of flows of desire, but they also speak at length of the ways in which movement is blocked, in which flows are restricted, regularized, encoded and channeled into circuits that are limited in their connections, exclusive in their disjunctions and fixed in their conjunctions. If desiring machines are everywhere deterritorializing flows, those same flows also are constantly being reterritorialized into organized patterns of recognizable objects and stable subjects. Hence, Deleuze and Guattari identify two poles of desiring production, "a paranoiac, fascisizing type or pole" that restricts and segregates flows, and "a schizorevolutionary type or pole that follows *lines of flight* of desire, breaks through the wall and makes flows move" (AO 329; 277). In *Anti-Oedipus*, they map the circuits of both poles, describing in their universal history three kinds of paranoiac social machines (primitive, despotic and capitalist), each with its characteristic means of limiting and organizing flows. Their critique of psychoanalysis is simply a part of this analysis, the Oedipal triangle of Papa-Mama-Me being but one component of a general system of restraints and controls in modern capitalist societies that regulate desire (in this case, by insisting that desire is primarily situated in the family, an ego-subject, whole and discrete organisms, and so on).

In *Kafka*, Deleuze and Guattari continue their attack on psychoanalysis by countering Oedipalizing readings of Kafka, but their main goal is to detail the workings of Kafka's writing machine in terms of the production, continuation and proliferation of movement. They identify three components of Kafka's writing machine: the letters, the short stories and the three novels.[18] The essence of the letters Deleuze and Guattari find in Kafka's correspondence with Felice Bauer, whom he courted by mail, eventually betrothed but never finally married. (All his letters are love letters of a sort, they claim: "there is always a woman on the horizon of the letters, she is the true addressee [*destinataire*], she is the one the father supposedly made him lose, she the one his friends hope he'll break with, etc." [K 53; 29].) After meeting Felice at Max Brod's, Kafka soon developed a regular correspondence with her, writing her daily and making her promise to respond as frequently in turn. Though they eventually became engaged, throughout their exchanges Kafka posed constant obstacles to their infrequent meetings and perpetual objections to their marriage. His procrastination led to the "tribunal in the hotel [*Der Gerichtshof im Hotel*]," as Kafka called it, an interview with Felice at the Askanische Hof in Berlin to determine his intentions. Later that day he apparently related the news of their failed engagement to her family, and as Kafka comments, "They agreed that I was right, there was nothing, or not much, that could be said against me. Devilish in my innocence [*Teuflisch in aller Unschuld*]" (Diaries II, 65). Felice and Kafka continued to write for awhile, but eventually the courtship and the correspondence came to an end.[19]

For Deleuze and Guattari, the letters "pose directly, innocently, the diabolical power of the literary machine" (K 52; 29). The love letters are a substitute for love, the product of a *diabolical pact* (at one point, he makes Felice promise to write him twice daily) that displaces the *conjugal contract*. Kafka is like Dracula, sending his batlike letters forth to suck life from Felice.[20] He doubles himself as the speaking subject [*sujet d'énonciation*] and subject of speech [*sujet d'énoncé*], the innocent speaking subject remaining at home, the equally innocent subject of speech venturing forth in the letters, attempting valiantly but in vain to overcome the obstacles to physical encounters. The object of the letters is to perpetuate the correspondence, to defer marriage and keep the libidinal writing machine operating. The danger, however, is that the writer will be trapped in his own machine, that the vampire will succumb to "the cross of the family and the garlic of conjugality" (K 54; 30). Ultimately, Kafka's letters do lead to the hotel tribunal, and the writer becomes caught in his own machine. "The formula 'diabolical in all innocence' has not been enough" (K 60; 33).[21]

Shortly after beginning his correspondence with Felice, Kafka produces his first mature story, "The Judgment," and soon thereafter "The Stoker" and "The Metamorphosis." The letters "are perhaps the motor force that, through the blood they bring, get the entire machine started," suggest Deleuze and Guattari, and the stories are written "either to figure forth the danger or to conjure it away" (K 63; 35). The short stories concern *lines of flight*, escape routes from traps, cages, prisons, dead ends, closed spaces and menacing machines. They trace pathways of possible movement, but also blockages that constrict and kill. In "The Judgment," Georg Bendemann finds no escape from familial and conjugal constraints and succumbs to the father's sentence. In "The Metamorphosis," Gregor Samsa explores a path of release from his enslavement to family and work by entering a process of becoming-animal. Gregor's line of flight, however, is consistently cut off, and three times he is driven back into his room. His sister encourages him in his becoming-insect by clearing his room of furniture, but Gregor clings in protest to the photo on the wall (portraits and photographs being consistently associated in Kafka with the imposition of social codes, according to Deleuze and Guattari). Thereafter, the sister's schizo-incestuous desire provides him no assistance in his efforts to escape. The apple of familial guilt, hurled by his father, rots in his body, and he finally dies.

Not all the short stories end in such fatal closure as "The Metamorphosis." The ape of "A Report to an Academy," for example, escapes his cage by embarking on a process of becoming-human. "'No, freedom was not what I wanted,'" he says. "'Only a way out; right or left, or in any direction; I made no other demand'" (Complete Stories 253–54). (In these words of the ape Deleuze and Guattari find the essence of becoming-animal and the line of flight—not absolute freedom, only a way out.) Yet though the ape escapes, no means exists to continue his flight, no connection affords an extension of the movement his becoming-human inaugurates. The problem of the writing machine is one of movement and connections, of syntheses that perpetuate a line of flight in specific yet open-ended circuits. In the short stories, lines of flight are either closed or left disconnected. The components of the stories form either a self-destructive machine or a machine that operates in a void. In some instances, one senses that some kind of machine is functioning, but it is hard to discern all of its parts or how they interact. In such cases, the stories provide *machinic indices* rather than fully constructed machines. The seven singing dogs of "Investigations of a Dog," for example, seem functional parts of a musical machine, but what kind of machine it is, and how the parts are related to other components, are uncertain. In other instances, a discrete and fully assembled machine is evident, but how its connections extend to other elements is undetermined. The penal colony torture machine is one such *abstract machine*, as is the mysterious Odradek of "The Cares of a Family Man," a flat star-shaped spool-like object, covered with broken-off bits of thread, with a small wooden crossbar sticking out of the star and a small rod joined to the crossbar at a right angle, the whole thing looking "senseless enough, but in its own way perfectly finished" (Complete Stories 428). Another such abstract machine appears in "Blumfeld, an Elderly Bachelor"—the "two small white celluloid balls with blue stripes jumping up and down side by side" (Complete Stories 185) that inexplicably arrive one day at Blumfeld's door. Besides this abstract machine, machinic indices are evident as well in Blumfeld's two assistants, whose strange antics seem somehow related to the bouncing celluloid balls, but in what ways, and as parts of what compound machine, one cannot determine.

It is only in the novels, the third component of Kafka's writing machine, that movement continues uninterruptedly, and that lines of flight are connected in specific circuits. Kafka's three novels remain unfinished, but in Deleuze and Guattari's analysis, this is only because the writing machine assumes its full functioning in these works. Max Brod says of *The Trial* that "Franz regarded the novel as unfinished," but Brod adds that "as the trial, according to the author's own statement made by word of mouth, was never to get as far as the highest Court, in a certain sense the novel could never be terminated—that is to say, it could be prolonged into infinity" (postscript to *The Trial*, p. 334).[22] Like *The Trial*, *America* and *The Castle* are also interminable, infinite and only unfinished in that they are machines that continue to operate without completely breaking down. And what makes possible their interminable function is the specificity and multiplicity of their connections. Although Deleuze and Guattari deal with all three novels, it is *The Trial* that best exemplifies the fully operational writing machine.

THE LAW MACHINE

In the penal colony torture apparatus we encounter an abstract law machine, but in the various episodes of *The Trial* we find the multiple *assemblages* of a completely formed, totally operational law machine, a social machine whose components are people, texts, institutions, practices, buildings, objects, and so on. *The Trial* may have few machines in the ordinary sense of the word (what Deleuze and Guattari refer to as "technical machines"), but the diverse elements of the Law, its officers, victims, servants, adjuncts, locales and accoutrements, function very much as a machine, even if one does not adopt *Anti-Oedipus'* broad definition of the machine as a system of cuts. We might note that in *Anti-Oedipus*, Deleuze and Guattari elaborate on the concept of a "social machine" by alluding to Lewis Mumford's analysis of the utilization of labor in the construction of the pyramids of Egypt. Mumford argues that the Pharaoh, his priests and bureaucrats, and the thousands of slaves who actually built the pyramids, together formed the first "megamachine." "If a machine be defined, more or less in accord with the classic definition of Franz Reuleaux, as a combination of resistant parts, each specialized in function, operating under human control, to utilize energy and to perform work, then the great labor machine was in every aspect a genuine machine: all the more because its components, though made of human bone, nerve, and muscle, were reduced to their bare mechanical elements and rigidly standardized for the performance of their limited tasks" (Mumford 191).[23] The law machine of *The Trial* is not as evidently a *labor* machine as the Pharaoh's pyramid construction apparatus, yet it does perform a certain kind of work and produce a specific kind of human commodity. But what is crucial is that Kafka's social machine is an *open-ended* social machine of *desiring* production.

In *The Trial*, everyone is connected to the Law, every place is a site of judicial activity. The three anemic young men who accompany the arresting officers are clerks in the bank, and in a storage room of the bank, K. later encounters the arresting officers being whipped because of K.'s complaints about them. K.'s uncle knows of the case before K. can tell him about it, and the uncle introduces K. to the lawyer. Leni, the lawyer's maid, seems intimately connected with defendants, lawyers and judges alike. The painter Titorelli is a court painter, the Cathedral priest proves to be the prison chaplain. As K. tells a manufacturer, who has also heard of his case, "'So many people seem to be connected with the Court!'" (*Trial* 169). Everywhere K. goes, the Law goes with him, and everywhere, the Law is eroticized. K. is first interrogated in Fräulein Bürstner's room, a fetishistic white blouse dangling from the window latch, and later K. pursues her and gives her a vampiric kiss on the throat. The court law books contain obscene drawings. K. finds himself attracted first to the apparently lascivious washer woman who shows him to the courtroom, and then to Leni, with whom he has sex during his first visit to his lawyer's quarters. An unmistakable masochistic eroticism pervades the whipping of Franz and Willem, and the faces of the young girls outside Titorelli's studio betray a "mixture of childishness and depravity" (*Trial* 178).

The Law, then, is an all-encompassing, eroticized social machine. Every person is an agent of the Law, every locale is a site of justice, and K.'s pursuit of his case leads from one assemblage of individuals, discourses, codes and objects to another, from the boarding house assemblage to the tenement/court assemblage, the bank assemblage, the law office assemblage, the studio assemblage, the Cathedral assemblage, and so forth. An open-ended series of connected components, all infused with an immanent desire. From the perspective of Kafka's activity as a writer, one can see how *The Trial* serves as an interminable desiring machine, a generator of syntheses that make possible an incessant and perpetual movement. But what is the point of this elaborate social machine? Is Kafka simply demonstrating the absurdity of the Law, showing the modern judicial apparatus to be a laughable Rube Goldberg machine or Beckettian stone-sucking machine? Kafka is often said to offer no critique of social institutions, but Deleuze and Guattari agree only if one means by "critique" an external commentary on social representations. They argue instead that Kafka offers an immanent critique by extracting "from social representations assemblages of enunciation and machinic assemblages and dismantling these assemblages" (K 85; 46). Writing, they say, "has this double function: to transcribe into assemblages, to dismantle assemblages. The two are the same thing" (K 86; 47). Kafka is "an author who laughs, profoundly joyous," yet also "from one end to the other he is a political author" (K 75; 41), and his political activity lies in this transcribing and dismantling of assemblages. Rather than commenting on social representations, Kafka experiments on them. *The Trial*, they argue, "must be considered as a scientific investigation, a report of experiments on the functioning of a machine" (K 80; 43–44), and the functioning of the machine is one with its dismantling. Thus Deleuze and Guattari say, "we believe only in a Kafka *politics*, which is neither imaginary nor symbolic. We believe only in one or several Kafka *machines*, which are neither structure nor phantasm. We believe only in a Kafka *experimentation*, without interpretation or significance, but only with experiential/experimental protocols [*protocoles d'expérience*]" (K 14; 7). We must now ask: In what sense is the transcription and dismantling of social representations a form of critique? How is such an operation a type of experimentation? And in what way are transcription and dismantling the same thing?

To transcribe social representations into assemblages means first of all to rewrite familiar codes and institutions in the unfamiliar terms of a social machine. As many have recognized, Kafka defamiliarizes the Law by depriving it of its conventional, commonsense logic. In *The Trial*, the Law is an empty form without content, charges are unspecified, guilt is automatically assumed.[24] An inaccessible authority issues judgments, and endless levels of judges, court officials and lawyers process the vague cases of randomly selected defendants. The familiar system of law, with its logic of rules, infractions, evidence, proofs and verdicts, is revealed to be a byzantine mechanism of power, unrelated to norms of justice and fairness, but regulated by a hierarchy of forces, a presumption of universal culpability and an inescapable network of punitive agents. Implicit in this mechanism is a culture of guilt, grounded in the religious tradition of an inscrutable God revealing His edicts through the execution of His sentences. In this sense, Kafka's transcription of the justice system as an elaborate machine constitutes a critique of law as power. Yet Deleuze and Guattari argue that this dimension of *The Trial*, undeniable as it is, serves only as a preliminary critique, for it presumes a conception of power confirmed and maintained by authoritarian social institutions themselves. What Kafka shows is that power is not inherently centralized and hierarchical, nor is it something that one either possesses or lacks. It is relational, pervading the circuits of the judicial machine and involving all individuals and components of the machine in a field of forces. In this regard, Deleuze and Guattari see Kafka's depiction of power as consonant with Foucault's analyses of power in *Discipline and Punish* and *The History of Sexuality, Vol. 1*. Further, Kafka shows that the circuits of power are also circuits of desire, that the Law is not only a machine for processing defendants, but a desiring machine in which power/desire is imbued through every circuit. What this suggests is that the problem of power is not simply one of oppressors and oppressed, of those who have power and those who don't, but of the libidinal investments that characterize all power relations, of the docility of the oppressed and their complicity in their own oppression, as well as the diffusive spread of a mentality of coercion throughout widening circles of disciplinary regulation.[25] This is not to deny the existence of genuine oppression, but simply to assert that the positions of oppressor and oppressed are secondary products of a primary circuit of power-desire: "Repression, from the perspective both of the repressor and the repressed, flows from this or that assemblage of power-desire, from this or that state of the machine. . . . Repression depends on the machine, and not the reverse" (K 103; 56).

But Kafka's transcription of the Law as a desiring machine is also a dismantling of the machine, an analysis of the ways in which the forces of domination and authority are undone, reconstituted and redeployed in unpredictable configurations. We recall that Deleuze and Guattari posit two poles in desiring production, a paranoiac pole of an exclusive, segregative division of flows and a schizophrenic pole of an inclusive, combinative synthesis of flows. Kafka presents a paranoiac view of the Law, centralized, remote, imperious, compartmentalized and administered through an intricate bureaucracy of officials, assistants and adjuncts, but he also details a schizophrenic deployment of the Law, a means of connecting components of the court system in unprescribed relations. The bank is connected to the punishment apparatus through the bank storage closet; Titorelli's studio and the courts are on opposite sides of the city, yet the back door of the studio issues directly into the court; the tenement building houses a tribunal, as well as a labyrinth of interchangeable offices. Fräulein Bürstner, the washer woman and Leni serve as connectors, sending K. down various paths in the surreal maze of the judicial machine. K. himself functions as a switching mechanism, exploring at every juncture the connections that might be made between heterogeneous elements of the Law. "If everyone belongs to justice, if everyone is an auxiliary of justice, from the priest to the little girls, it is not by virtue of the transcendence of the law, but the immanence of desire" (K 92; 50).

It is important to note, however, that the paranoiac and schizophrenic poles are both poles of desire, and that the exclusive, segregative application of the Law and its inclusive, combinative use are always active together in the social field. "These two coexisting states of desire are the two states of the law: on one hand, *the transcendent paranoiac Law* that never ceases to agitate a finite segment, to make it a complete object, to crystallize this or that; on the other hand, *the immanent schiz-law*, which functions like a justice, an antilaw, a 'procedure' that dismantles the paranoiac Law in all its assemblages" (K 108–9; 59). Everywhere in *The Trial*, hierarchical, authoritarian regulations are being imposed, while at the same time disruptive, mutant connections are being established. To transcribe social representations in terms of assemblages is to display the immanence of the schiz-law within the paranoiac Law, to show that the familiar, commonsense elements that make up the legal system are actually components of a megamachine, which is constantly constructing itself as a paranoiac, hierarchical Law and at the same time dismantling itself through a schiz-law process that forms connective, disjunctive and conjunctive syntheses between components of the machine. In this sense, then, "it is the same thing—the discovery of assemblages of immanence, and their dismantling" (K 109; 59).

But there is another way in which the operations of transcription and dismantling are the same thing. If Kafka transcribes the social representations of the Law in terms of the assemblages of a ubiquitous legal machine, he does not simply rewrite the realities of the Austro-Hungarian Empire in an unconventional form. If art is a mirror, Kafka tells Janouch, it is a mirror "which goes 'fast', like a watch—sometimes" (Janouch 143). In a certain sense, argue Deleuze and Guattari, Kafka's art is a mirror of the future, and in the judicial machinery of *The Trial* one can discern the *"diabolical powers that are knocking at the door"* (K 74; 41).[26] Deleuze and Guattari identify those powers as the bureaucratic states of capitalist America, Stalinist Russia, and Nazi Germany. Others have commented on Kafka's prescient understanding of modern police states, totalitarian regimes and anonymous bureaucracies, but Deleuze and Guattari are not arguing that Kafka is simply an astute prognosticator. Instead, they assert that in works such as *The Trial*, he is disclosing *virtual* vectors of unfolding relations that exist in his world but that only later become *actualized* in the concrete forms of capitalist, Stalinist and fascist bureaucracies. There is, one might say, a generalized bureaucratic, police-state, totalitarian "function" at work in the Prague of the Austro-Hungarian Empire (and specifically in the Worker's Accident Insurance Company where Kafka was employed), what Deleuze and Guattari will call an "abstract machine" in *A Thousand Plateaus*.[27] This generalized bureaucratic function is actualized in the concrete assemblages of the Austro-Hungarian Empire, but it coexists with those assemblages as a virtual plane of "lines of flight," tendencies, becomings, directions of movement toward potential actualizations of various sorts. The actual assemblages of a given social order, such as the Austro-Hungarian Empire, presuppose the existence of this generalized bureaucratic function, with its vectors of tendencies and becomings, and take form along the lines traced by this virtual function, or abstract machine. At the same time, this generalized function fulfills a "pilot role," as Deleuze and Guattari say of the abstract machine. "An abstract or diagrammatic machine does not function in order to represent, even something that is real, but it constructs a real to come, a new type of reality" (MP 177; 142). That "real to come" can take various forms—in this case, those of the bureaucracies of capitalist America, Stalinist Russia and Nazi Germany, though these are not the only forms that could have been produced by this generalized bureaucratic function.

One of the complications of this model arises from the coexistence of the paranoiac and schizophrenic poles in desiring production. Every social order (at least in the modern era) comes into existence through the modification, eradication, redefinition or reconfiguration of a preceding order. The bureaucracy of the Austro-Hungarian Empire takes shape only through a complex series of metamorphoses of social relations, reinscriptions of codes, redeployments of material objects and practices. However static, monumental, compartmentalized and hierarchical that imperial bureaucracy may appear to be or may present itself as being, its formation takes place through a double process of deterritorialization and reterritorialization, of erasure and rewriting of codes and relations. The virtual vectors of a generalized bureaucratic function serve a pilot role in the formation of this actual imperial bureaucracy, opening paths of deterritorialization that are simultaneously reterritorialized in the rigid, stratified forms of the bureaucratic apparatus. Virtual vectors of deterritorialization, however, remain in existence, immanent within the imperial bureaucracy, and they serve a pilot role for metamorphoses of the imperial bureaucracy toward other social forms, which themselves will be constructed along lines of simultaneous deterritorialization and reterritorialization. What specific forms those virtual vectors of deterritorialization and reterritorialization will take cannot be determined in advance. They might eventuate in diverse "diabolical powers of the future," but they might just as well issue in social orders that are better than the present one.

It is from this vantage that one must consider the revolutionary function of Kafka's writing machine. Deleuze and Guattari reject any notion of revolutionary action as aimed toward the realization of a plan or design of an ideal society. Rather, revolutionary action proceeds through metamorphosis, change and becoming, through the transformation of a present intolerable situation toward some unforeseeable future. The lines of metamorphosis are always present in the real in the form of virtual vectors of deterritorialization, and revolutionary action simply induces their actualization through an intensification of destabilizing, deforming and decoding forces that are being stabilized, formed and coded by the particular social system. Kafka's political strategy, according to Deleuze and Guattari, is not to protest oppressive institutions or propose utopian alternatives, but to accelerate the deterritorializing tendencies that are already present in the world.

"Since the collective and social machines bring about a massive deterritorialization of human beings, [Kafka] will go even further along that route, to the point of an absolute, molecular deterritorialization. Critique is completely useless. It is much more important to espouse the virtual movement that is already real without being actual (conformists, bureaucrats are always stopping movement at this or that point)" (K 107; 58). There is no guarantee that such an accelerated deterritorialization will yield positive results. There is no clear differentiation between good and bad desire, between paranoiac and schizophrenic desiring production, for "desire is such a soup, such a segmentary porridge, that the bureaucratic or fascist pieces are still or already within the revolutionary agitation" (K 109-10; 60). Hence, "since one cannot precisely make a division between the oppressors and the oppressed, nor even between different kinds of desire, one must carry all of them into an all too possible future, hoping that this movement will *also* disengage lines of flight or parade, even if they are modest, even if they are trembling, even—and above all—if they are asignifying" (K 107-8; 59).

In *The Trial*, then, Kafka starts with the social representations of the complex of relations inherent in the juridical system of the Austro-Hungarian Empire and transcribes them in terms of the multiple assemblages of a social machine. The familiar system of Law is shown to be a proliferating mechanism of power that spreads into all aspects of life, and its functioning is shown to be directed simultaneously by paranoiac, territorializing restrictions and codifications of relations and by schizophrenic, deterritorializing reticulations and decodifications of relations. In this sense, the social machine both constructs and dismantles itself, and in this regard one can say that transcribing and dismantling the machine are the same process. Yet Kafka also accelerates the deterritorializing movements of the machine and multiplies the connections between its heterogeneous elements. In so doing, he reveals metamorphic tendencies that eventuate in the "diabolical powers of the future," but also revolutionary possibilities that remain to be actualized. Rather than commenting on social institutions or proposing alternatives, he experiments on the virtual lines of flight immanent within his world. He adopts a "method of active dismantling" which consists of "prolonging, accelerating a whole movement that already traverses the social field: it operates in a virtual domain, already real without being actual" (K 88–89; 48). Neither "an interpretation nor a social representation," this method is "an experimentation, a social-political protocol" (K 89; 49). Dismantling, then, which is one with transcription, is also experimentation, and in this regard *The Trial* may be seen as "a scientific investigation, a report of experiments on the functioning of a machine" (K 80; 44).

ART AND LIFE

Kafka's writing machine has three components, the letters, the short stories and the novels. Kafka's problem is to keep the machine operating, to create and sustain movement through the formation of open-ended circuits of desiring production. It would seem, though, that there is a fundamental difference between perpetuating the flow of letters to one's fiancée and writing stories and novels about the perpetuation of flows. Yet Deleuze and Guattari insist that there is no opposition between life and art in Kafka. They find it "so irritating, so grotesque, to oppose life and writing in Kafka, to suppose that he sought refuge in literature through lack, weakness, impotence in the face of life. A rhizome, a burrow, yes, but not an ivory tower. A line of flight, yes, but not at all a refuge" (K 74; 41). Deleuze and Guattari point out that the letters, short stories and novels communicate with one another through multiple transverse connections, the mechanism of the trial appearing in all three components, a becoming-dog of Felice connecting the letters to the short stories, a bureaucratic apparatus from the novels informing the machinic indices of a short story, and so on. One might argue that this simply demonstrates the mutual influence of life and art in the writer's consciousness, but Deleuze and Guattari's point finally is that writing for Kafka is itself a "machining" activity within the extended social machine of which he is a part, both when he writes "real" letters and when he writes fiction. Kafka surveys the social field, charting the interconnections between components of various machinic assemblages, and "he knows that all the links attach him to a literary machine of expression, of which he is at once the gears, the mechanic, the operator, and the victim" (K 106; 58). Just as everyone is connected with the Law in *The Trial*, so is Kafka himself situated within networks of relations—judicial, bureaucratic, political, commercial, artistic, familial, and so forth—all functioning as assemblages of

machines, and his writing machine too is enmeshed within those social   **87**
machines, whether he is writing letters to Felice or novels about K.

When Kafka writes, he acts, for writing is an action within a broad
field of social action, and in that field, the discursive and the nondiscursive are intertwined in mutually affecting patterns of practice, movement and modification. Hence, Kafka's writing is not simply a mental
representation of an external world, nor is it a superstructural aesthetic
commentary on a foundational economic reality: "Let no one say that
this line [of deterritorialization] is present only in the mind [*en esprit*].
As if writing were not also a machine, as if it were not an act, even independent of its publication. As if the writing machine were not also a
machine (no more superstructural than any other, no more ideological
than any other), now taken up in capitalist, bureaucratic or fascist
machines, now tracing a modest revolutionary line" (K 109; 60). When
Kafka writes, he does not retreat from the world, but acts within it: "far
from being a writer retired in his room, his room offers him a double
flow: that of a bureaucrat with a great future before him, plugged into
the real assemblages that are in the process of forming themselves; and
that of a nomad in the process of fleeing in the most current and actual
manner [*en train de fuir à la façon la plus actuelle*], who plugs himself into
socialism, anarchism, social movements" (K 75; 41).

In *Proust and Signs*, Deleuze regards the *Recherche* as a machine, an
entity that does not have meaning so much as it functions. In *Kafka*,
Deleuze and Guattari treat Kafka's writings as a tripartite machine
enmeshed within a world of machines. As they argue at length in *Anti-
Oedipus*, the essence of the machine is to form connective, disjunctive
and conjunctive syntheses, to cut/connect flows, to overlap flows in
inclusive disjunctions, to permutate flows in nomadic fluctuations of
intensity. Machines "machine," they fashion circuits of which they are
a part. This is the essence of the machines that Deleuze and Guattari
find in Kafka. His genius, they say, "is in considering that men and
women are part of the machine, not only in their work, but even more
so in their adjacent activities, in their rest, in their loves, in their protes-
tations, their indignations, etc." (K 145; 81). For Kafka, "desire never
ceases to make a machine in the machine [literally, "make machine in
the machine," *faire machine dans la machine*], and to constitute a new gear
alongside the preceding gear, indefinitely, even if these gears seem to
oppose one another, or to function in a discordant manner. That which

makes the machine [*Ce qui fait machine*], strictly speaking, are the connections, all the connections that guide the dismantling" (K 146; 82).

In *Proust and Signs*, Deleuze shows that the *Recherche* is a multiplicity, a machine whose whole is produced as an added part alongside its other parts. Proust likens his work to a cathedral and to a dress, but Deleuze stresses that the cathedral is unfinished and the dress a patchwork forever in the process of being stitched together. The "oneness" of this multiplicity is formed through transversals that put divergent series and closed vessels in communication with one another. Kafka's machine, by comparison, is even more clearly a multiplicity, his works forming a burrow, like the habitat of the molelike creature of "The Burrow," a maze of interconnecting tunnels with no clear entrance or exit and multiple points of possible escape. The burrow is a rhizome, like crabgrass, a decentered proliferation of points, any one of which may be connected to any other. Kafka's letters, short stories and novels are the tunnels of this burrow, the nodes of the crabgrass rhizome, and the diaries "are the rhizome itself," "the element (in the sense of milieu) that Kafka declares he does not want to leave, like a fish" (K 76; 96). The letters, short stories and novels are interconnected, and each component functions by forming connections, initiating and continuing movement. The writing machine is at once a tunneling machine and the tunnels it digs, a "rhizoming" machine and the rhizome it forms. And the more successful the machine, the more incomplete it is. The flow of letters ceases when the conjugal trap closes; in the short stories, lines of flight are blocked ("The Metamorphosis"), only vaguely indicated through indices of an unspecified machine ("Investigations of a Dog"), or isolated in the abstract working of a machine disconnected from the social field ("In the Penal Colony"); but in the novels, the machine functions fully, the connections multiply and spread indefinitely. The unified, "well-formed" short stories, such as "The Metamorphosis," are so many dead ends in the burrow, whereas the unfinished novels are properly operational burrowing machines that continue interminably to burrow. The function of the machine is to machine, and while it machines it necessarily creates an open multiplicity. The fully formed, complete machine is an engine of incompletion. As Deleuze and Guattari say of Kafka's writing machine, "never has one made so complete an *oeuvre* out of movements that are all aborted but all communicating with one another" (K 74; 41).

Kafka's writing machine is not to be interpreted, but described. It does not mean so much as it functions, and its functioning makes of itself an open multiplicity, a sprawling burrow or spreading rhizome. The writing machine is embedded in and traversed by social machines, its operation interconnected with the processes of a universal desiring production. In this regard, it is immediately political, its functioning taking place within a collective field of activity. What remains to be specified is the way in which language functions within such a machine. Deleuze and Guattari regard Kafka as a practitioner of "minor literature," an immediately political literature whose language is affected by a high level of deterritorialization and articulated through collective assemblages of enunciation. As we shall see in the next chapter, minor literature entails a minor usage of language, and such a usage is crucial in the functioning of the minor writing machine.

Chapter Four

MINOR LITERATURE

Deleuze and Guattari subtitle their study of Kafka *Pour une littérature mineure*, "For (or Toward) a Minor Literature," and in some ways Kafka's work can be seen as simply the occasion for Deleuze and Guattari's development of the broad concept of minor literature, one suggested by Kafka, exemplified in his writings, but characteristic of several other writers of diverse practices and tendencies. Central to the concept of minor literature is a particular use of language, a way of deterritorializing language by intensifying features already inherent within it. Such a minor use of language proceeds via a collective assemblage of enunciation and functions as a political form of action. Precisely how the elements of minor literature are related to one another, and in what ways they are manifest in language per se, are questions that require careful elucidation. Deleuze and Guattari detail the elements of minor literature in *Kafka* and elaborate on the concept in *A Thousand Plateaus*, offering in both cases occasional examples of a minor usage of language in authors other than Kafka. And in a 1979 essay on the Italian playwright Carmelo Bene, "One Less Manifesto" (SP), Deleuze extends the concept to the theater. What these texts suggest is that minor literature is above all linguistic action, and that the theater is a paradigmatic instance of such action in its incorporation of speech within gesture in a pragmatic context.

Deleuze and Guattari find inspiration for their theory of minor literature in an extended diary entry of Kafka's, dated December 25, 1911.
Earlier that year, Kafka had begun attending performances of a Yiddish
theatrical troupe from Lemberg (the capital of Galicia, the most north-
easterly province of the Austrian Empire, near the Russian border), and
he had formed a close friendship with one of the actors, a Polish Jew
named Jizchok Löwy. From Löwy's accounts of Jewish literature in
Warsaw and Kafka's own exposure to Czech literature, Kafka had
begun reflecting on the dynamics of minor literatures (literally "small
literatures," *kleine Literaturen*), and in this dense and at times opaque
diary entry Kafka developed what Ritchie Robertson rightly calls "nothing less than an essay on the sociology of literature."[1]

Kafka first lists the many benefits that literature may bring to a
nation or a people, even if such a literature is not that of an especially
large group. Literature stirs minds and spirits, provides a unifying
national consciousness that is often lacking in public life, and gives a
nation pride in the face of a hostile environment. It brings about "the
assimilation of dissatisfied elements [*die Bindung unzufriedener
Elemente*]" (Diaries I, 191), and through the incessant activity of literary
magazines, it produces "a constant integration of a people with respect
to its whole" (Diaries I, 192). It makes possible the discussion "of the
antithesis [*des Gegensatzes*] between fathers and sons," as well as the
presentation of national faults in a way that is "liberating and deserv-
ing of forgiveness." In such a cultural environment, one finds "the birth
of a respect for those active in literature" and "the beginning of a lively
and therefore self-respecting book trade and the eagerness for books"
(Diaries I, 192). Literature becomes an immediate and vital force, not a
matter for distanced evaluation, but a "keeping of a diary by a nation
[*Tagebuchführen einer Nation*]" which is something entirely different from
historiography and results in a more rapid (and yet always closely scru-
tinized) development" (Diaries I, 191).

In a small nation, these "benefits of literature" may be gained and
perhaps even heightened, not in spite of, but because of, the size of the
culture. Generally minor literatures have no towering individual figures
who dominate the field, such as a Shakespeare in English literature or
a Goethe in German, and the absence of such figures has several positive consequences. No great artist silences others, and "genuine compe-

tition on the greatest scale has a real justification" (Diaries I, 192). The competing writers maintain their mutual independence, since there is no dominating presence under whose sway they may fall, and the untalented are discouraged from writing, since they have no fashionable great model they can mindlessly mimic. When a small nation begins to write its literary history, the absence of dominant figures makes possible a stable canon that does not fluctuate with tastes. This is because the writers' undeniable influence "becomes so matter of fact that it can take the place of their writings" (Diaries I, 193). Even when an influential work of the past is actually read, what readers encounter is not the work itself but the aura of its reputation and its position in the national tradition. In a major literature, there are so many influential works that some are forgotten as tastes change, and others are resurrected as new generations of readers experience the power of neglected masterpieces. But in a minor literature, the influence of key works cannot be forgotten, and "the writings themselves do not act independently upon the memory," since they are one with their reputation. As a result, "there is no forgetting and no remembering again. Literary history offers an unchangeable, dependable whole that is hardly affected by the taste of the day" (Diaries I, 193). Further, since a small nation has fewer works to consider in formulating its literary history, it "can digest the existing material more thoroughly." Not only will the works be more fully assimilated, but national pride will assure that they be adamantly supported and defended, for in a small nation, "literature is less a concern of literary history than of the people, and thus, if not purely, it is at least reliably preserved" (Diaries I, 193).

Finally, in a small nation there is an intimate link between literature and politics. Here Kafka's remarks grow especially obscure, and the logic behind this link is not entirely certain. Kafka notes that since "the interconnected people" [*die zusammenhängenden Menschen*] are lacking, "interconnected literary action" [*die zusammenhängenden litterarische Aktionen*] is also absent, by which he seems to mean that in a small nation the literati do not form a self-contained, interrelated group whose judgments of works are primarily literary. Even when a work is considered calmly, its "boundary" is not determined by its connection with "similar things" (i.e., other works of literature), but with politics. Indeed, the political connection is seen "everywhere," and often "one even strives to see it before it is there." Yet Kafka does not worry that literature in such a context serves as mere propaganda, for "the inner independence of the literature makes the external connection with politics harmless" (Diaries I, 194). The result is that literature in small nations is held fast in political slogans [*sie sich an den politischen Schlagworten festhält*], but it is thereby disseminated throughout the country [*die Litteratur sich dadurch im Lande verbreitet*]. Kafka also suggests that in minor literatures there is an interpenetration of the personal and the political, since "insults, intended as literature," are an open and vital part of the debates among writers and readers. "What in great literature goes on down below, constituting a not indispensable cellar of the structure, here takes place in the full light of day, what is there a matter of passing interest for a few, here absorbs everyone no less than as a matter of life and death" (Diaries I, 194).

Kafka summarizes his reflections in a closing "character sketch of the literature of small peoples [*Schema zur Charakteristik kleiner Litteraturen*]": "1. Liveliness: a. Conflict. b. Schools. c. Magazines. 2. Less constraint: a. Absence of principles. b. Minor themes. c. Easy formation of symbols. d. Throwing off of the untalented. 3. Popularity. a. Connection with politics. b. Literary history. c. Faith in literature, can make up their own laws" (Diaries I, 195). His conclusion, then, is that minor literatures are invigorated by lively conflict, unconstrained by great masters and intimately involved with the life of the people. Kafka examines the peculiar conditions of small nations that give rise to these characteristics, yet it should be evident that his interests go beyond those of empirical observation and sociological explanation. Kafka is describing Czech and Warsaw Jewish literature, but he is also forming a portrait of an ideal literary community of which he would like to be a part, as is suggested in the entry's final sentence: "It is difficult to readjust when one has felt this useful, happy life in all one's being" (Diaries I, 195). Such an ideal community may be fostered in small nations, but it is not necessarily dependent for its existence on such contingent circumstances. Minor literature for Kafka, finally, is literature as it should function in the world, and this is the sense in which Deleuze and Guattari take the term. What they stress in Kafka's remarks is that minor literature is thoroughly political, "less a concern of literary history than of the people"; that it subsumes the personal within the political, making individual conflicts a communal "matter of life and death," as well as opening to public discussion familial disputes between fathers and sons; and that it centers not on great individual figures but on multiple writers engaged in a vibrant collective enterprise.

DETERRITORIALIZED LANGUAGE

Deleuze and Guattari add to this description of minor literature two characteristics Kafka does not mention: In it, language "is affected by a high coefficient of deterritorialization" (K 29; 16), and the writer operates via a "collective assemblage of enunciation" (K 33; 18). They find linguistic deterritorialization evident in Kafka's practice as a Prague Jew writing in German. As Klaus Wagenbach argues at length in his study of Kafka's early years, Prague Jews at the turn of the century were in a peculiar linguistic situation. Most spoke German and attended German schools. Many, like Kafka, were raised by parents who had abandoned their rural roots and native Czech language to embrace city life and the tongue of Prague's prestigious linguistic minority. (Wagenbach estimates that 80 percent of Prague's citizens were speakers of Czech, 5 percent well-to-do ethnic Germans and the rest German-speaking Jews [Wagenbach 28, 65, 191].) Kafka was reared in a German-speaking home, yet he was unusual among his Jewish contemporaries in mastering Czech (Wagenbach 181). The linguistic atmosphere of Kafka's Prague was further complicated by the presence of "Kuchelböhmisch," a mixture of German and Czech, and "Mauscheldeutsch," a sort of Germanized Yiddish that influenced Jewish speech to a limited extent. Kafka's father occasionally made use of popular *Mauscheldeutsch* expressions, and the father's German, notes Wagenbach, "was far from correct" (Wagenbach 80).

Prague German was an impoverished tongue, claims Wagenbach, "a sort of ceremonial language subsidized by the state," a mere "foreign body, dry and colorless like paper" (Wagenbach 87).[2] As Heinrich Teweles, the editor of *Bohemia* lamented, "In Prague, we do not have an ethnic German group encouraging the ceaseless renewal of the language; we are all only Germans by education" (cited in Wagenbach 77). Not only was this paper language ungrounded in an established community, but it also was affected in pronunciation, syntax and vocabulary by its constant contact with the Czech language. Many speakers of Prague German had a decidedly Czech accent, and the nonstandard turns of phrase that typified their speech often betrayed the influence of Czech grammatical constructions. Wagenbach cites as chief among these characteristics the incorrect use of prepositions (*darauf denken, daran vergessen*), the misuse of pronominal verbs (*sich spielen*) and the omission of articles (*Wir gehen in Baumgarten, Eingang in Garten*). Typical of Prague German as well was a general impoverishment of vocabulary, induced in part by the constant necessity of simplifying the terms of communication between speakers of Czech and German, but also by specific Czech practices. For example, Prague speakers of German often used the simple verb *geben* (to give) in lieu of the verbs *legen, setzen, stellen* and *abnehmen* (to lay, to set, to put, to remove), a usage parallel to that of the Czech *dati* (to give).

In Deleuze and Guattari's terms, Kafka's Prague German was a deterritorialized German. Separated from a naturalizing, integrating ethnic German speech community, it had undergone numerous deformations through its proximity to Czech, and its impoverishment had forced a limited vocabulary to assume multiple functions, each term taking on an intensive and shifting polyvocality. Wagenbach notes that many Prague writers responded to this linguistic "floating" and "verbal indigence" with a compensatory "verbal profusion" (Wagenbach 80), a language overloaded with similes, metaphors, oniric symbols, neologisms, arabesques, circumlocutions, and so forth. Kafka, by contrast, responded to this linguistic floating and indigence through what Wagenbach describes as "a very personal Prague German, divested of almost all local influences" (Wagenbach 80), a language that is "correct, cold, impassive, unadorned, constructed with the greatest logic" (Wagenbach 76), informed by a "purist tendency" and a "way of 'taking words at the letter of the word'" (Wagenbach 86, 87). What Deleuze and Guattari find in this cool, impassive, minimalist style is an acceptance of Prague German's linguistic poverty and an intensification of its tendencies through ascetic limitation, that is, a deliberate exacerbation of the deterritorializing forces already present in the language.

In this regard, they see Kafka as following the course of linguistic deformation he himself speaks of in his remarkable "Introductory Talk on the Yiddish Language," delivered before a performance by Löwy's theatrical troupe, February 18, 1912. Kafka approaches Yiddish as an offshoot of German, whose "idiom is brief and rapid," "a spoken language that is in continuous flux." Its words "are not firmly rooted in it, they retain the speed and liveliness with which they were adopted.

(*Dearest Father* 382). It is a "linguistic medley of whim and law," which "as a whole consists only of dialect, even the written language" (*Dearest Father* 383). Its proximity to German assures that "everyone who speaks the German language is also capable of understanding Yiddish," though the close ties between the two languages make translation impossible: "The fact is Yiddish cannot be translated into German. The links between Yiddish and German are too delicate and significant not to be torn to shreds the instant Yiddish is transformed back into German" (*Dearest Father* 384–85). What allows ready understanding, Kafka tells his audience, is that "apart from what you know there are active in yourselves forces and associations with forces that enable you to understand Yiddish intuitively" (*Dearest Father* 385). Yiddish, in short, is like Prague German, only to a greater degree—a hyperdeterritorialized German, in continuous flux, brief and rapid, traversed by great migrations, a medley of whim and law, an amalgam of dialects with no standard speech, a field of forces that is less known than intuitively understood.

Kafka's Yiddish, in Deleuze and Guattari's view, is not so much a language as a way of inhabiting language, a minority's means of appropriating the majority's tongue and undermining its fixed structures. Yiddish speakers, like Prague Jews, make a *minor* use of language, a destabilizing deformation of the standard elements of German that sets it in motion and opens it to forces of metamorphosis. This minor use of language Deleuze and Guattari see as consonant with Kafka's vision of a properly functioning literary community, and they argue that emergent in Kafka's practice as a writer, his understanding of Yiddish and his analysis of "small literatures," is a conception of literature as a convergence of linguistic experimentation and political action. Such a literature is minor, finally, not because it is the literature of a restricted group (though the political dimension of literature is often most evident in "small literatures"), nor because it is the literature of a minority (though the effects of linguistic deformation are often striking in the speech and writing of minorities), but because it is the literature of minor usage, of a "minorization" of the dominant power structures inherent in language. We must now turn to Deleuze and Guattari's remarks on language in *A Thousand Plateaus* to see in what sense linguistic experimentation has a directly social and political effect.

LANGUAGE AND POWER

Language for Deleuze and Guattari is a means of action, a way of doing things. As speech-act theorists have long pointed out, there are certain expressions that in their enunciation clearly constitute an action, such as "I thee wed" when pronounced by a minister. Deleuze and Guattari see in such *performatives* the paradigm of all language and argue that linguistics should be regarded as a subdivision of a general pragmatics, or theory of action. The function of language is not primarily to communicate, they argue, but to impose order—to transmit what they call *mots d'ordre* ("slogans," "watchwords," literally "words of order") (MP 96; 76). Every language encodes the world, categorizing entities, actions and states of affairs, determining their contours, specifying their relations, and so on. With the inculcation of a language comes the organization of reality according to a dominant social order, and everywhere speech-acts take place a dominant social order is confirmed and reinforced. Language operates by inducing "incorporeal transformations" (MP 102; 80) of the world, speech-acts changing things, acts, states of affairs, and so on, through their codification, in the same manner as the groom and bride are transformed into husband and wife with the phrase, "I now pronounce you man and wife."[3] Such incorporeal transformations presuppose regular patterns of action and organized configurations of entities, and it is via socially sanctioned networks of practices, institutions and material entities that the codification of language is enacted. These complex networks are comprised of "assemblages" (*agencements*), collections of heterogeneous actions and entities that somehow function together.[4] Two broad categories of assemblages may be distinguished, the first consisting of nondiscursive *machinic assemblages* of bodies, "of actions and passions, an intermingling of bodies reacting to one another," the second of discursive *collective assemblages of enunciation*, "of acts and statements, of incorporeal transformations attributed to bodies" (MP 112; 88). Machinic assemblages are the various patterns of practices and elements through which a world's entities are formed, and collective assemblages of enunciation are the patterns of actions, institutions and conventions that make possible linguistic statements. When the judge pronounces the defendant "guilty," for example, her verdict presupposes all the regularities of the legal code, of judicial, legislative and executive institutions, the conventions of behavior in court rooms, and so forth, all of

which function together as a collective assemblage of enunciation.
Entities of this assemblage are also formed through nondiscursive practices, the court building, the gavel, the judge's robes, and so on, being produced through multifarious networks of actions that function as machinic assemblages. Although the two kinds of assemblages are intermingled, they remain separable processes, collective assemblages of enunciation functioning as a level of expression, and machinic assemblages as a level of content. Expression and content, however, are not related to one another as signifier to signified, but as distinct patterns of actions and entities interfering with one another, intervening in each other's functioning: "In expressing the noncorporeal attribute, and at the same time attributing it to a body, one does not represent, one does not refer, one *intervenes* in a certain manner, and that is an act of language" (MP 110; 86).

Linguists generally analyze language in terms of constants and invariants, whereas Deleuze and Guattari argue that the standard, fixed forms of language are secondary effects produced by regular patterns of action. Primary for Deleuze and Guattari are variables, which exist in a virtual dimension comprised of multiple "lines of continuous variation," and which assemblages actualize in specific, concrete instances. Consider the statement "I swear!," for example. Phonemically, one may view variations in the pronunciation of "swear" as insignificant deviations from a standard phonemic unit, but Deleuze and Guattari look on all the possible pronunciations of "swear" as forming a continuum of sounds, a line of continuous variation, which has a virtual existence, real without being actual. Each speaker actualizes a particular portion of that continuum, and the regulating patterns of action of a dominant social order determine which point along the continuum counts as the "correct" pronunciation and which points are "incorrect," "nonstandard," "deviant." A similar continuum underlies the syntax of "I swear!," a line of continuous variation containing "I do swear," "Me swear," "So do I swear," "Swear I," and so on, norm and deviations again being enforced through regular patterns of action. Finally, a semantic line of continuous variation passes through "I swear!" Commonly, the semantic content of a statement is seen as a stable, denotative core that takes on various nuances of meaning in diverse contexts. But Deleuze and Guattari regard each speech act as the actualization of a particular point on a continuum of semantic variables. When the son swears before his father, the fiancé before his betrothed or the defendant before the judge, in each instance "I swear!" is a different speech-act with a different semantic content. Each performance is an actualization of a continuum of virtual "I swears!," the variable nuances of meaning receiving sanction as standard or deviant, literal or figurative, serious or whimsical, and so on, according to the dominant practices of the social order.

All the lines of continuous variation of a language are parts of an "abstract machine," which also includes as complementary parts the variable trajectories of the nondiscursive patterns of action that shape entities in the world. Collective assemblages of enunciation and nondiscursive machinic assemblages actualize the abstract machine, and the abstract machine puts the two assemblages in relation with one another. The regular practices of a given social order control and restrict variables, but lines of continuous variation remain immanent within assemblages, making possible nonstandard actualizations that destabilize norms and rules. Hence, the various "errors" of Prague German and the deformations of German produced within Yiddish are so many actualizations of points along lines of continuous variation, variables that undermine the regularities of standard German and thereby destabilize as well all the assemblages of practices, institutions, entities and states of affairs that those linguistic regularities presuppose. One can see, then, why Deleuze and Guattari regard the deterritorialization of language as political action, for language is itself action shaped by structures of power, and a minor use of language, such as that made of German by Prague Jews, necessarily engages power relations as it counters the restrictive controls of standard usage and sets nonstandard variables at play within the language.

THE MINOR USE OF LANGUAGE

Deleuze and Guattari assert that Kafka makes a similar minor use of language in his own writing, intensifying the deterritorializing impoverishment of Prague German in his ascetic, unadorned style. His strategy is "to be a foreigner *within* his own language" (K 48; 26), "to make use of the polylingualism in [his] own language, to make of this a minor or intensive usage, to oppose the oppressed-character of this language to its oppressor-character, to find points of non-culture and underdevelopment, linguistic third-world zones through which a language escapes, an animal grafts itself, an assemblage plugs in" (K

49–50; 26–27). What Deleuze and Guattari mean concretely by "being a foreigner in one's own language" they seldom specify, but from hints they supply in *Kafka* and other works, one can get a preliminary sense of what they have in mind. They provide no strictly stylistic examples of Kafka's minor use of German in *Kafka*, but they do cite a few instances of other writers' deterritorialization of language. They allude briefly to Artaud's "cries-breaths [*cris-souffles*]" (K 49; 26), which Deleuze examines in *The Logic of Sense*, the "breath-words [*mots-souffles*], cry-words [*mots-cris*] in which all the literal, syllabic and phonetic values are replaced by *values that are exclusively tonic* and non-written" (LS 108; 88) (see chapter 1). They also mention the usage Céline makes of French in *Guignol's Band*, "following another line, exclamatory to the highest point" (K 49; 26). (A random sample: "Boom! Zoom! . . . It's the big smashup! . . . The whole street caving in at the water front! . . . It's Orléans crumbling and thunder in the Grand Café! . . . A table sails by and splits the air! . . . Marble bird! . . . spins round, shatters a window to splinters!" [*Guignol's Band* 6].) In *A Thousand Plateaus* they offer e. e. cummings's lines "he danced his did" and "they went their came" as instances of minor "agrammaticality," "the line that puts grammatical variables in a state of continuous variation" (MP 125; 99). And Gherasim Luca's "Passionément," they cite as an example of stammering in language (MP 124; 98). ("Passionné nez passionnem je/ je t'ai je t'aime je/ je je jet je t'ai jetez/ je t'aime passionnem t'aime." Deleuze says of this poem in "He Stuttered," "The entire language spins and varies in order to disengage a final sonic block, a single breath at the limit of the cry I LOVE YOU PASSIONATELY [*JE T'AIME PASSIONNÉMENT*]" [CC 139; 110].) They mention Beckett frequently as a minor stylist, and in "The Exhausted" Deleuze offers two examples of Beckett's minor practice, the first whereby "short segments are ceaselessly added to the interior of the phrase in an effort to break the surface of words open completely" (E 105; CC 174) ("folly seeing all this— / this— / what is the word— / this this— / this this here— / all this this here— / folly given all this— / seeing— / folly seeing all this this here—" [Beckett, "What Is the Word," in *As the Story Was Told* 132]); the second in which "punctuation marks riddle the phrase in order to ceaselessly reduce the surface of words" (E 106; CC 174) ("Less best. No. Naught best. Best worse. No. Not best worse. Naught not best worse. Less best worse. No. Least. Least best worse" [Beckett, "Worstword Ho," in *Nohow On* 118]).

Such clear deviations from standard usage as these—*cris-souffles*, exclamatory shouts, fragmented phrases, syntactic hybrids, self-dividing sentences, obsessive iterations—must seem far removed from the calm prose of Kafka, and indeed, Kafka critics have generally rejected this portion of Deleuze and Guattari's analysis, countering that Kafka was a linguistic purist who went to great lengths to be sure that he wrote in a strictly standard style.[5] But we must be cautious in assuming that a minor usage of language is simply incorrect usage. The object of minor writing is to make language vibrate, to induce disequilibrium, to activate from within the language itself the lines of continuous variation immanent within its grammatical, syntactic and semantic patterns. "Masterpieces are written in a sort of foreign language [*une langue étrangère*]," remarks Proust, and each great writer invents his or her own foreign language within a language, his or her own means of making language strange. "To be a foreigner [*un étranger*], but in one's own language, and not simply as someone who speaks a language other than his or her own. To be bilingual, multilingual, but in a single and same language, without even dialect or patois. . . . One only arrives at this result through sobriety, creative subtraction. Continuous variation has only ascetic lines, a little herb and pure water" (MP 125; 98–99).

Kafka creates "a unique and solitary writing," following the line of deterritorialization of Prague German, "but in the sense of a new sobriety, a new unheard-of correctness, a pitiless rectification. . . . Schizo politeness, drunkenness from pure water" (K 47–48; 25–26). Deleuze and Guattari quote Kafka's contemporary Franz Blei, the editor of the journal *Hyperion*, who says of Kafka's prose that it "has the air of the cleanliness of a child who is taking care of his person" (cited in Wagenbach 82). Hence, part of the strangeness of Kafka's language, suggest Deleuze and Guattari, is a certain hypercorrectness, a stark purity that admits of no direct violation of standard usage. But its starkness also echoes the "verbal indigence" of Prague German, the impoverishment of vocabulary that overloads individual words with diverse functions and tonalities, such as the verb *geben*, which must serve as well for *legen, setzen, stellen* and *abnehmen*. The reduction of vocabulary pushes each word a few steps closer toward an inarticulate extreme, toward a vanishing point at which all sense must be expressed in a single sound.[6] It is in this way that Kafka wrests from Prague German "all its points of underdevelopment" and makes it "cry with a cry so sober and rigorous" (K 48; 26).

A minor usage of language, then, may manifest itself through direct violations of linguistic norms and rules, but also by more indirect means that leave basic conventions intact. The intensity and strangeness of Kafka's style, it would seem, is primarily in its rigor, simplicity and coldness. Yet a minor usage is an "asignifying *intensive usage* of language" (K 41; 22), and Deleuze and Guattari do insist that Kafka at times treats words as asignifying bits of sound. They cite as evidence passages from Kafka's diaries in which he notes sonic disturbances in his own writing: "Almost every word I write jars against the next, I hear the consonants rub leadenly against each other and the vowels sing an accompaniment like Negroes in a minstrel show" (Diaries I, 33); "I live only here and there in a small word in whose vowel . . . I lose my useless head for a moment. The first and last letters are the beginning and end of my fishlike emotion" (Diaries I, 61–62). They allude to a diary passage in which Kafka recalls a childhood experience of repeating a phrase until it became nonsense, as well as a letter to Milena in which Kafka makes free associations with the sound of her name. But the only examples of sonic disturbances in Kafka's fiction that they mention are the strange asignifying sounds that recur in his works—the ubiquitous buzzing of "The Burrow," Gregor's insect twittering in "The Metamorphosis," the canine choir's amusical music in "Investigations of a Dog," the whispering of the mice in "Josephine the Singer, or the Mouse Folk," Franz's shriek in *The Trial*. These, however, are sonic effects described in the narratives, not effects manifest in Kafka's own language. It would appear that Deleuze and Guattari are making a fundamental category mistake at this point, confusing a verbal representation of sound (the phrase "he twittered") with the sound itself (an actual twittering). If we pursue this apparent confusion, however, we may eventually arrive at a more complete grasp of the relation between sound and sense in a minor usage of language.

Deleuze and Guattari divide their discussion of asignifying sound into two numbered paragraphs (K 38–41; 21–22), the first of which posits the existence of such sounds in Kafka (the evidence for this argument we examined above), the second of which concerns the difference between metaphor and metamorphosis and the relation between sound and sense in the process of "becoming-animal." They open their discussion of metaphor and metamorphosis by concurring with

Wagenbach that in Kafka "the *word* reigns supreme, it directly gives birth to the image" (Wagenbach 88). They then ask, by what means does this take place, through what "procedure" (K 39; 21) does the word give birth to the image? Every human language "implies a deterritorialization of the mouth, tongue and teeth" (K 35; 19), a detachment of certain oral activities from such animal functions as eating, drinking, howling, humming, and so on. Sounds, once detached from their animal function, are reterritorialized in sense (*sens*: sense, meaning), "and it is sense, as proper sense, that presides over the assignment of the designation of sounds (the thing or state of things that the word designates), and as figurative sense, that presides over the assignment of images and metaphors (the other things to which the word is applied under certain aspects or certain conditions)" (K 37; 20). What is crucial about a minor usage of language is that it deterritorializes sound, "detaches" it from its designated objects and thereby neutralizes sense. The word ceases to mean and becomes instead an arbitrary sonic vibration. Yet something does subsist from the sense, a means of directing lines of flight. In a becoming-insect, for example, a line of flight passing through the terms "human" and "insect" subsists from the sense of the words, but it is a line of flight in which there is no longer a literal or a figurative sense to the words. The thought of becoming-insect is not a question of metaphor, of a literal designation of things by words and a metaphorical extension of one literal designation to another (the human like an insect, the insect like a human). Instead, words and things form "a sequence of intensive states, a scale or a circuit of pure intensities that one can traverse in one direction or another" (K 39–40; 21–22). A passage emerges between what had formerly been designated "human" and "insect," a continuum of intensive states in which words and things can no longer be differentiated. At this point, "the image is this passage itself, it has become becoming" (K 40; 22). The process of becoming is one of metamorphosis rather than metaphor. "Metamorphosis is the contrary of metaphor. There is no longer either proper or figurative sense, but a distribution of states in the range of the word. The thing and the other things are no longer anything but intensities traversed by the sounds or deterritorialized words following their line of flight. It's not a matter of a resemblance between the behavior of an animal and that of a man, even less of wordplay. There is no longer man or animal, since each deterritorializes the other, in a conjunction of flows, in a continuum of reversible intensities" (K 40; 22). When the image becomes becoming, "the animal does not speak 'like' a man, but extracts from language tonalities without signification; the words themselves are not 'like' animals, but clamber on their own, howl and swarm, being properly linguistic dogs, insects or mice" (K 41; 22).

One might be puzzled when turning from this phantasmagoric account of becoming to the staid and rather lucid narrative of "The Metamorphosis," but what Deleuze and Guattari are describing is more a compositional process than a completed text. Their point, it would seem, is that Kafka invents through metamorphosis rather than metaphor, and that metamorphosis proceeds through a dissolution of sense. In essence, a deterritorialization of meaning, whereby a word becomes a mere sonic disturbance detached from its sense, functions much as the diagram does in Francis Bacon's paintings. As Deleuze observes in *Francis Bacon: The Logic of Sensation*, Bacon often starts a composition based on a representational image of some sort—a bird, a face, a bed. But in the process of painting, he deliberately introduces into the image a nonrational, tactile blotch, a swipe of a sponge or a spasmodic brushstroke. This blotch he calls a diagram, and in its chaotic disturbance of the representational image he finds indications of directions for metamorphosing the image and developing mutative forms that he could not have anticipated before the occurrence of the chaotic blotch. Bacon's diagram is a locus of catastrophe, a point at which common distinctions and ordinary representations break down. From the diagram issue compositions whose contours are suggested by the diagram in the guise of tendencies, vectors or movements toward new elements and states of affairs. The diagram is a synthesizer, a kind of pulverizing-machine into which conventional representations are fed and out of which emerge the figures, contours and fields of Bacon's canvases. The diagram, however, does not cover the entire painting; the catastrophe is limited, and in certain works it is not even immediately observable in the composition itself. In a similar manner, in Kafka's writing a sonic disturbance suspends sense, deterritorializing literal and figurative linguistic designations. The asignifying sound serves as a diagram, a local catastrophe that guides invention, in the case of a becoming-insect along the lines of flight that pass through what were formerly designated "human" and "insect." What emerges from this diagram is "The Metamorphosis." The diagram itself appears only in Gregor's twittering and in the evenly distributed ascetic intensity of Kafka's stripped-down, impoverished style. In Gregor himself we meet a Bacon-like figure, a self-deforming form that captures the forces of a metamorphic passage between forms, a zone of human-insect imperceptibility that is neither human nor insect.

A similar process may be presumed to take place in *The Trial*, in this case a continuum of speech-acts serving the same function as the passage between human and insect in a becoming-insect. To be accused, to investigate, to testify, to defend, to prosecute, to be judged, and so forth, entail multiple speech-acts within a judicial setting. Related speech-acts exist in other spheres—financial, industrial, religious, familial—but segregated from one another, regulated and organized according to common sense distinctions. Through a sonic disturbance, sense is suspended and a diagram emerges. Within that diagram, intensive continua of "I swear!," "Guilty!," "Defend yourself!," "Under arrest!," and so on, emerge, suggesting passages between ordinarily separated realms, connections between actions, institutions and entities that produce strangely composite structures and associated practices, bank-torture chambers, tenement-bureaucracies, boarding house-detention centers, cathedral-prisons. *The Trial* emerges from this diagram, K.'s movements tracing the paths opened up by its continua of speech-acts, but the diagram itself is evident only in characters' occasional non sequiturs, the scream of a flogging victim and the ascetic simplicity of the narrative's language.

In one regard, then, Deleuze and Guattari's apparent confusion of sound and the representation of sound simply highlights the paradoxical nature of the linguistic diagram, in which sense is suspended, and pathways of becoming-other and continua of speech-acts blend word and thing in circuits of pure intensities. The diagram discloses a virtual dimension, immanent within language, that consists solely of lines of continuous variation, vectors of intensities. It is the dimension of the abstract machine, which "operates through *matter*, and not through substance; through *function* and not through form. Substances and forms are either 'of expression' *or* 'of content.' But the functions are not yet 'semiotically' formed, and the matters are not yet 'physically' formed. The abstract machine is a pure Function-Matter—a diagram independent of the forms and substances, the expressions and contents it will distribute" (MP 176; 141). In the compositional process, a deterritorialization of sense detaches sounds from the things they designate, opening up an immanent Function-Matter that is neither linguistically nor physically shaped. As the writing proceeds, the trajectories of this amorphous Function-Matter distribute expression and content in separable elements and make possible a new configuration of their relation, a completed composition that is a genuine invention.

But the confusion of sound and the representation of sound also suggests a complex relation between expression and content, one especially elusive in writers such as Kafka. A passage from Deleuze's "He Stuttered," a brief essay on stammering in one's own tongue, points toward the nature of that relation. In the realistic novel, Deleuze notes, authors commonly present direct discourse with varied phrases, such as "he said," "she replied," "she gasped," "he stuttered." They also occasionally represent stammering in direct speech itself ("b-, b-, but I, I, I . . . "). It would seem that the first practice is distant from the act of making language itself stutter, but this may not always be the case, Deleuze claims.

> For when the author is content with an external indication which leaves intact the *form of expression* ("he stuttered"), its efficacity would be poorly understood if a corresponding *form of content*, an atmospheric quality, a milieu that serves as a conductor of words [*un milieu conducteur de paroles*], did not itself gather up the tremble, the murmur, the stutter, the tremolo, the vibrato, and make the indicated affect reverberate over the words. This at least is what happens with great writers like Melville, in whom the din of the forest and the caverns, the silence of the house, the presence of the guitar testify to the murmur of Isabelle and her sweet "foreign intonations" [in *Pierre, or the Ambiguities*]; or Kafka who confirms the twittering of Gregor through the trembling of his feet and the oscillations of his body. . . . The affects of language here form the object of an indirect effectuation, but close to that which takes place directly, when there are no longer any characters other than the words themselves. (CC 135–136; 107–8)

In Artaud, Céline, Luca and Beckett, the words themselves are affective intensities, asignifying stutterings within language that directly disrupt linguistic conventions. In Melville and Kafka, deterritorialized sounds appear indirectly in the form of content—the description of the sounds of the forest, house and guitar that echo Isabelle's speech, the description of Gregor's twittering that resonates with his twitching body.

What allows the communication among sounds and vibrations in Melville and Kafka, the *echo* of forest, house, guitar and speech, the *confirmation* of the twittering in the trembling feet and oscillating body, is an atmospheric quality, a milieu *"conducteur de paroles,"* both a conducting directional force for discourse and an electrical conductor that transmits affective reverberations *"sur les mots,"* over, above, across, through the words. Such a communication takes place in "great writers," those who are able to create an atmosphere that gathers within itself the various vibrations. Deleuze does not say what distinguishes great writers from those lesser talents who simply evoke foggy settings and emote vague feelings, but it would seem that in Melville and Kafka, at least, there is an answerable style that forms part of the atmosphere, an adequation between the peculiar strangeness of each writer's use of his language and the objects described. Kafka's spare, ascetic use of German is not simply a fitting vehicle for the narration of Gregor's dreamlike transformation, it is an inseparable atmospheric medium that pervades the story, just as conversely, the peculiar quality of the prose of "The Metamorphosis" is inseparable from the strange transformations represented in it. The echoes between the twitterings of Gregor and the elements of Kafka's prose, then, may be seen not simply as the residual effects of a compositional process of becoming-animal, but also as evidence of the atmosphere within which represented affects communicate with one another over, above and through the words.

THE COLLECTIVE ASSEMBLAGE OF ENUNCIATION

It might seem odd that Deleuze refers to Kafka as a "great writer," since Kafka is a practitioner of minor literature, in which "talents do not abound" and "the conditions are not given for an *individuated enunciation,* which would be that of some 'master' and could be separated from the *collective enunciation"* (K 31; 17). One might wonder too why Kafka is said to create "a unique and solitary writing" (K 47; 25) if in minor literature "everything takes on a collective value" (K 31; 17). In his diary remarks on "small literatures," Kafka is struck by the advantages that accrue to a literary community lacking in great masters; for Deleuze and Guattari, however, what is crucial is not a quantitative paucity of talent but the absence of a particular kind of writer, the towering *individual,* who articulates "an *individuated enunciation.*" Major and minor literatures are characterized by their respective usages of language, a major usage leaving intact dominant social codes, a minor usage dismantling them. In the broad cultural context with which Deleuze and Guattari are concerned in *Kafka*—the culture of Western capitalism—the ruling social order stresses individualism and the separation of the personal and the political.[7] Hence, they assert that in a major literature, "the *individual concern* (familial, conjugal, etc.) tends to join with other no less individual concerns, the social milieu serving as an environment or background," whereas in a minor literature "each individual concern is immediately plugged into the political" (K 30; 17). A great writer is not necessarily a major writer, and a minor writer may be great—simply not a great *individual* writer, in the sense of an autonomous figure distanced from the political sphere.

Yet it should be clear from Deleuze and Guattari's general approach to language that major and minor are not simply opposed to one another as the individual to the collectivity. Every language presumes collective assemblages of enunciation, nondiscursive machinic assemblages and an abstract machine that distributes and interrelates these assemblages. Strictly speaking, "there is no subject, *there are only collective assemblages of enunciation*" (K 33; 18). In part, Deleuze and Guattari are simply making the rather unexceptional observation that language is a social creation, whose rules, conventions, vocabulary, and so on, are invented by groups rather than individuals (even in the case of a term coined by a specific person, since the term's formation takes place within a collective context, and its inclusion within a language depends on its acceptance by a community of speakers). A collective assemblage of enunciation is operative in both a major and a minor usage of language, and in neither does a writer act as an independent agent creating *ex nihilo*. The difference between the two is that in a major usage the writer accepts and confirms the role of depoliticized individual that the social order assigns the artist, whereas in a minor usage the writer rejects that assigned function and directly engages the collective assemblage of enunciation.

The problem for the minor writer is that the present configuration of the social order is unacceptable, and an alternative collectivity does not yet exist. Literature is a concern of the people, but as Paul Klee remarks, "the people are lacking" (Klee 55). Literature therefore must take on "this role and this function of collective and even revolutionary enunciation: it is literature that produces an active solidarity, despite skepticism; and if the writer is in the margins or off to the side of his or her fragile community, that situation puts him or her that much more in a position to express another potential community, to forge the means of another consciousness and another sensibility" (K 31–32; 17). To *express* a different potential community, we should note, is not to *describe* something that is fully formed; rather, it is to "forge the means" of a different consciousness and sensibility, to open the way toward a new community. The minor writer's task is to "extract from social representations the assemblages of enunciation and the machinic assemblages and to dismantle these assemblages" and thereby "make the social representation take flight" (K 85; 46–47). Literature "expresses these assemblages, under conditions that are not given outside, and that exist solely as diabolical powers to come or as revolutionary forces to construct" (K 33; 18).

For Deleuze and Guattari, to invent something new is necessarily to invent something whose shape cannot be foreseen. The new emerges through a process of metamorphosis whose outcome is unpredictable. If writers find existing configurations of social relations unacceptable, their only option is to induce a metamorphosis of the established forms of the social field, with no guarantee that the result will be a more acceptable community. It is for this reason that in a minor literature expression precedes content: "it is expression that outdistances or advances, it is expression that precedes contents, either in order to prefigure the rigid forms into which they are going to flow, or in order to make them take off along a line of flight or of transformation" (K 152–53; 85). In a major literature content precedes expression; "a content being given, in a given form" the major writer seeks "to find, to discover or to see the form of expression which suits it" (K 51; 28). The major writer leaves undisturbed the regular codes and organized practices established in language, seeking simply an adequate expression for a preshaped content. For the minor writer, by contrast, "expression must break forms, mark new ruptures and branchings. A form being broken, reconstruct the content that will necessarily be in rupture with the order of things" (K 52; 28). Since the "good sense" of conventional codes is part of the enactment of coercive power relations, the minor writer must suspend sense and develop "a *machine of expression* capable of disorganizing its own forms, and of disorganizing the forms of contents, in order to liberate pure contents that mingle with expressions in a single intense matter" (K 51; 28). By treating words as asignifying sounds, the minor writer suspends sense. Metaphor then gives way to metamorphosis, and the image becomes becoming, a passage of intensities in which word and thing are indistinguishable. The result of this metamorphic process will be a reconstructed content "necessarily in rupture with the order of things" (K 52; 28), one that serves either as a prefiguration of the diabolical powers of the future, such as those of the fascist, Stalinist or capitalist bureaucracies, or as an opening toward new social and material relations that can only take on a specific and definite form through their enactment at some time to come.

In the absence of a people, writers who are marginalized and solitary may be in the best position "to express another potential community" (K 32; 17), but if they do so, it will not be as individual subjects, for "the most individual literary enunciation is a particular case of collective enunciation" (K 150; 84). "When a statement is produced by a *Célibataire* or an artist singularity, it is only as a function of a national, political and social community, even if the objective conditions of that community are not yet given at that moment outside the literary enunciation" (K 149; 83–84). Indeed, the situation of the writer working in anticipation of a people is common enough for Deleuze and Guattari to make it a defining characteristic of literature: "It's even a definition: a statement is literary when it is 'assumed' by a *Célibataire* who outdistances the collective conditions of enunciation" (K 150; 84). This does not mean, however, that the "people to come" somehow function as an identifiable subject of speech. "No more than the *Célibataire*, the collectivity is not a subject, either a subject of enunciation or a subject of the statement. But the actual *Célibataire* and the virtual community—both of them real—are the pieces of a collective assemblage" (K 150; 84).

In sum, then, the actual writer, existing as a concrete entity unfolding in the world, makes use of language, which functions via collective assemblages of enunciation and machinic assemblages, discursive and nondiscursive patterns of heterogeneous practices, institutions and entities that inform relations of power. Immanent within language are lines of continuous variation, virtual continua of variables—sonic, morphemic, grammatical, syntactic, semantic—that are actualized in specific enunciations. All the virtual lines of continuous variation of a language, together with lines of continuous variation immanent within the nondiscursive circuits of machinic assemblages, form the abstract machine, a pure Function-Matter of vectors and trajectories without semiotic or physical organization. In a minor usage of language, the actual writer engages the virtual lines of continuous variation and causes the language itself to stammer, to enter a process of metamorphosis that follows the trajectories of the specific lines of continuous variation activated in a given instance. Those virtual lines of metamorphosis *are* the "people to come," the virtual collectivity that functions together with the actual writer as a new and metamorphic collective assemblage of enunciation. Each writer discovers his or her own way of making language stammer and hence his or her "unique and solitary writing" (K 47; 25), but only through an experimentation on a language's collective assemblages of enunciation, which in a given social context actualize specific circuits of power, and through an activation of the virtual lines of continuous variation immanent within the language, which open vectors of transformation toward a people to come.

The concept of minor literature cuts across at least three different categories: the literature of numerically small nations and groups; the literature of oppressed minorities; and the literature of the modernist avant-garde. In some cases, the first two categories coincide, but not in all. Small groups may be comprised of relatively autonomous, homogeneous populations, whose literary aspiration is simply to create great works that rival those of major literatures. In such cases, small groups have little in common with oppressed minorities. Conversely, oppressed minorities may be numerically small, but they may also form a statistical majority, for as Deleuze and Guattari argue (MP 133–35; 105–6), minorities are defined by their deviance from the norm rather than their actual numbers. Worldwide there may be relatively few white male adults, but nonwhites, women and children remain minorities nonetheless. Linguistically minorities may form a separate, small group, speaking their own ethnic tongue, but in other cases they may be differentiated from the larger population only through their particular use of a common language. The latter instances are what interest Deleuze and Guattari, and their concern with "small literatures" is restricted to those that involve a minor usage of language. It is through the concept of a minor usage of language that Deleuze and Guattari bring together the linguistic inventions of a minority inhabiting a majority's tongue and the experimentations with language of the modernist avant-garde. A minimal justification of this conjunction is that these minority usages and these artistic practices both represent deviations from a linguistic norm, but one might question whether in fact minority speech communities have much in common with experimental writers. Deleuze and Guattari's purpose, however, is not to erase the distinction between the two groups, nor is it simply to provide an analytic schema for their empirical description. Rather, it is to modify the notions of minority literature and modernist literature and to invent possibilities for future literary endeavor. Modernism is often seen as an apolitical movement, and experiments with language are commonly treated as mere formal innovations. But in linking minority and modernist practices, Deleuze and Guattari insist that such writers as Artaud and Beckett are political writers, that *cris-souffles* and fragmenting iterations are forms of social invention and interactions with power. Minority literatures, for their part, are frequently conceived of in terms of group identity, and Deleuze and Guattari's effort here is to support experimental tendencies within the writings of minorities and to critique sentimental appeals to a lost ethnic unity or a future homogeneous totality. Yet finally their aim is to issue a manifesto for a new literature, one in which linguistic experimentation is combined with the invention of a people to come. Kafka provides Deleuze and Guattari with provocation for their theorization and material for the elaboration of their concepts, but their aim is not primarily to formulate a definitive interpretation of his life and work. There is no doubt that their reading of Kafka's diary entry on small literatures is selective and unconcerned with such issues as Kafka's state of mind or degree of artistic development in 1911. Nor is their treatment of Kafka's style such as to convince one that Kafka consciously followed the line of linguistic experimentation suggested by Yiddish, that he purposely deterritorialized German or that he explicitly tied avant-garde stylistics to minority politics. Yet their use of Kafka does emphasize aspects of his work that have only recently received full attention—specifically those of the social and political critique implicit in much of his writing and the complex influences of Prague Jewish culture on his fiction. Their insistence on Kafka's humor serves as a refreshing corrective to the reductively psychologizing readings of his works, and their "machinic" analyses of the functional relations between elements of his *oeuvre* help counter the symbolic and mystical appropriations of his texts common in early Kafka criticism.

Deleuze and Guattari's handling of Kafka's style is perhaps the most confusing aspect of their analysis, in part because they offer no concrete examples of the linguistic effects they posit, but also because their object is to include him in a category with writers whose practices seem quite different from his own—Artaud, Céline, cummings, Luca, Beckett. At times, it seems as if Deleuze and Guattari are merely willing Kafka into being the writer they want him to be, yet finally their inclusion of Kafka with Artaud, Beckett, and others, in a single classification points toward an extended sense of what the category "minor literature" is all about. Kafka experiments on language, but not necessarily in the obvious ways of the modern avant garde. His ascetic, sober use of German suggests that a minor style may leave basic linguistic conventions intact and yet induce a strangeness within the language. An experimentation with language entails a *compositional* practice that suspends sense and engages a process of becoming-other, but the work produced through this process need not be manifest directly in the form of expression per se. And in Deleuze and Guattari's understanding of language, a reconfiguration of the representations of the social world is itself an experimentation on language, since the semantic dimension of language is as much a part of the immanent field of lines of continuous variation as the phonemic, grammatical, morphemic and syntactic elements. Hence, to build a law-desire machine with multiple connections between courtroom, tenement, bank, bedroom, atelier and cathedral is to experiment on language, to activate lines of continuous variation that pass through diverse speech-acts and establish new relations between them. Sound and sense may separate in *cris-souffles* at the edge of the articulable, but they may also reconvene in stories of talking dogs or interminable trials. And the elusive qualities of a style—its peculiar cadences, rhythm, diction, syntactic turns—may constitute an atmospheric medium in which form and content, sound and sense are inseparable, but in a fashion that renders them strange, foreign—new. As Proust says, "Les chefs-d'oeuvre sont écrits dans une sorte de langue étrangère."

Chapter Five

KLEIST, BENE, AND MINOR THEATER

In 1978, Deleuze and the Italian actor, playwright and filmmaker Carmelo Bene published under their names a modest volume in Italian titled *Sovrapposizioni*. The next year, a French version of the text appeared as *Superpositions* [*Superimpositions*]. The first part of the book presents the script of Bene's drama *Richard III, or the Horrible Night of a Man of War*. The second consists of Deleuze's "One Less Manifesto [Un manifeste de moins]," an essay on Bene, the theater and its relation to minor literature. Besides providing Deleuze's most extended commentary on drama, the book offers an intriguing example of the kind of contemporary writing Deleuze sees as fulfilling literature's project of a minor usage of language. The book's superimposition of Bene's play and Deleuze's essay invites as well an analysis of the relation between the two texts, a relation that is largely complementary but framed in different vocabularies that require a delicate and rather involved translation of terms. Deleuze sees the figure of Shakespeare's Richard III as a "man of war" engaged in a "becoming-woman," and Bene treats Richard similarly in his dramatic appropriation and transformation of Shakespeare's script. To understand Deleuze's unorthodox reading of Richard, one must look first at Kleist and his *Penthesilea*, for only in this drama is the relation Deleuze finds between the warrior and becoming-woman made clear. To make sense of Bene's *Richard III*, one must penetrate the cryptic comments scattered throughout his play and situate them within his equally idiosyncratic dramatic theory. Once so glossed, Bene's drama and Deleuze's essay prove to promote a common vision of the theater, a "minor theater" that sets all the variables of the stage in continuous variation.

KLEIST AND THE WAR MACHINE

Bene and Deleuze's collaborative project seems to have coalesced in 1977, sometime during the months of September and October when the Carmelo Bene Company was in residence in Paris, staging performances of Bene's *Romeo and Juliet* and *S.A.D.E* at the Opéra-Comique for the annual *Festival d'automne*. In his highly stylized and rather cryptic autobiographical "Romeo and Juliet in Paris" (in *Sono apparso alla Madonna* [*I Have Appeared to the Virgin*, 1983]), Bene reports meeting with Deleuze after one of his Paris performances in 1977. "He is an autodestructor, Gilles Deleuze. He smokes too much and can't do without it, this human *computer*. He reads as much as he writes and *vice versa*." He is "the greatest thinking machine, I believe, in this chasm of our times" (*Opere* 1165). When a friend of Bene's whispers to Deleuze that *Le Monde* would like a full-page portrait of Bene from Deleuze's hand, Bene grows enthusiastic and describes his project for *Richard III*. Deleuze then exclaims, "'I'm writing a book, who cares about newspapers!'"

> And he writes it, without having seen the performance. And he writes *me*. And I write the text he will see in my final Roman performance at the Teatro Quirino: four months after the publication of his essay. And at the end he embraces me in the dressing room, sits down tired in the armchair, the expected enthusiasm in his eyes:
>
> "*Oui, oui, c'est la rigueur.*"
> And that's all. (*Opere* 1166)

Deleuze, for his part, appears to have been reflecting on *Richard III* around the same time, as can be seen in the following passage from his 1977 *Dialogues*:

The man of the State, or man of the court, is a deceiver, but the
man of war (not the marshal or general) is a traitor. . . .
Shakespeare brought on the stage many deceiver kings, who came
to power through deception, and who proved finally to be good
kings. But when he encounters Richard III, he rises to the most
novelistic of tragedies. For Richard III does not simply want
power, he wants treason. He does not want the conquest of the
State, but the assemblage of a war machine: how can one be the
only traitor, and betray everything at the same time? The dialogue
with Lady Anne, which commentators have judged 'improbable
and overdone,' presents two faces which turn away from one
another, and Anne, already consenting and fascinated, has an inti-
mation of the tortuous line that Richard is in the process of tracing. And nothing reveals treason better than the *choice of object*.
Not because it is a choice of object—a poor notion—but because it
is a becoming, it is the demonic element *par excellence*. In his
choice of Anne, there is a becoming-woman of Richard III. (D 53;
41–42)

Deleuze's identification of Richard III as a "man of war" is echoed in
the subtitle of Bene's play, "the Horrible Night of a Man of War," and
the motif of "becoming-woman" is of central importance in Bene's
drama. To what extent this convergence of interests is the result of one-
way or mutual influence (or chance) is difficult to tell, but it is certain
that the concepts of the war machine, betrayal and becoming-woman
occupy Deleuze at several points in *Dialogues* and eventually receive
detailed treatment in various sections of *A Thousand Plateaus* three years
later. If anything, Richard III seems in these works a very small component of a larger, ongoing investigation, a brief example among many of
a complex of concepts related to war, betrayal and becoming-woman—
and by no means the clearest instance of this complex. In fact, Kleist's
Penthesilea, which Deleuze discusses in conjunction with Richard III in
Dialogues and *A Thousand Plateaus*, provides a much better example of
these concepts, and one that helps make sense of Deleuze's reading of
Shakespeare.

In *Kafka*, Deleuze and Guattari mention Kleist briefly, differentiating Kafka's central question, "what is a minor literature?" from Kleist's
problem, "what is a literature of war?" This question, they remark, is

"not without relation to the question of Kafka, but it is not the same" (K 101; 55).[1] In *A Thousand Plateaus*, they comment that "all of Kleist's work is traversed by a war machine invoked against the State" (MP 328; 268). There is a fundamental incompatibility between the war machine and the State, they argue, the anarchic, chaotic tendencies of the one always threatening to disrupt the order of the other. To wage war, the State must make use of a "war machine," but *the State by itself has no war machine*; it will only appropriate the war machine in the form of the military institution, which will never cease to cause it problems" (MP 439; 355). Deleuze and Guattari point out that Georges Dumézil finds that the tensions between the war and State function throughout Indo-European mythology in the contrasting figures of the warrior and the king, the warrior in many traditions being guilty of various "sins" against social order and in this regard being "in the position of betraying everything" (MP 438; 354). Yet the war machine does not have war per se as its direct object, as Deleuze explains:

> we define the "war machine" as a linear assemblage which is constructed on lines of flight. In this sense, the war machine does not at all have war as its object; it has as its object a very special space, *smooth space*, which it composes, occupies and propagates. *Nomadism* is precisely this combination "war machine-smooth space." We try to show how and in what case the war machine takes war for its object (when the apparatuses of the State appropriate the war machine which does not initially belong to them). A war machine tends to be revolutionary, or artistic, much more so than military. (PP 50–51; 33)

Smooth space is a space of becoming, flux and metamorphosis, as opposed to striated space, which is stable and clearly demarcated. The war machine is "a pure form of exteriority" (MP 438; 354), a force of deterritorialization fashioning assemblages that follow and disclose lines of flight. It is in this sense that Kleist's writing is everywhere traversed by a war machine.

Yet, though the war machine does not have war as its direct object, war and warriors do play an important part in Kleist's work, and in this regard his drama *Penthesilea* is especially significant. This aspect of Kleist is developed at length by Mathieu Carrière in his *For a Literature of War, Kleist,* a text Deleuze and Guattari make use of in virtually all of their comments on Kleist.[2] Carrière says of Kleist that "war is the dynamic, the matrix which determines all his experiences" (Carrière 36). Kleist came of a long aristocratic line of Prussian officers, and between the ages of fifteen and twenty-one he served in the elite King's Guards Regiment in Potsdam, resigning at the rank of second lieutenant in 1799. In 1803 he attempted to join Napoleon's army, and in 1808–9 he wrote a series of war propaganda pieces. Many of his works have war, violent struggle or insurrection as their setting—*The Schroffenstein Family, Robert Guiscard, Penthesilea, Michael Kohlhaas, Käthchen of Heilbronn, The Battle of Teutoburg Forest [Der Hermannsschlacht],* "The Betrothal in Santo Domingo," *The Prince of Homburg.*[3] But Carrière sees these facts as mere indications of a larger concern. War for Kleist, he claims, is a "climate of infection," infection being "the invasion of a multiplicity of bodies by another multiplicity; its project is the disorganization, the deterritorialization of the affected body. . . . Infection is the encounter of at least two enemy populations on the same territory, on the field of battle. It is a form of affective encounter" (Carrière 9–10). In an age obsessed with "sentiment," Kleist pursues "affects," nonpersonal atmospheric states that ignore the distinction between exterior and interior, defy rational control and disrupt logical time. The enemy populations in war's climate of infection are clashing forces, multiplicities that may be as much actual external bodies as internal states of a given individual. War, in short, is the encounter of deterritorializing affective forces.

The master figure of the affect in Kleist is that of the point of intersection of two infinite lines, the "abstract point where two comets, two chains of events, cross" (Carrière 13). This point is "at the same time the center of immobility and the trace of the most frightening speeds" (Carrière 13). From such an immobile point highly graceful movements may issue, as Kleist's "On the Marionette Theater" makes clear. In this brief essay, a dancer interested in the movement of puppets explains that each movement has a "center of gravity" which the puppeteer need only engage to induce in the marionette a dance of the utmost grace. The puppet's line of movement is in one sense a simple function of mechanical forces, but in another it is "something very mysterious," for "it is nothing less than *the path of the dancer's [i.e., the puppeteer's] soul*" (*An Abyss Deep Enough* 212). The grace of the marionette's dance comes in part from its lack of consciousness, as the dancer-narrator explains in an anecdote of a bear who can parry the thrusts of the greatest swordsman, the bear's superior grace of movement arising from its animal unconsciousness. The dancer concludes that in the organic world grace increases as reflection decreases, but "just as two intersecting lines, converging on one side of a point, reappear on the other after their passage through infinity, . . . so will grace, having likewise traversed the infinite, return to us once more, and so appear most purely in that bodily form that has either no consciousness at all or an infinite one, which is to say, either in the puppet or a god" (*Abyss* 216).

Grace issues from an immobile point, a center of gravity, through which pass unconscious yet mysterious forces, mechanical yet divine. An affect is such an immobile point, and from a psychological perspective it is experienced as a break in continuity, a gap in consciousness, a jump or leap into a hole. (Kleistian heroes frequently fall into trances, walk in their sleep, and so on.) The affective point is at once the juncture of forces colliding at maximum acceleration and a motionless, catatonic seizure. Though graceful movements may arise from the affective point, its violent, spasmodic advent can induce an appearance of ineptitude, clumsiness and boorishness (hence the appropriateness of the seemingly oafish bear as image of eminent gracefulness). The affect is a break in the continuity of rational consciousness and a hiatus in the regular flow of chronological time. In such a moment of atemporal disequilibrium, no sense of self exists, no separation of inside and outside. All that remains is a "violent, immobile, graceful climate" (Carrière 18), a "silent tempest, from which lightning flashes from time to time" (Carrière 23).

WAR AND PENTHESILEA

The climate of affects is a climate of war, a dimension of forces that penetrates psychological depths and spreads across social fields. In Kleist's drama *Penthesilea* (1807), the personal and political aspects of war are intertwined, the forces of affective intensities and physical violence meeting in unstable relations of love and combat. The play opens on the plains of Troy, Odysseus discussing with his troops the consternating presence of the Amazons, who have fought against the Trojans but now battle the Greeks. The Amazons fight for no known cause.

They seem a pure force of destruction unallied to either side of the ongoing Trojan War, an anarchic war machine set loose against the State machines of Greece and Troy. In actuality, however, the Amazons do have their own form of State organization, and they do wage war with a purpose. The Amazons, as Penthesilea later explains to Achilles, are descendants of Scythians who had been conquered by Vexoris, king of Ethiopia. The Ethiopians had killed all the male Scythians and planned to rape all the women, but when the Ethiopian men came to the Scythian women's beds, the women stabbed the men, "And all that race of murderers with knives/ In that one night was tickled to the shades" (*Penthesilea* 379). In that moment of violence, "A nation [had] arisen, a nation of women, . . . A folk that gives itself its own just laws,/ Obeys its own decrees" (*Penthesilea* 379). When the high priestess expressed doubts that women could permanently fend off hostile male forces, Tanais, the Amazons' founding queen, tore away her right breast and seized the ritual bow of Scythian state authority, all Amazon women thereafter removing their right breasts to adapt themselves to the bellicose function of shooting the bow and arrow. (At this point in Penthesilea's narration, Achilles asks if they are all "barbarously, inhumanly, deformed" [*beraubt, unmenschlich, frevelhaft, Penthesilea* 381].) To procreate, the Amazons adopted a practice of waging sporadic wars with surrounding tribes, capturing the strongest men and returning to their homeland to mate with them. It is for this purpose that the Amazons have descended on the combatants at Troy.

The Amazons, then, have a State, one founded on the death of male conquerors and on self-mutilation for the purposes of war. Their institutions "are weak," however, and "their social structures are still young and unstable" (Carrière 82). The Amazons observe two rites, both of which unleash forces that threaten to run out of control. The Feast of Flowering Virgins inaugurates the hunt for men. The warrior-virgins are declared Brides of Mars, and "like the fiery hurricano's blast" (*Penthesilea* 383) they descend upon their prey. The priestess names the people to be attacked, but no one is allowed to select an individual opponent. The Feast of Roses marks the return of the warrior-virgins, when the male captives are adorned with roses and invited to join in orgiastic pleasures with their conquerors. In the first ritual, an anonymous force of violence is set loose, in the second, an equally anonymous libidinal force. Both rituals are institutions that regulate deterritorializing forces, and both are in constant danger of collapsing into an unrestricted play of violence and eros.

Penthesilea focuses on the tragic love/combat of Achilles and Penthesilea, virgin queen of the Amazons, a conflict of motives complicated by the fact that Penthesilea's mother on her deathbed has sworn Penthesilea to seek out and take Achilles as her husband, and thereby violate the law that forbids the choice of an opponent in the Amazons' ritual war. But as Carrière argues, the drama is less one of destiny or tragic necessity than one "of jumping from one affect to another" (Carrière 79). When Penthesilea is initially described, she is on horseback at the head of her troops, "immobile," "with blank unseeing eye,/ Expressionless" until "suddenly her eye falls on Achilles" for the first time. With a "sudden spasm" she leaps from her horse "And she herself, unconscious, infatuate,/ Stands drinking in the Peleid's gleaming form" (*Penthesilea* 316–17). Soon thereafter Penthesilea undergoes another affective jump, another moment of immobility, spasmodic movement and unconscious intensity. In the midst of the ensuing battle she sees Achilles being attacked by the Trojan Deiphobus. "The Queen, death-colour, two whole minutes long/ Hangs limp her arms. . . . Then down as from the firmament itself/ She drives her blade into the Trojan's neck" (*Penthesilea* 319–20). A catatonic stutter, followed by a rush of violent speed. Achilles for his part grows "Infatuate since he's flushed such noble game/ So strange, so lovely" (*Penthesilea* 321). Later, he pursues Penthesilea, but "suddenly before his horses' hoofs/ A chasm gapes, and down from giddy height he gazes, frozen, into yawning depths." As he falls into the chasm, "in chaos of tangled harness lie/ Chariot and steed," and he rests "Powerless as lion in the hunter's snare" (*Penthesilea* 322), literally immobile in a chaotic gap. Penthesilea spots Achilles, presses "her tiny hands,/ As though now giddy, to her forehead," and then "in furious ardour," "in fierce desire," "quite bereft of judgment" (*Penthesilea* 323), she vainly tries to reach Achilles. ("A foaming-jawed hyena! 'Tis no woman!" Antilochus exclaims [*Penthesilea* 324].) Once Achilles escapes this chasm, he refuses Agamemnon's order to retreat to Troy and swears to fight Penthesilea. "Until I first have had my sport with her,/ And then, her brow adorned with bleeding gashes,/ Shall drag her by the feet behind my car" (*Penthesilea* 333–34).

At this point, Penthesilea and Achilles have both betrayed their States, the one by choosing her enemy, the other by disobeying his commander and giving himself over to "these women and their crazy war" (*Penthesilea* 334), as Odysseus puts it. Henceforth, the two are engaged in their own struggle. "Together, Achilles and Penthesilea form the assemblage of affective war" (Carrière 95), a climate of clashing forces that threatens destruction but also holds out the utopian promise of an uncoded, intensive love, and hence of a fulfillment of "Kleist's great desire—to live as two in madness" (Carrière 102). When the two finally meet in direct combat, Penthesilea is struck unconscious by a blow and captured by Achilles, who shows a growing attachment to her. Prothoe, Penthesilea's sister, convinces Achilles that Penthesilea cannot survive the shame of defeat, so he agrees to pretend that she has won their battle when she awakes. After she is revived, Penthesilea becomes ecstatic at her supposed victory, but soon the truth is revealed. She reacts in horror to her defeat, and the two combatants part to their respective camps. Achilles, however, has fallen in love, and he abandons his plan of taking Penthesilea as a captive bride to his native Phthia. Instead, he challenges her to combat with the intent of losing the fight and becoming her prisoner. Unfortunately, she has embraced Ananke in the meantime, and "in wild ecstasy" and "with every sign of madness" (*Penthesilea* 395) she summons her hunting dogs. When she meets Achilles on the battlefield, "with maniac tread among her hounds/ With foam-flecked lip she goes and calls them sisters,/ Who howl and howl" (*Penthesilea* 401). The dogs attack Achilles, and she shoots him through the throat with an arrow. When he cries to her, "'Penthesilea! What dost thou? My beloved!/ Is this the Feast of Roses thou didst promise?,'" she "Strikes deep her teeth into his snowy breast,/ She and the dogs in ghastly rivalry," "black blood . . . dripping from her mouth and hands" (*Penthesilea* 404–5).

In the end, Achilles gives himself over to a process of becoming-woman, but Penthesilea is engaged in a process of becoming-animal. As she merges with the multiplicity of the pack, "the assemblage of gracious war becomes the machine of fascist war; the war of love becomes the war of Mars, the destroyer god" (Carrière 71). Affects are junctures of transformation, moments of metamorphosis. As a result, "catastrophe inhabits each thing; it is the intimate point of every center of gravity; it is the capacity of each thing to transform into another, the tendency toward disintegration" (Carrière 71). Becoming-other holds creative promise, but it also entails danger. The affect of desire may easily change into an affect of destruction. Such is the case in *Penthesilea*, and so too in Kleist's *Hermannsschlacht*, where the Roman Ventidius arranges a secret tryst with Thusnelda, the wife of Hermann, the German commander. As Ventidius extends his lips to kiss Thusnelda in the dark, a ravenous captive bear is set loose upon him and he is devoured. A becoming-bear of Thusnelda, a becoming-dogs of Penthesilea, the lips of love turning into the teeth of destruction.

In *Penthesilea*, Deleuze and Guattari find a revealing analysis of war and its relation to the war machine. The war machine is opposed to the State, the Amazons "surging forth like lightning, 'between' the two States, the Greek and the Trojan. They sweep everything away in their passage" (MP 439; 355). The war machine is a force of metamorphosis that disrupts stable codes and social relations. Hence, the warrior is inevitably a traitor, that is, one who betrays "the world of dominant significations and the established order" (D 53; 41). Achilles defies his commander and the Greek social order in pursuing Penthesilea, and she violates "the collective law of her people, that law of the pack that forbids the 'choice' of an enemy" (MP 440; 355). The metamorphoses of the war machine induce in subjects a process of becoming-other, a passage between the binary poles of stable oppositions. Achilles' becoming-woman and Penthesilea's becoming-animal are but two instances of the general process of becoming-other that belongs to the war machine. That process operates through affective intensities, apersonal, nonrational junctures of force, at once immobile and speeding out of control. "Succession of catatonias, and extreme speeds, faintings and arrows. . . . No form develops, no subject is formed, but affects are displaced, becomings are catapulted and form a block, like the becoming-woman of Achilles and the becoming-dog of Penthesilea. Kleist marvelously explains how forms and persons are only appearances, produced by the displacement of a center of gravity on an abstract line, and by the conjunction of lines on a plane of immanence" (MP 328; 268). In *Penthesilea*, affects are not internal states, but a form of exteriority: "sentiments are torn from the interiority of a 'subject' so they may be violently projected into a milieu of pure exteriority that instills in them an incredible speed, a catapulting force: love or hatred are no longer sentiments but affects. These affects are so many instances of the becoming-woman, the becoming-animal of the warrior (bear, dogs). Affects traverse the body like arrows, they are arms of war. The deterritorialization speed of the affect" (MP 440; 356). The war machine is not exclusively destructive, but the forces it activates are dangerous and potentially self-annihilating. Hence, Kleist celebrates the war machine's struggle against the State, but always in a "combat that is lost in advance" (MP 440; 355). In all his works, he poses the question: "Is it the destiny of the war machine, when the State triumphs, to fall into the alternative: either to be nothing but the disciplined, military organ of the State apparatus, *or to turn against itself* and become a suicide machine for two, for a solitary man and a solitary woman?" (MP 440; 356).

If we turn now from *Penthesilea* to Shakespeare's *Richard III*, we can see clearly what Deleuze means when he calls Richard a "man of war," and perhaps we may better understand how Deleuze can read Shakespeare as he does. It might seem improbable to say of the power-mad Richard that "he does not simply want power, he wants treason" (D 53; 42), but Deleuze means by this that Richard is a traitor to all social codes, and as a result he embraces forces that eventually undermine all State order. Readers have long recognized the gusto with which Richard pursues his nefarious designs and the openness with which he declares his intentions: "And therefore, since I cannot prove a lover/ To entertain these fair well-spoken days,/ I am determined to prove a villain/ And hate the idle pleasures of these days" (I, i, 28–31). Though he feverishly seeks the crown, he does so with an energy that stems as much from a delight in destruction as a desire for control over others. And though he never says that he wants treason, he does end up betraying everyone, including his loyal confidant Buckingham. Richard's zeal and diabolical humor arise from the anarchic war machine he activates, and though he reaches the throne, the uncontrolled forces he engages inexorably lead to his demise.

As a man of war, Richard enters into a process of becoming-other—specifically, a becoming-woman that manifests itself in his bizarre courtship of Lady Anne in Act I. As Deleuze notes, the scene is often judged "improbable and overdone *[peu vraisemblable et outré]*," but these are precisely the characteristics of a becoming-other, a process that defies regular expectations and the measured control of good taste. (One might judge much of *Penthesilea* similarly "improbable and overdone.") Lady Anne reviles Richard as a "foul devil" (I, ii, 50) and a villain who "knowst no law of God nor man" (I, ii, 70). She spits in his face and wishes him dead, yet by the end of the scene she accepts his ring and his suit of love. He who is so "Deformed, unfinished" that dogs bark at him (I, i, 23), who "cannot prove a lover" and hence determines "to prove a villain" (I, i, 28, 30), is able to woo the widow of a man he has murdered. "Upon my life," he exclaims, "she finds (although I cannot)/ Myself to be a marv'llous proper man" (I, ii, 253–54). In this improbable and over-done encounter, Richard's deformity acquires its own grace, like the grace of Kleist's marionettes tracing an abstract line through a center of gravity or like the bear who parries every thrust of the sword. Lady Anne, "already consenting and fascinated," has a presentiment of "the tortuous line that Richard is in the process of tracing" (D 53; 42). He, like Penthesilea, has made the choice of an object. "In his choice of Anne, there is a becoming-woman of Richard III" (D 53; 42), a becom-ing-other that is not an imitation of the feminine but an engagement with graceful, affective forces of metamorphosis.

Deleuze's comments on *Richard III* are brief and largely unspecific, and one might ask whether Richard's encounter with Anne in Act One is germane to the rest of the play. Is there a continuing becoming-woman in the drama? Can one conceive of the tragedy in terms of Richard's relationship to the feminine? These are questions Bene addresses in his *Richard III*.

BENE'S RICHARD

Carmelo Bene was an actor, director, playwright, author and filmmaker whose projects often involved the remaking of famous works by other authors. Born in 1937 at Campi Salentina in the Puglia region of the southern Italian province of Lecce, Bene formed his own company in 1961, producing that year versions of Camus's *Caligula*, Stevenson's *Strange Case of Dr. Jekyll and Mr. Hyde*, Collodi's *Pinocchio* and Shakespeare's *Hamlet* (the first of seven different Hamlets he created,[4] some after Shakespeare, some after Shakespeare and Jules Laforgue, whose 1887 story "Hamlet, or the Consequences of Filial Piety" Bene particularly admired). Subsequent productions of the 1960s included versions of Marlowe's *Edward II* (1963), Wilde's *Salome* (1964), Prèvost's *Manon* (1964) and *Arden of Feversham* (1968). Between 1968 and 1973 Bene devoted himself to the cinema, his chief films being *Our Lady of the Turks* (a 1968 version of his own 1964 novel), *Capricci* (a version of *Arden of Feversham*, 1969), *Don Giovanni* (1971), *Salome* (1972) and *One Less*

Hamlet (after Laforgue, 1973). After 1974 he produced versions of Byron's *Manfred* (1979), Goethe's *Egmont* (1983), Musset's *Lorenzaccio* (1986) and Kleist's *Penthesilea* (1989 and 1990), as well as treatments of Shakespeare's *Romeo and Juliet* (1976), *Richard III* (1977), *Othello* (1979) and *Macbeth* (1983).[5] Bene died in 2002.

To say that Bene is simply a director of others' dramas would be inaccurate. Not only does he adapt stories and novels for the stage (and dramas, operas and novels for film) but he also writes scripts that in some cases have only a loose relation to the earlier works whose titles they bear. Yet in many instances it would be problematic to call Bene the author of his plays, as he himself recognizes in his frequent reference to his productions as "by *author x*" "according to C.B. [*secondo C.B.*]." Such is the case with his *Richard III*, which Bene describes as "*secondo C.B.*" in the bibliography of his *Opere*, and which he subtitles in the *Opere* "Italian Version and Re-elaboration of William Shakespeare from *Sovrapposizioni* by Carmelo Bene and Gilles Deleuze." With the exception of two passages taken from *Henry VI, Part III*, virtually all of the lines spoken by the actors are translations of lines from Shakespeare's *Richard III* (albeit in an often free and occasionally melodramatic translation). If one were to look only at the actors' lines, one might regard Bene's *Richard III* as merely a severely truncated performance script of the original play. But Bene's script includes as well extensive stage directions and comments, which detail an action that has little to do with the plot of Shakespeare's tragedy. And no one attending a performance of the play would mistake its strange goings-on for a simple production of Shakespeare. Rather, Bene's *Richard III* is both a critical commentary on Shakespeare and a creative response to the play, a performance event extracted from the text, latent within it and yet alien to it.

The only characters who appear on the stage are Richard and the principal women from Shakespeare's play, the Duchess of York (Richard's mother), Margaret of Anjou (Henry VI's widow), Elizabeth (Queen to Edward IV) and Lady Anne (widow of Edward, Prince of Wales, and future bride of Richard). (Bene adds to the cast two female characters, a chambermaid, whom Richard "insists on calling Buckingham" [SP 10], and a silent Mistress Shore.) The First Part of the play begins with a portion of Richard's final soliloquy from *Henry VI, Part III* (V, vi, 61–83), in which he speaks of his deformities and his possession of "neither love, nor pity, nor fear." Richard attempts to continue with his famous opening line, "Now is the winter of our discontent," but he is silenced by the grieving women. After a pause "of at least fifteen minutes" (SP 15), Richard and his mother discuss his brother Clarence's imprisonment (I, i, 43–80, the Duchess taking the lines assigned to Clarence in Shakespeare), and Richard declares his intention of murdering Clarence (I, i, 117–21). Then follows a somewhat streamlined version of Act I, scene iii, in which Queen Elizabeth expresses concern at her husband's illness, Richard protests that Elizabeth has slandered him, and Margaret curses Elizabeth, the Duchess and Richard. The Duchess then recites Clarence's nightmare of shipwrecks and corpses (I, iv, 9–33), after which ensues virtually all of that "improbable and overdone" scene of Richard's courtship of Lady Anne (I, ii, 5–263). At the conclusion of his Act I, scene ii soliloquy, Richard moves directly into his opening speech (I, i, 1–41) and then continues with portions of the Act III, scene ii soliloquy from *Henry VI, Part III* (153–95), in which he speaks of his deformities and his murderous plans to attain the crown. The Second Part of Bene's play contains brief views of Richard's rise to power and demise in Shakespeare's Acts II through V, largely handled through monologue, interspersed with scenes involving the female characters. Richard mentions Clarence's death (II, i, 80–84), asks that Hastings be sounded out regarding his plot to take the throne (III, i, 161–64, 172–85, 188–96), inquires about strawberries (III, iv, 31–33), plants rumors of the illegitimacy of Edward's children (III, v, 72–94), seeks the citizens' reaction to his prospective kingship (III, vii, 1–2, 21–24), feigns disinclination to the crown (III, vii, 141–65), accepts the crown (III, vii, 223–26), tells Buckingham he wants the bastard children dead (IV, ii, 5–18), turns on Buckingham (IV, ii, 32–115), recites Tyrrel's account of the children's murders (IV, iii, 1, 10–14, 26–29), dreams of the ghosts of his victims (V, iii, 178–82, 201–2, 213, 210), reacts to news of the battle at Bosworth Field (V, iii, 272–302) and calls for a horse (V, iv, 7–13). Amidst this sequence of vignettes are the laments of the Duchess and Elizabeth over their losses (II, ii, 40, 47–54, 55–88), the reactions of the women to Lady Anne's journey to join Richard (IV, i, 13–103), and most of Act IV, scene iv (9–465), in which the Duchess and Elizabeth renew their laments, Margaret rejoices in their suffering and Richard asks Elizabeth for her daughter's hand.

Such is the play's configuration of lines, a heavily cut, and occasionally rearranged, version of Shakespeare's script. But the characters' actions suggest another plot entirely. Bene describes the set as "totally funereal: everywhere coffins and mirrors" (SP 9). Mistress Shore is lying on a large white bed, and Lady Anne weeps by the coffin of Henry VI. "Everywhere there are drawers" (SP 9) containing gauze, white bands of cloth and prosthetic limbs of various sorts with which Richard will adorn himself. A clock "as in Poe" (SP 9) ticks loudly, and flowers cover the floor, "in such great numbers that one stumbles on them" (SP 9). Center stage is a mannequin of the haggard and sickly Edward IV. From time to time, a skull on a platter is illuminated by a spotlight. Throughout the play, Richard fondles the chambermaid, at one point removing her clothes and caressing her "lazily and obscenely" (SP 27). All the women in fact "comport themselves in a truly strange manner" (SP 20), undressing and dressing, exposing a shoulder, a breast, a thigh, buttocks, and so on. Richard at times delivers his lines with "the articulations of a troglodyte . . . in stammerings" (SP 15); he frequently stumbles, falls and slides to the ground. During his scene with Lady Anne, Richard pulls various prosthetic limbs from the drawers on the stage, and at a certain point "artificial human members, contorted and deformed, . . . rain down upon him" (SP 36). Richard unrolls the winding sheet of Henry VI and wraps diverse prosthetic devices to his own body. As his artificial deformities multiply, Lady Anne grows increasingly aroused; "hotter and hotter," "truly debauched," she "undresses and dresses continually" (SP 40–41). In the Second Part, Richard gradually removes his prostheses, and the women slowly lose interest in him, eventually dressing and behaving in a more conventional fashion. At the close of the play, Margaret makes and remakes the royal bed, throws sheets and pillow cases on the stage (the ghosts of Richard's nightmare), then drags behind her "the great train of dirty sheets" (SP 83) as she leaves Richard alone on the stage.

"The entire first part," says Bene, "is debated between Richard and the *women*: between the 'imbecility' of the unique (impossibility of the *different*, etc.) and the *obscene* of the feminine in *history*" (SP 10). To a degree, Bene derives these themes of difference and the feminine from Shakespeare. In Act V, scene vi of *Henry VI, Part III*, Richard states, "I have no brother, I am like no brother;/ And this word 'love,' which grey-beards call divine,/ Be resident in men like one another,/ And not in me. I am myself alone" (ll. 80–83). These lines Bene presents at the beginning of his *Richard III* in the following form: "I have no brother at all, I resemble no one, I . . . And the word 'love' that is said to be divine goes off with all those who are made for one another . . . I . . . I am *different!*" (SP 14). And the importance of women is suggested early in Shakespeare's *Richard III*, when Richard remarks, "Why this it is, when men are ruled by women" (I, i, 62), a line Bene renders as "It's always thus! But of course! When men are women" (SP 17). Richard also tells Clarence that one must wear the Queen's livery to advance at court (I, i, 80), an observation Bene alludes to in Richard's line, "We . . . serve . . . you . . . and we wear only your . . . emblem [*devise*] . . . of . . . *woman!*" (SP 18). Yet what Bene means by the "'imbecility' of the unique," "the impossibility of the *different*," and "the obscene of the feminine in *history*" can scarcely be discerned through Shakespeare's texts.

Bene speaks frequently of the impossible when discussing his theater. "In the theater, for me, what counts solely is that which creates a fact and liquidates an anecdote. I am tempted only by texts that are impossible to represent" ("L'énergie" 65). Like the painter Francis Bacon, he seeks the immediacy of the "brutality of fact" through the disruption of conventional narratives that mediate experience. Thought is the enemy, for as "Aristotle has said: thought is the thought of the thought. But, from the instant that the thought of the thought commences, grace is lost, the immediate is lost. The life of the immediate is unthinkable [*La vie de l'immédiate est impensable*]" ("L'énergie" 74). The immediate is unthinkable "because it is a discourse; it is like what in the theater I call the non-representable, *in the immediate*" ("L'énergie" 74). Bene is a great admirer of certain unconventional saints, "Saint Joseph of Copertino [1603–1663, a slow-witted ecstatic known for his feats of levitation and flying], the imbeciles, the idiot saints, Saint Francis of Assisi, who dances before the Pope" ("L'énergie" 74), all of whom live in the immediate and hence in a state of grace. "Each time that we live outside the immediate, we are in disgrace" ("L'énergie" 74), though by the world's standards we may seem gracious, conforming to the norms of harmonious, regular and proper behavior. But culture begins the moment the idea is examined rather than lived, from the instant the idea is outside us. "If *we* are *the idea*, then we can dance the dance of Saint Vitus and we are in a state of grace. We begin to be wise precisely when we are 'disgraced'" ("L'énergie" 74), that is, when we lack worldly grace, the grace of culture, and attain the grace of "imbecility," of the unthinkable, of the impossible, nonrepresentable immediate.

Every human being is unique, Bene asserts, but the unique individual does not imply the existence of a self. "No *I*. The *I* is the subject, be careful! The unique, Unique. The inimitable. . . . The subject does not exist" (L'énergie 81). Thus the "'imbecility' of the unique," it would seem, refers to the unthinkable immediacy of the individual human being living in a state of grace, outside the norms of culture and the narratives of self and world. The unique is difference, but difference that is not framed in conscious thought. Citing Deleuze, Bene says that *"Repetition is difference without concept.* Whoever understands this doesn't need the pathetic theater of conflict [i.e., traditional theater]" (*Opere* 1167). Bene's project is to "liquidate anecdotes" and "create facts," to disrupt the stories of received codes and engage in an "eternal undramatization as undoing" (*Opere* 1167). Bene says of himself that "C.B. is something entirely other. *From the rest and not from himself"* (*Opere* 1168). "C.B. is only *different* in *sameness.* . . . Thus C.B. can only [do] what he cannot [do]. He can only [do] the impossible" (*Opere* 1168). His plays stage a "theatrical *impasse,* the necessity and impossibility of doing theater" ("L'énergie" 64), an impasse that involves "the total impossibility of communication" ("L'énergie" 70). Everywhere in the modern world there is communication of a sort, Bene admits, but this "communication is a corruption" ("L'énergie" 73), a mere circulation of clichés, received ideas and tired values. Audiences come to the theater expecting confirmation of what they already know, what they already think, feel and believe. But his plays present an impasse in such communication, a presentation of the nonrepresentable, of difference as the unthinkable immediate.

OBSCENE HISTORY

The action of Bene's *Richard III,* then, involves Richard's "otherness," his difference from dominant conventions and established codes. In Shakespeare, Richard is a deformed monster, separated from the rest of humankind. In Bene, his deformities open him to the impossibility of difference. His repeated stumbling, slipping and falling are part of his St. Vitus dance of grace, his "imbecilic" discovery of the immediate. As he attaches various prosthetic limbs to his body, he embraces deformity as an undoing of the body, a deformation of the natural and the given. His physical "disgrace" creates genuine grace, and when he surrenders his artificial limbs, he loses that true grace and attempts to return "to the regularity of nature" (SP 57). But Richard's deformation, we must note, is also inseparable from "the obscene of the feminine in *history*." The obscene Bene defines as "the excess of desire" and as "continual transgression" (SP 10). The references to excess and transgression of course recall Bataille, and that association is indirectly confirmed in Bene's interview comments on "the idea of luxury" (*l'idée de luxe*, with a clear allusion to the Latin *luxuria*: luxury, luxuriance, extravagance, excess). Bene explains that his "discourse is *Sadean. Completely*" ("L'énergie" 81). "I start from this proposition: I alone exist, nothing exists outside myself; and whatever does not produce or procure pleasure does not interest me" ("L'énergie" 81). Work is a restricting and controlling of energy, and hence antithetical to the idea of luxury. "In short, in every work situation there is no room for luxury, nor is there any place for eroticism, which, in my opinion, represents the human" ("L'énergie" 81). The worker, Bene claims, is not a human being. Luxury is the human, yet in the contemporary world "*homo eroticus* has become a luxury" (L'énergie 82), a superfluity. When asked how one should gain a living, Bene answers, "Kill. Massacre. Plunder. Steal. Give play to your life [*Joue ta vie*]. Never take a job" (L'énergie 82). Bene means to shock, of course, but his point is clear: The erotic is a transgressive force of excess, one that disrupts social order and ignores all practical considerations. The erotic necessarily undoes stable political relations, and hence for Bene, "eroticism and politics are the same thing" ("L'énergie" 77). To live luxuriously, in excess, is to live tragically, says Bene, and "to live tragically means also that one risks suicide or madness" ("L'énergie" 82). But to live tragically means as well that one enters into utopian possibilities of social transformation. Thus, when Bene speaks of revolution, he refers to a "utopia of the revolution" ("L'énergie" 63). In his native Campi Salentina, he remarks, after the election of communists to the local government, the people embarked on a festival of anarchy, celebration and destruction. "What a revolution! *The* revolution!" It "was utopian, that is, impossible" (L'énergie 62). Bene's erotic politics, then, is one of utopian revolution, an impossible, impractical politics of luxury and transgressive excess that may manifest itself in the most personal and the most public of spheres.

The link between the obscene and Richard's progressive deformation is clear: both are a form of excess, a disruption of norms, regularities and limits. Through his relationships with the women of the play

Richard gains access to an erotic politics of self-mutation, in which
desire and decoding are one. As Richard trips and stumbles, as he
becomes more and more unnatural and deformed, the women find him
increasingly attractive and the interactions between Richard and the
women become more and more openly erotic. Conversely, as he
removes his prostheses, the women gradually lose interest in him and
eventually leave him alone. In the long scene with Lady Anne the connection between deformation and desire is most explicitly shown, and
here as well Bene suggests the dynamics of excess that inform the
action. It is during this scene that Richard constructs his artificial body,
and at each stage of the assemblage Richard and Anne grow increasingly aroused. Their passion, however, is also steeped in violence and
destruction. At one point "they hold each other like Tristan and Iseult
in the fatal scenes" (SP 34), and at another, as Richard offers to stab
himself, "Lady Anne, truly debauched—let us not separate despair from
the obscene—as a not at all convincing Judith—is tempted by an equally
beautiful blade and would truly kill him, but as in the final moments
of a turbulent night of love" (SP 40). Yet this potentially murderous
Liebestod is also utopian. At one juncture in the action, Bene comments
in the stage directions that Richard and Anne "are united for a few
instants," and "that which brings them together, I would say, is the
unique possibility of living, as on an island forever, a little like Miranda
and Caliban if the action had been different in that 'Tempest'" (SP 39).
What unites the two "is the idea of the different, but without posing
the problem, etc." (SP 39). Clearly, the excesses of the erotic unleash
forces of metamorphosis that have destructive and creative potential.
Clearly as well, the utopian moment of erotic excess is a moment of
grace, of life in the immediate, for the immediate is difference without
concept, "the idea of the different, but without posing the problem,"
that is, living the idea without thinking it. (If the idea is not outside us,
"if *we* are *the idea* then we can dance the dance of Saint Vitus and we are
in a state of grace" ["L'énergie" 74].) Like Tristan and Iseult, Judith and
Holofernes, and Miranda and Caliban (and, one might add, Penthesilea
and Achilles), Richard and Anne are joined in an affective becoming of
forces, a climate of war (in the Kleistian sense) whose dangers and
promises issue from the same metamorphic disruptions of difference.

Bene ties difference to "the obscene of the feminine," but he adds

as well that "the obscene of the feminine" is "in *history*." The relationship between the obscene and history is complex, for the obscene is
both the way into and the way out of history. Bene exclaims of the
utopian revolution of Campi Salentini that it was "so antihistorical,"
"so insane" ("L'énergie" 62). And when pressed during an interview to
recognize the exigencies of history, Bene remarks "I mean . . . I am an
antihistoricist" ("L'énergie" 73). Bene's *storia* (like the French *histoire*)
means both "history" and "story," and any break in the conventions of
stable society necessitates a disruption of the narratives that shape such
a world. Bene's impossible revolution, then, is antihistorical in that it
puts an end to comforting narratives, but it is also antihistorical in that
it disrupts rational time. The moment of the immediate is ahistorical,
an event that cannot be subsumed within history's chronological
sequence of regulated instants. Yet Bene's play is about Richard's ties to
history, and in the Second Part of the drama, says Bene, "feminine history abandons Richard (and it is unfortunately abandoned)," Richard
descending into "the boring phase of alcoholism, the strange malaise of
those dawns when, dull and empty, one looks for a horse in order to
return home and disappear" (SP 10). It would seem that here "history"
has a somewhat different sense than that of "narrative," and Bene confirms this suspicion later in the play when he writes, "Obscene is history [*Oscena è la storia*], political action, whatever it may be. . . . " (SP 39).
Shakespeare's *Richard III* is a history play, a play of political action, and
though Bene removes much of the overtly political content of
Shakespeare's drama, one of his purposes is to clarify the nature of
political action. All political action is obscene—that is, all political
action proceeds through an excess of desire. Richard's initial decision
to embrace his deformities and pursue the women is his "'political
choice'" (SP 15); his walk with Elizabeth is "a 'political' promenade" (SP
22). The essence of history as political action, then, is to be found in
Richard's relationship with the play's women, that is, with the excess of
desire. Richard makes "his fortune in politics thanks to his acquired
defects," and when he throws off those "artificial defects, one by one,"
he indulges an "impolitic dream" and attempts "to rid himself of his
proper history" (SP 56–57). He "wants at all costs to defy History: this
is why he not only takes off his false limbs, but at the same time begins
to make himself attractive, to arrange his hair, to throw in the air a pile
of very elegant masculine evening clothes" (SP 60). In returning "to the

natural, to the regularity of nature" (SP 57), he "seeks at all costs an autonomy" (SP 60), a separation from the women and from the excesses and deformities of desire. At the end of the play, Richard "is alone, truly alone: no more women-history . . . no more anything: not even dresses, women's shoes, or anything like that" (SP 78). He begins to recite his lines "like the 'I' itself [*lo stesso 'Io'*], like every tyrant outside history" (SP 79). He rushes around in circles, frantically seeking something, anything. "Now it is different. . . . Different also is Richard. Different from himself. . . . It is delirium. It is 'the tale told by an idiot signifying nothing'" (SP 78).

The tyrant is outside history, disconnected from desire and the other. He presumes a false autonomy, a set identity; he speaks with the voice of the "I," the ego-self. The result is not stability and order but delirium, a descent into a black hole. In the "few instants" when Richard and Lady Anne were united like Caliban and Miranda on the island of an alternate *Tempest*, they were outside history, in a utopia of difference without concept, "the idea of the different, but without posing the problem" (SP 39). But the impossible difference of this ahistorical event was a difference *à deux*, a difference in desire, a deforming becoming-other that involved a social relation. Richard's final difference, by contrast, is self-referential and delusional, a moment of "historical-fetishistic masturbation" (SP 78) in which desire continues, but as a closed circuit of meaningless self-images in frantic pursuit of one another. His escape from history is an effort to defy history, that is, to defy desire and its deformities. The result is delirium and isolation. Richard becomes "delirious with battles" (SP 80), he throws rags "into the void" (SP 81), he addresses his final lines "to nothingness [*al nulla*]" (SP 83). As Margaret, "the synthesis of the historical feminine," leaves him alone on the stage, Bene comments ominously: "It grows truly somber on this island. . . . " (SP 80).

Official history is a coherent narrative in logical time, a confirmation of established values, norms and conventions. By contrast, lived history, or the domain of concrete political action, is obscene, excessive, nonrational. When the women engage in competitive laments over their misfortunes, Bene says they realize that "crowns fly from head to head without any feminine reason—which is however the only history which one can undergo" (SP 48). Official history is dead, whereas the history of excessive desire is vital. When Lady Anne first grows attracted to Richard, Bene comments: "Here is all the importance of history, which serves only those who advance it. . . . I repeat: a deformed being is preferable to dead heroes! What could Lady Anne do with a cadaver?" (SP 38). Bene's set is "entirely funereal," a mannequin of a dying king center stage, a dead king's corpse to the side. Only the deformed man of war remains to lure the women from their mourning and initiate the metamorphic process of desire. Engaging that process makes possible an escape from official history into a utopian difference without concept; defying it, however, leads to the void of delirious self-absorption.

The action of Bene's play forms a commentary on the history of Shakespeare's *Richard III*, but at the same time it constitutes a presentation and demonstration of the theater's utopian function. Throughout the script, Bene remarks on the actors' motives and reactions as performers on the stage. The actor playing Richard "in his petty normality" (SP 14) thinks he can "make himself accepted as he is" (SP 16) and attract the attention of the other actors. They silence him, however, and only when he begins tripping and stumbling do they respond to him. Hence, when Richard falls and Elizabeth exposes a breast to the audience, she does so "to come to the aid not of a character but of her stage partner" (SP 22). Initially, the actor playing Richard understands "nothing of his fortuitous incidents: slipping, falling, etc." (SP 30), but during his scene with Lady Anne "the actor Richard becomes aware [of his effect on her], he begins to begin to understand, that is, to explain it to the audience" (SP 31).[6] What the actor begins to understand and to explain to the audience is that his graceless fumblings constitute his grace, and his artificial deformities make up his charm. But he also demonstrates that he is an actor constructing himself as an unnatural, disunited body. His prostheses are "fakeries [*trucchi*]" (SP 37); he is "a king 'made of pieces and fragments'" (SP 57); and when he discards his false body parts, the stage is littered with "those cursed fake members of this theater king [*quei maledetti arti truccati di quel re da teatro*]" (SP 67). Yet the point is not that all is illusion and trumpery, but that the actor's denaturalizing and undoing of his body is a way of making present on the stage a body of desire. Bene's is a theater of the impossible, a staging of the unthinkable immediate, a presentation of the nonrepresentable, a communication of the impossibility of communication.[7] The theater's purpose is to create in the performance space the event that the characters are enacting in the plot and the actors are discovering in their interplay—the obscene event of the excess of desire. Hence, at the close of the First Part of the play, Bene adds to Richard's soliloquy from *Henry VI, Part III* a few key words (here italicized): "Atrophied like a dry branch!, *an obvious theatrical superpolitical hump! [una gobba evidente plateale strapolitica!]* . . . Disproportionate . . . chaotic . . . (*and here he weeps, but with joy), dissimilar . . . pitiable! . . . Theater!!!*" (SP 46). Thus, this "theater king," here complete in his assemblage of fake "pieces and fragments," simultaneously comments on his character's situation, enunciates his realization as an actor and makes present an event of difference—the disproportionate, the chaotic, the dissimilar—an event that is *strapolitica*: hyperpolitical, surpolitical, metapolitical. The theater in a sense is outside the world, an artificial, self-enclosed space like the utopian island of Caliban and Miranda, the site of a surreal politics and a metapolitical clarification of desire, but it is also an intensification of the world, a hyperpolitical space in which an erotic politics can be produced in all its impossibility.

DELEUZE'S BENE

At the beginning of "One Less Manifesto" ["*Un Manifeste de moins*"], Deleuze cites Bene's comment that his *Romeo and Juliet* is "a critical essay on Shakespeare" (SP 87; 204), which leads Deleuze to ask in what way Bene's theater may be seen as a form of critique. In one sense, Bene's is a theater of subtraction, says Deleuze, a theater "of less" [*de moins*], just as his Hamlet is *One Less Hamlet* [*Un Hamlet de moins, Un Amleto di meno*].[8] In his *Romeo and Juliet*, Bene "subtracts" Romeo by removing him from the play; in his *S.A.D.E.*, he "subtracts" the Master from the Sadean Master-Slave pair, reducing the omnipotent Master to a masturbatory tic. And in *Richard III*, he "subtracts" all the male characters save Richard. Yet this subtraction involves construction as well. In *Romeo and Juliet*, Mercutio, "a mere virtuality in Shakespeare's play" (SP 88; 204–5), grows to giant proportions once Romeo is removed. In *S.A.D.E.*, the subaltern servant becomes the dominant figure in the Sadean couple. And in *Richard III*, the women and Richard take on an alternate constitution. In each case, the subtraction of characters brings with it the construction of other characters, and it is in this dual process of subtraction and construction that Deleuze finds the essence of Bene's theatrical critique. Each play "involves in the first place the fabrication of the character, his preparation, his birth, his stammer-ings, his variations, his development. This critical theater is a consti-tuting theater, Critique is constitution" (SP 88; 205). In this regard, Bene's critique is a form of "theater-experimentation" (SP 89; 205). His task is to subtract something from a play, observe what emerges, and from that see what new constructions can be formed. His role is not that of an "author, actor or director" but "an operator" (SP 89; 205), a "controller" or "mechanic" (SP 92; 206). Like a midwife, he helps "to give birth to a monster, or a giant. . . . " (SP 92; 206).

What Bene subtracts in *Richard III* is "the whole royal and princely system" (SP 90; 205), and the monster he gives birth to is Richard, the man of war, who "less covets power than he wants to reintroduce or reinvent a war machine" (SP 90; 205). Deleuze observes that the man of war, like Achilles in *Penthesilea*, has a special relation to the feminine (SP 91; 206), and in Bene's play "as the women at war enter and leave," Richard "forms himself, or rather deforms himself, following a line of continuous variation" (SP 91; 206). Here of course we recognize the reading of Shakespeare's *Richard III* Deleuze offered in *Dialogues*, but Deleuze does not stress in Bene the theme of war per se so much as Bene's implicit critique of power and the notion of deformation as con-tinuous variation. The war machine opposes the State and its fixed power relations, and what Deleuze finds consistently "subtracted, amputated, neutralized" in Bene's theater are "the elements of Power, the elements that make or represent a system of Power" (SP 93; 206). Deleuze treats Bene as a minor writer, in the sense developed in the last chapter, and in Bene's subtractive critique Deleuze finds a minor usage of major structures. In a major power system, "from a thought one makes a doctrine, from a way of living one makes a culture, from an event one makes History. One thus claims to recognize or admire, but in fact one normalizes" (SP 97; 208). Conversely, to "minorize" the major is "to disengage becomings against History, lives against culture, thoughts against doctrine, graces or disgraces against dogma" (SP 97; 208). Clearly, Bene's critique of Shakespeare's *Richard III* is a minoriza-tion of the major, a subtraction of Shakespeare's official State repre-sentatives that disengages becomings and dis/graces in Richard's metamorphosis. But Deleuze links Bene's critique of power to the forms of the theater as well. The elements of power in the theater, Deleuze argues, assure both "the coherence of the subject treated and the coherence of the representation on the stage" (SP 93; 207). The critique of power, in other words, necessarily entails a critique of representation, for the conventional codes of language, interaction, gesture, comportment, and so forth, are saturated with the power relations of the dominant social system. Thus, in order to critique power,

> you begin by subtracting, cutting out everything that constitutes an element of power, in language and in gestures, in representation and in the represented. . . . Next, you will cut out or amputate history, because History is the temporal marker of Power. You will cut out structure, because it is the synchronic marker, the totality of relations between invariants. You will subtract constants, stable or stabilized elements, because they belong to a major usage. You will amputate the text, because the text is like the domination of language [*langue*] by speech [*parole*], and bears witness again to an invariance or a homogeneity. You cut out dialogue, because dialogue transmits to speech [*parole*] the elements of power, and makes them circulate: it's your turn to speak, in such-and-such codified conditions (linguists try to determine the 'universals of dialogue'). Etc., etc. (SP 103–4; 211)

It would seem that nothing would remain in such a theater, yet Deleuze insists "everything remains, but under a new light, with new sounds, new gestures" (SP 104; 211).

In what way does Bene's *Richard III* subtract the elements Deleuze enumerates—history, structure, dialogue, text and linguistic constants—and what arises in their place? As we have seen, Bene excises much of the plot of Shakespeare's history, such that without a thorough familiarity with the original script, the lines retained by Bene relate no coherent story, yet what remains are the becomings of Richard and the female characters (history, in other words, is "minorized" into events). The structure of Shakespeare's drama is destroyed by Bene's drastic cuts and transpositions of speeches and scenes, but in its place arises the action of Richard's prosthetic articulation and disarticulation. (It would seem that it is not structure *in toto* that is subtracted, but simply the conventional structure of a standard narrative.) Dialogue is disrupted in part through Bene's cuts and transpositions, but also through various performance practices—stammerings, screams and

KLEIST, BENE, AND MINOR THEATER

whispers of the actors; electronic distortions of their voices; overlapping deliveries of exchanges; blockings, postures and actions that contradict the text's implicit interlocutory relationships, and so on. "It's curious, how there is no dialogue in the theater of CB; for the voices, simultaneous or successive, superimposed or transposed, are taken up in this spatio-temporal continuity of variation" (SP 105; 211). What replaces conventional dialogue is a kind of music of interactions, a complex of layerings, syncopations, alternations and hesitations that suggest relations between the voices outside those coded in the logic of the characters' verbal exchanges. As for the subtractions of text and linguistic constants, these require more extended consideration.

By the subtraction of the text Deleuze means the elimination of the hierarchy of written script over performance practice—in other words, the subversion of the concept of a "faithful" re-presentation of an authorial and authoritative original. In part what Deleuze is pointing toward is Bene's appropriation of Shakespeare's lines for new purposes, and the relative autonomy with which he pursues his own dramatic ends. But Deleuze notes as well the way in which Bene's own written script "subtracts" or counteracts the conventional notion of the text. Virtually all of the characters' lines of Bene's *Richard III* are from Shakespeare, but fully half the play consists of Bene's comments, directions, observations and analyses. To call them "stage directions" hardly seems adequate, since stage directions are generally subordinate to the principal text. A "text" is present in Bene's play—the Shakespearean lines—but they have become a "simple material for variation" (SP 105; 105), and Bene's remarks are "non-textual and yet interior" to the text, written indications that function "as operators, expressing each time the scale of variables through which the statement passes, as in a musical score" (SP 105-6; 212). What Bene invents is "a writing that is neither literary nor theatrical, but truly operational, and whose effect on the reader is very strong, very strange" (SP 106; 212). All of Bene's theater "must be seen, but also read, even though the text properly speaking is not essential. This is not contradictory. It's rather like deciphering a score" (SP 106; 212). Bene's written comments, we might say, stand *between* Shakespeare's text and the performance event. Bene's handling of Shakespeare's script is such that the script is dismantled, de-composed and turned into a material for continuous variation. The raw material is then processed through the operations detailed in

Bene's comments, the result being a given performance of the play. **141**
Bene's writing is neither literary nor theatrical, for it is midway between
the written script and the performance event, and it is subordinate neither to the literary end of enhancing the written text nor to the theatrical end of guiding its faithful performance. Bene's comments have a
kind of viral relation to Shakespeare's text, as if they were an infection
that had attained a kind of participation in the original, yet without
assimilation. Bene's remarks are operators, and in this sense disposable
once they have done their job and helped generate a performance, yet
his written compositions, like the printed *Riccardo III*, have a kind of
force and strangeness of their own. His plays "must be seen, but also
read" (SP 106; 212).

When Deleuze speaks of subtracting constants that belong to a
major usage, he refers of course to the minor use of language discussed
at length in *Kafka: Toward a Minor Literature*. In *Superpositions* Deleuze
reiterates the argument that the supposed constants and invariants of
language are actually power relations that a minor usage sets in continuous variation, and he asserts that Bene, like Kafka, Beckett, Godard and
Luca, is a foreigner in his own tongue who invents ways of making language itself stutter. Yet once again, as in *Kafka*, he provides few concrete
instances of a minor style per se and no examples from Bene's writings
of a minor use of Italian. What becomes especially clear in *Superpositions*,
however, is that Deleuze's concept of a minor usage of language necessarily extends well beyond that of a writer's manipulation of words on a
page, and that the *performance* of language provides Deleuze with the
fullest instance of a minor style. It is significant that in citing his favorite
example of minor writing, Luca's "Passionément," Deleuze advises that
one "read *or listen* to the poem" (SP 108; 213, emphasis added). "Never
has one attained such intensity in a tongue, such an intensive usage of
language. A public reading of poems by Gherasim Luca is a complete
and marvelous theatrical event" (SP 108; 213). When Deleuze reiterates
his argument that the semantic units of language are not constants that
undergo a secondary modification in varying contexts, he offers for
illustration of this point Lady Anne's remark to Richard "You horrify
me!" It is not the same statement when screamed by a woman at war, by
a child shrinking from a toad or by a young woman feeling faint stir-
rings of pity and desire. Each "You horrify me!" is a different speech act,
and each is an actualization of a virtual line of continuous variation that

passes through all possible instantiations of the phrase. Deleuze argues that Bene induces a minor usage of "You horrify me!" by having Anne "pass through all these variables": He has her "rise up as a woman at war, regress to a little child, return to life as a young woman, on a line of continuous variation, and as fast as possible" (SP 105; 211). To "minorize" the phrase, then, she must shift rapidly between different modes of delivery, each involving a variation in tone of voice, accent, facial expression, posture, gesture, movement, and so on.

Conventionally, these variables have the status of para- or extra-linguistic elements, but in the final analysis, they all are components of Bene's minor style. In his theater, "all linguistic and sonic components, indissolubly language [*langue*] *and* speech [*parole*], are placed in a state of continuous variation," and they have an effect on "the other non-linguistic components, actions, passions, gestures, attitudes, objects, etc." (SP 109; 213). Variables of language/ speech internal to language are placed in reciprocal relation with external variables, "in the same continuity, in the same flux of continuity" (SP 110; 213). Deleuze cites Corrado Augias's observation that Bene's theater exhibits a general "aphasia" in language and a parallel panoply of "impediments" that affect gestures and things. The actors whisper, scream or moan, their voices are distorted electronically in diverse ways, and at the same time objects interfere in the actors' regular movements, the most notable impediments in *Richard III* being the clothes the women constantly don and remove and the various props which Richard stumbles against and falls over. The aphasic distortions of language and speech create a continuum of linguistic and sonic variations, while the impediments create a parallel continuum of variations, Richard's ceaseless stumblings forming an oscillating "gesture in perpetual positive disequilibrium" (SP 111; 214), the women's dressing and undressing inducing a constant "variation of the clothing" (SP 112; 214).

One may make a rough distinction, then, between "the continuous variation of gestures and things" and the "continuous variation of language and sounds," but in Bene's theater and his cinema "the two variations must not remain parallel. In one way or another they must be *placed within one another*" (SP 115; 216). They must "*form a single and same continuum*" (SP 116; 216). Early in *Richard III*, the continua of language/sounds and gestures/things remain distinct, the Duchess's variations in voice and tone answering Richard's "troglodyte" stammerings in one continuum, the serving woman's movements corresponding to Richard's stumblings in a second. In the "improbable and overdone" scene with Lady Anne, however, the two continua come together. As Richard "gains his political choice, he constitutes his deformities, his war machine" (SP 117; 216). Lady Anne for her part "weds a war machine" and "enters herself into a variation that weds that of Richard" (SP 118; 216–17). Eventually, "the vocal variations of the one and the other, phonemes and tonalities, form a more and more tightly drawn line, which slides into the gestures, and *vice versa*. The spectator must not only understand, but hear and see the goal that the stammerings and stumblings have been pursuing from the beginning, without one's knowing it: the Idea become visible, sensible, the political become erotic" (SP 118; 217).

In Bene's language, the goal of "the political become erotic" is manifest in the "obscene," the excess of desire that disrupts codes and conventions. In Deleuze's terms, the goal is that of a generalized becoming, a continuous variation of all the components of drama, parallel to the "generalized chromaticism" Deleuze calls for in music (SP 100; 209; see also MP 123; 97). Indeed, Deleuze implies that the generalized becoming of Bene's drama renders it an essentially musical theater. Deleuze notes Bene's remark that in traditional drama the word destroys song, whereas in his works the actor must "sing incomprehensible words" ("L'énergie" 78), and Deleuze finds in Bene's treatment of the actor's voice "a sort of *Sprechgesang*" (SP 105; 211), midway between the regularities of conventional speech and singing, a continuous oscillation between the two modes that blurs them into one another. Deleuze points out as well that Bene aspires in his cinema and drama to make "music for the eyes," a kind of "music of images" ("L'énergie" 71). Ultimately, the music of Bene's theater is one in which language, sounds, gestures, movements, lighting, sets and props are as so many materials for a single composition, whose principle of construction is that of speeds and intensities. As the various components are put in continuous variation, they lose their fixed identities, their stable shapes and configurations. They become mere metamorphosing movements in perpetual transition, mutating processes that can be described only in terms of their velocities and their surges and declines in intensity. It is through this general principle of continuous variation that "the writing and gestures of CB are musical: it is because every form is deformed by modifications of speed, such that one does not pass twice by the same gesture or the same word without gaining different temporal characteristics. It is the musical formula of continuity, or of form in transformation [*forme à transformation*]" (SP 113; 215).

This form in transformation, or self-transforming form, may just as well be described as a deformation, or undoing of fixed and stable form, and here the theme of Richard's deformities and the drama's formal/structural deformations come together. Yet deformation is not to be construed as simply transgressive and negative, a point Deleuze indirectly makes in his citation of a group of fourteenth-century scholastic writers, chief among them Nicolas Oresme, who developed a geometry of *difform* movements and qualities, "based on the distribution of speeds between different points of a moving object, or the distribution of intensities between different points of a subject" (SP 114; 215). In the language of this medieval geometry of speeds and affects, difformity is simply the contrary of uniformity. Difformity is the state of having diverse forms as opposed to a single form, and further, difformity is a function of movement in time. Hence, Nicolas Oresme speaks of qualities that are "uniform," unchanging in time, others that are "uniformly difform," changing in a constant fashion over time; and still others that exemplify "difform difformity," either simple or composite, in which qualities change at varying velocities.[9] *Deformation*, we might say, stresses the critical function of an undoing of conventional forms, and *transformation* stresses the creative function of a production of new continua of metamorphosis (one can no longer speak of "new forms"), whereas *difformation* stresses both functions. Hence, what Deleuze identifies initially as Bene's "subtractions" and "constitutions" we can identify as so many *difformations*, conversions of language, sound, action, costume and stage into varying continua of speeds and intensities that serve as the constituents of an abstract music of relations.

The critique of power, then, requires a critique of representation, and in the theater, such a critique entails a difformation of all the components of traditional dramatic representation, including those of history (that is, conventional plot), structure, dialogue, text and language. In Bene's theater, the critical difformation of language extends first from *langue* (language system) to *parole* (language performance), then from the continuum of language/sounds to the continuum of gestures/things, until all elements of the stage production become constituents of a musical "composition in speeds and intensities." We should note, however, that though in one sense Bene's "minorizing" difformation of the non-linguistic elements of dramatic representation simply proceeds from a general critique of power, in another it follows logically from the nature of language itself as Deleuze conceives it. If language is action, the semantic content of an utterance does not precede its performance but is generated in its enunciation. Though Deleuze avoids a pan-textualism and insists on the distinction between the discursive and the nondiscursive, he recognizes as well that linguistics is a subset of pragmatics. Words do not mean by themselves but only in a context of action, and though one may differentiate words from things, words only mean in relation to a world of nonlinguistic entities. When Lady Anne sets "You horrify me!" in continuous variation, she destabilizes action-contexts, which contain both discursive and nondiscursive elements. She alters the semantic content of the phrase through variations in tone of voice, accent, emphasis and articulation, all of which are part of the vocal performance of language, but also through facial expression, posture, gesture and movement, as well as her interaction with the material elements surrounding her body—clothing props, sets, lighting.

It is significant, then, and perhaps not surprising, that Deleuze often seems vague when discussing the narrowly linguistic characteristics of a minor style. Style in general he defines as "precisely the procedure of a continuous variation" (MP 123; 97), and style in literature involves a continuous variation of all the elements of language. His sense of a minor usage of language inevitably leads to an emphasis on the performance of language, on its enactment in a dramatic situation. Thus the theater, rather than being a specialized or hybrid form of literary endeavor, may be seen as one of literature's paradigmatic spheres of activity. The general chromaticism that sets all the components of drama in continuous variation we may regard as a staging, an enactment, of the intricate and multiple connections between words and things, and the minor style of Bene's theater we may see as an explicit demonstration of what is implicit in any minor usage of language—a difformation of action/contexts across discursive and nondiscursive zones alike.

THE THEATER AND THE PEOPLE

To what extent does Deleuze's "One Less Manifesto" provide an adequate account of Bene's theater and his *Richard III*? Deleuze views

Shakespeare's Richard through the lens of the "man of war," the individual who engages a war machine of universal betrayal and becoming-woman. That view itself is shaped by Deleuze's understanding of Kleist's "literature of war" and his *Penthesilea*, a drama that develops fully the war/State opposition and the connection between violence and desire as affective intensities engaged in a process of becoming-woman and becoming-animal. Bene subtitles his play "The Horrible Night of a Man of War," but otherwise says little about war and nothing about the war machine. Yet he does make the telling comment late in the play that "Margaret unmakes and remakes the bed on which she tried to love so great a war" (SP 80), a remark that suggests a close tie between war and Bene's central theme of the feminine excess of desire in history. Bene's reference to Richard as a "man of war," it seems clear, then, is not simply a casual salute to Deleuze but rather the sign of a basic compatibility between their two projects and their views of Shakespeare's Richard. Deleuze might not be comfortable using Bene's vocabulary of "excess," "transgression" and the "impossible," and Bene may not adopt the language of "war machines" and "becoming-woman," but both see in Shakespeare's Richard an atypical king with a peculiar relation to women and politics—a man of war, in Deleuze's terms—and both regard the progressive deformation of Shakespeare's character as a means of critiquing the fixed power relations of the original drama and inducing creative metamorphoses that follow lines opened up by the play's female figures.

Yet if Deleuze and Bene both treat Richard as a man of war whose deformations constitute a becoming-woman, Deleuze offers only a partial reading of Bene's play, concentrating most of his attention on the First Part's climactic scene between Richard and Lady Anne and ignoring virtually all of the Second Part of Bene's drama. In one of the few critical treatments of "One Less Manifesto," Mark Fortier notes this fact and argues that Deleuze misreads Bene's *Richard III*, attributing a prevailing optimism to "a basically tragic work" (Fortier 7). Fortier rightly observes that Richard is abandoned by the feminine in the Second Part and that as he removes his prostheses he becomes "the perpetrator of a great error, a great masochism and self-mortification" (Fortier 7). In Fortier's reading, Richard's failed metamorphosis is symptomatic of Bene's jaundiced view of the theater and its potential for political transformation. Just as Richard's excess of desire leads only to a temporary undoing of power relations, so the theater also can only momentarily unsettle power relations before they return in all their rigor and severity. In concentrating only on the first half of *Richard III*, argues Fortier, Deleuze ignores the play's central lesson and appropriates the work for an optimistic politics that Bene ultimately does not embrace.

Deleuze does indeed speak at times as if the play ended with part one, and his lone comment on the second half provides no clear evidence of how he reads Richard's eventual narcissistic isolation.[10] But it is not at all obvious that Bene's *Richard III* teaches a tragic moral, nor that Bene's view of the political role of the theater is largely pessimistic. Bene's *Richard III*, like his *Romeo and Juliet*, is a "critical essay on Shakespeare" (SP 87; 204), and though Bene's critical operation of "subtraction" removes a good bit of Shakespeare's text, Bene chooses to retain sufficient portions of the text to trace the course of Richard's fortunes from Act One through Act Five. Hence, the given for Bene, his starting point, is the story Shakespeare tells. Bene's challenge is to extract from Shakespeare's play the latent possibility of an action that can be developed both as a commentary on the original story and as an action of significance in its own right. The course of action Bene traces in his play—from Richard's engagement with the women and his prosthetic self-assemblage in the First Part to his isolating abandonment of the feminine and his deformities in the Second Part—parallels that of Shakespeare's play, functioning as a commentary on the original story of Richard's exuberant, nihilistic rise to power and his eventual decline into a morose, haunted, narcissistic isolation. If there is a moral to Bene's story per se, it is not that the revolutionary metamorphosis of excessive desire and self-deformation inevitably fails, but that there are dangers in becoming-other and that without caution one can fall into a black hole of disconnected delirium and isolation. In this matter, Bene and Deleuze are in accord, for Deleuze makes the same point in *Dialogues*, where he says an intensity may "become dangerous" if "enough precautions" are not taken; a supple, molecular line may "rush into a black hole from which it will not emerge," and lines of flight may "turn into lines of abolition, of destruction, of others and of oneself" (D 167–68; 138–40).

As for Fortier's assertion that Bene's theater politics is more pessimistic than Deleuze's, it is true that in interviews Bene downplays the theater's potential for social transformation. The theater, says Bene, can only create a temporary "scandal," not a genuine "crisis," for it is unlikely that an audience will leave the theater and put into practice the deformations of codes and norms that have been enacted on the stage; hence, "the theater has no utility. It is absolutely gratuitous" ("L'énergie" 75). Remarks such as these, though, seem less categorical statements of principle than expressions of distaste for the self-congratulatory posturing of some proponents of the radical avant-garde. As Deleuze observes, such comments stem from an "extreme modesty," a recognition that "the theater obviously does not change the world and does not make the revolution" (SP 120; 217–18), at least in any direct and simplistic way. Yet Bene does continue to perform as if his plays might make a difference, and he does claim to engage in a form of popular theater (though he prefers to call it "ethnic"). The problem with a "theater of the people," Bene explains, is that it presumes the existence of a genuine people, but "it is the people that are lacking [c'est le peuple qui manque]" ("L'énergie" 76). This problem is one Deleuze frequently poses via the same memorable phrase from Paul Klee. And it seems that Bene means by the phrase much what Deleuze does—that the practices and institutions of power are so pervasive that both rich and poor, dominant and subordinate, are structured by the same hierarchical and asymmetrical codes and norms, and as a result, an autonomous, uncompromised collective consciousness of the oppressed does not exist. When Bene says that the theater addresses "an audience of slaves," of "rich slaves or poor slaves, it makes no difference" ("L'énergie" 84), he simply points out that the fundamental conflicts of the social field, as Deleuze puts it, "are already normalized, codified, institutionalized. They are 'products'" (SP 122; 218). The only solution is to invent a new people, to create what Bene calls an "ethnic" people that does not yet exist. And the only means of creating such a people is through an undoing of the codes of power, which inhere in the forms of conventional theatrical representation as well as in their contents.

Bene speaks often of various "impossibilities" of the theater, but his project is to "do the impossible." A genuinely popular theater, an "ethnic" theater that promotes a people to come, is in a similar sense impossible—hence his seemingly pessimistic remarks about the uselessness of the theater—yet it is an impossibility he strives to create. Deleuze and Bene, finally, do not differ in their understanding of the theater's political function. It is not to represent the plight, the perspective or the consciousness of a specific group, but to undo social representations and activate becomings that anyone may have access to. Says Deleuze, "This anti-representational function would be to trace, to constitute in some way a figure of the minoritarian consciousness, as the potentiality of everyone. To render a potentiality present, actual, is totally different from representing a conflict" (SP 125; 219). The theater Bene and Deleuze envision is one "which represents nothing, but which presents and constitutes a minority consciousness, as becoming-universal, constructing alliances here or there as the case may be, following lines of transformation that leap out of the theater and take on another form, or which are reconverted into theater by a new leap" (SP 130; 221–22).

In *Kafka* a distinction is made between Kleist's "literature of war" and Kafka's "minor literature," but it would seem the two converge in Bene's *Richard III*. The subtraction of the plot of State power from Shakespeare's history brings to the fore a "man of war," whose progressive deformation combines with a becoming-woman in a single process of open-ended metamorphosis (albeit one that eventually falls into a black hole). Bene extends the subtraction of power to the forms of representation, undoing conventions of plot, structure, dialogue, text and language, and turning the components of the stage performance into so many materials for a musical composition of mutative lines of continuous variation. Bene makes a minor usage of all the elements of drama, his minor style inevitably affecting the various dimensions of the speech/action situation—words, voice, sound, gestures, costumes, lighting, sets, and so forth. And through his experimentations on the forms of drama he furthers minor literature's end of inventing a people, not through the representation of a prospective identity, but through the "sudden emergence of a creative variation, unexpected, sub-representational" (SP 122; 218).

Bene's theater, we have seen, stages language's interconnections with the nonlinguistic world. In the next chapter we will examine another mode of linguistic enactment and another dimension of language's interface with the world, focusing on the visual and sonic limits to language, what Deleuze calls "visions" and "auditions," and the use they are put to in Beckett's television plays.

Chapter Six

LIFE, LINES, VISIONS, AUDITIONS

In the preface and opening chapter of *Critique et clinique* (1993), Deleuze suggests that the theme uniting that collection of essays is the relationship of literature to life and the outside. His initial conception of the critical/clinical project, as we saw in chapter 1, focused on symptomatology as a common ground for literary and psychoanalytic investigation, Sade and Masoch providing semeiologies of contrasting scenes, Carroll and Artaud offering topologies of qualitatively distinct worlds. But in his return to the motifs of *critique* and *clinique*, Deleuze extends his concern with specific affinities between literature and medicine to a broad consideration of literature as health, the clinical aspect of his enterprise bearing simply on those instances in which literature fails to make connections that further the activities of life. To write is "to invent a new language within language," to invent "a *process* carrying words along from one end of the universe to the other" (CC 9; lv). Writing is a "voyage, a journey" (CC 10; lvi), a trajectory toward an outside when healthy, a blocked path when sick. Yet the invention of a new language connects literature not only to the outside world, but also to the outside of language itself, to "visions and auditions that are nonlinguistic, but that language alone can make possible" (CC 9; lv). When the writer is a "seer and hearer," an inventor of visions and auditions, literature attains its goal of "the passage of life into language" (CC 16; 5). The object of this chapter is to delineate what Deleuze regards as the proper relation between literature and life, that is, between writing and the outside, both as outside world and outside of language. I will look first at Deleuze's meditations on literature, life and lines of flight in *Dialogues* and *A Thousand Plateaus*, in which literature's connection with the outside world may be discerned, and then at his scattered remarks on visions and auditions in *Critique et clinique*, in which literature's relation to the outside of language may be traced. A brief concluding examination of the theme of visions and auditions in "The Exhausted," Deleuze's 1992 study of Beckett's television plays, will bring us to issues midway between those of the pragmatics of theater and the images of cinema.

THE LINE OF FLIGHT

In the second chapter of *Dialogues* (1977), "On the Superiority of English-American Literature," Deleuze addresses the topic of literature and writing at length. He cites "Thomas Hardy, Melville, Stevenson, Virginia Woolf, Thomas Wolfe, Lawrence, Fitzgerald, Miller, Kerouac" (D 47–48; 36) as creators of a literature superior to that produced by most French authors, for these English and American writers, unlike their French counterparts, are able to fulfill writing's highest function—that of tracing a line of flight. Deleuze's main inspiration for this opposition of English-American and French literature comes from D. H. Lawrence's *Studies in Classic American Literature*, particularly the final chapters on Melville and Whitman. There Lawrence discerns in Melville a controlling obsession with escape: "To get away, out of our life. To cross a horizon into another life. No matter what life, so long as it is another life" (D. H. Lawrence 142). Melville "instinctively hated human life, our human life, as we have it," but he was also "passionately filled with the sense of vastness and mystery of life which is non-human" (D. H. Lawrence 142). In Whitman, Lawrence identifies a complementary obsession with "the Open Road," which is "Whitman's essential message" (D. H. Lawrence 183), the "message of American democracy" (D. H. Lawrence, 186). What Whitman discovers is a moral function for art, that of forcing the soul to inhabit the body rather than withdrawing from it, and "to go down the open road, as the road opens, into the unknown, keeping company with those whose soul draws them near to her, accomplishing nothing save the journey, and the works incident to the journey, in the long life-travel into the unknown, the soul in her subtle sympathies accomplishing herself by the way" (D. H. Lawrence 182). Rather than merging with other beings, the soul enters into a relationship of sympathy with them, "feeling with, not feeling for" (D. H. Lawrence 183). The soul encounters other souls on the open road, "And for one and all, she has sympathy. The sympathy of love, the sympathy of hate, the sympathy of simple proximity; all the subtle sympathizings of the incalculable soul, from the bitterest hate to passionate love" (D. H. Lawrence 186). Despite Whitman's frequent lapses into mystical fusion and solipsistic narcissism, says Lawrence, "the exultance of his message still remains. Purified of MERGING, purified of MYSELF, the exultant message of American Democracy, of souls in the Open Road" (D. H. Lawrence 186–87).

In Melville and Whitman, Lawrence hears "a new voice in the American classics" (D. H. Lawrence 7), and of course, that voice is as much his as it is theirs. The voice Deleuze hears is that of becoming and the line of flight, and when he speaks of English-American literature it is primarily in reference to those writers who share Lawrence's project in one respect or another. What Lawrence articulates in his studies of Melville and Whitman is a conception of literature as escape, but always as an escape across the horizon to a different world, a world that is antithetical to the human realm, yet filled with a nonhuman life. The path of flight is an open road, a "long life-travel into the unknown," whose goal is merely the process of the journey. The open road is selfless yet not amorphous, purified both of merging and of self, and its mode of relation is that of sympathy, a "feeling with" that includes within it the sympathies of love and hate—in short, a general affectivity that pervades a process of open-ended movement. All these motifs—flight, the open-ended journey, nonhuman life, selfless identity, general affectivity—enter into Deleuze's characterization of writing in *Dialogues*.

What does it mean to write? Deleuze offers one equivalent after another in *Dialogues*—to write is to flee, is to betray, is to become, and so on—each infinitive signaling networks of concepts we have come upon before. "To flee is to trace a line, lines, an entire cartography" (D 47; 36), "To write is to trace lines of flight" (D 54; 43). A *ligne de fuite* is a line that converges on the vanishing point (*point de fuite*) in perspectival representation, a line leading beyond the horizon. Quite literally Melville traces a line of flight in his sea stories, a path crossing "a horizon into another world" (D. H. Lawrence 142), but all writing does the same. A flight "is a kind of delirium" (here we recall Carroll, Artaud and the becoming of non-sense as opposed to the good sense [*le bon sens*] of the right direction), and "To be delirious is exactly to go off the track" [*Délirer, c'est exactement sortir du sillon*, the word *sillon* having the sense of "furrow," "track," "trail" (of a wheel), "wake" (of a ship), "path" (of a projectile), "railroad track"] (D 51; 40). To flee, then, is to trace an uncharted course and depart the paths of conventional sense and preexisting codes. Hence, too, "there is always treason in a line of flight" (D 52; 40), a betrayal of "the world of dominant significations and established order" (D 53; 41; here we recall *Richard III* and *Penthesilea*). To flee, however, is not just to escape, but also "to make something flee" [*faire fuir quelque chose*], "to make a system leak [*faire fuir un système, fuir* having the sense of both "to flee" and "to leak"] as one breaks a pipe" (D 47; 36). To go off the track is also to alter the track and create a new one, to derail/shunt, unroute/reroute, misdirect/redirect. To be a traitor to dominant significations and established order "is difficult," for "it is to create" (D 56; 45).

Deleuze characterizes the creative deformation that makes something flee as becoming—the becoming-woman, becoming-child, becoming-animal, becoming-imperceptible we have encountered in his discussions of Proust, Kafka, Kleist and Bene. "To write is to become, but not at all to become a writer. It is to become something else" (D 54; 43). In a becoming, something passes between two terms such that both are modified. "Not that the two terms are exchanged, . . . but one becomes the other only if the other becomes something else again, and if the two terms are effaced. . . . Melville's sailor becomes albatross, when the albatross itself becomes an extraordinary whiteness, pure vibration of white (and the becoming-whale of Captain Ahab forms a block with the becoming-white of Moby Dick, pure white wall)" (D 88–89; 73). All becomings efface stable identities and hence tend toward a becoming-imperceptible; for this reason, "the aim, the finality of writing" is "becoming-imperceptible" (D 56; 45). By being effaced, the terms in a becoming are rendered mere vectors, directions, movements—what Deleuze and Guattari speak of as "flows" in *Anti-Oedipus*. Thus, "To write has no other function: to be a flow that conjoins with other flows—all the becoming-minoritarian of the world" (D 62; 50). To conjoin flows is to form assemblages, collections of heterogeneous elements that somehow function together, not through a unifying principle but through "'sympathy,' symbiosis" (D 65; 52). Whitman's "sympathy" of the Open Road, then, is the general affectivity that provides assemblages with their "consistency," their cohesion as conjoined flows of multiplicities.

To form assemblages is "to be in the middle, on the line of encounter of an interior world and an exterior world" (D 66; 52). To write is to open a line of encounter between a becoming-imperceptible of the writer and a general becoming of the outside. Deleuze sees a complementary relationship in the notions that life is something personal and that the literary work "is supposed to find its end in itself, either as total work, or as work in the process of formation, which always goes back to a writing of writing" (D 60–61; 49). The autonomous author and the autonomous work are concepts that obscure the nature of writing and life. To write is to trace a line of flight, and to flee "is to produce the real, create life" (D 60; 49). As the writer's identity is effaced, a conjunction of flows connects writing with nonwriting. "In truth, *to write does not have its end in itself, precisely because life is not something personal.* Or rather, the goal of writing is to carry life to the state of a non-personal power [*puissance*]" (D 61; 50). The conjunction of flows of a becoming-other produces a general deterritorialization, which "liberates a pure matter, it undoes codes, it carries away expressions and contents, states of things and statements [*énoncés*], on a zigzag, broken line of flight" (D 88; 72–73). The life that traverses a deterritorialized pure matter is nonpersonal and nonorganic, a vital passage of lines abstracted from persons, organisms and all other stable entities. To write, finally, is to engage the abstract line of this nonpersonal, nonorganic life, and in this regard, writing is no different from creation in the other arts. "So, what is it, to paint, to compose or to write? It's all a question of line, there is no considerable difference between painting, music, and writing. These activities are distinguished by their respective substances, their codes and their territorialities, but not by the abstract line they trace, which flies between them and carries them toward a common destiny" (D 89; 74).

LINES

To write is to flee, to make flee, to be delirious, to leave the track, to betray, to become, to conjoin flows, to form assemblages, to deterritorialize—but above all, to trace a line of flight, for the line of flight is the line of creation and "experimentation-life" (D 59; 47), and whether "individuals or groups, we are made of lines" (D 151; 124). In what way, though, are we "made of lines," and how might we treat writing in terms of lines? These are the topics of Plateau Eight of *A Thousand Plateaus*, "1874: Three *Nouvelles*, or 'What Happened?'." Here Deleuze and Guattari discuss lines and writing's line of flight primarily through analyses of three texts, Henry James's novella "In the Cage" (1898), F. Scott Fitzgerald's essay "The Crack-Up" (1936) and Pierrette Fleutiaux's short story "Histoire du gouffre et de la lunette" (The Story of the Abyss and the Spyglass, 1976). Deleuze and Guattari's object in part is to detail the lines that traverse these literary works, but ultimately their aim is to develop a discourse of lines that encompasses literature and the world as a whole. "For we are made of lines. We do not want to speak only of lines of writing, lines of writing conjoin with other lines, lines of life, lines of fortune and misfortune [*chance et malchance*], lines that make up the variation of the line of writing itself, lines that are *between the lines* that are written" (MP 238; 194).

How might we see the world in terms of lines? The line of flight is the line that leads to the vanishing point, the line that tends beyond the horizon. To traverse a horizon is to trace a line, to create a path—the wake of a ship, the track of an animal, the trail of an army—to proceed on a route that may subsequently be mapped with a line. But to trace a line of flight is also to "go off the track," *sortir du sillon*, which suggests that the routines of daily life are also lines, railways of prescribed activities, ruts of habit, coded career paths, programmed highways and byways of socially sanctioned interaction. The flows Deleuze and Guattari describe at such length in *Anti-Oedipus* may also be seen as lines, each flow connecting machines in an open-ended additive circuit, the sum of circuits traversing the body without organs like a network of gradients crisscrossing the surface of an ovum. In *A Thousand Plateaus*, circuits of flows are characterized in terms of assemblages, and these, too, may be regarded as lines. The collective assemblages of enunciation and the machinic assemblages of bodies that shape language are organized patterns of force, regular arrangements of practices, institutions and material entities that string together heterogeneous elements in a sympathetic cofunctioning. We recall as well that immanent within the assemblages are "lines of continuous variation," immanent, virtual continua of variables that assemblages actualize in specific forms and shapes. Lines finally may be thought of as melodic lines, which Deleuze and Guattari use as a figure for interacting patterns of nature, or "refrains," which bring the various species of the natural world together in a vast contrapuntal symphony of relations.[1] Hence, as "individuals or groups, we are traversed by lines, meridians, geodesics, tropics, zones [*fuseaux*, as in *fuseaux horaires*, time zones], which do not beat to the same rhythm and do not have the same nature" (MP 247; 202).

Two features of this model are crucial to keep in mind: Lines are dynamic and abstract. Always in motion, never static, lines may leave lingering traces, but they are vectors, trajectories, courses of movement and becoming, some so predictable in their journeys that they may be charted, demarcated by intersecting regular trajectories, graphed by grids of coordinated vectors, but others as erratic as the line of flight, a vital, nonorganic zigzag passing between things. Lines may be conceived of as moving from a point of origin to an endpoint, but the dynamic passage of the line is always between points, in the middle, and at any juncture of its passage it may swerve from its path (or conversely, return from its zigzag into a regular course of movement). As processes and movements, lines are also abstract, not the outlines and delineations of stable things but the tracings of their surges, flows and wakes. Further, lines are abstracted from things, determined by characteristics selected and separated from other characteristics. And lines often pass through things, connecting components and constituents of entities in assemblages that have only the abstract form of circuits and flows (not a mother and baby, but a flow of milk passing through a breast-machine to a mouth-machine).[2]

Deleuze and Guattari open Plateau Eight's discussion of lines by distinguishing between *contes* and *nouvelles*, the *conte* designating a story in which the reader constantly asks, "what's going to happen?" (*qu'est-ce qui va se passer?*), the *nouvelle* a story which poses the question, "what happened?" (*qu'est-ce qui s'est passé?*).[3] Although one might see here a simple opposition of future and past, the distinction is somewhat more subtle. The *conte* is always oriented toward a *discovery*, the *nouvelle* toward a *secret*, such that in a *conte* even the past and present are pulled toward a future, whereas in a *nouvelle* the present and future are experienced as already past. The temporality of the *nouvelle* is such that "one enters a room, and one perceives something as already there, having just taken place, even if it has not yet occurred. Or one knows that what's in the process of occurring is already for the last time, that it's over. One hears an 'I love you' and knows that it's for the last time" (MP 238; 194). The *nouvelle* has a fundamental relation with the secret, though "not with a secret matter or object to be discovered, but with the form of the secret, which remains impenetrable" (MP 237; 193). The form of the secret is that of something hidden that requires opening, unfolding, explication, but that can only be opened after the fact, *après coup*, even if it may be sensed as already present before it happens. The *nouvelle* "puts us in relation with an unknowable or an imperceptible" (MP 237; 193), with the *form* of the secret as unknowable or imperceptible, even if the contents of a specific secret should eventually become known or perceptible. *Contes* and *nouvelles* both "treat a universal matter" (MP 238; 194), that of lines, but *nouvelles* have specific ways of handling lines that are intimately related to this retrospective temporality of the imperceptible.

Deleuze and Guattari first detail the lines of the *nouvelle* through a reading of Henry James's "In the Cage" (James calls this 150-page novella a "Tale" [James, Preface, v]). The story involves a telegraph operator who apparently uncovers the secrets of Lady Bradeen and Captain Everard, two of her aristocratic customers who are having an affair. The telegraphist is engaged to a grocer, Mr. Mudge, but she postpones her marriage as she becomes increasingly attached to her two customers, especially to Everard. She begins walking by his lodgings after work and one evening runs into him. They engage in a lengthy conversation, during which she obliquely confesses her interest in his situation and swears, "'I'd do anything for you'" (James 442). Later, he comes to her telegraph cage in a panic, worried that an earlier wire from Lady Bradeen might have compromised the lovers. The telegraphist is able to recall from memory the precise wording of the earlier message, and to his great relief, Everard learns that the text in question will cause no damage. He departs and eventually marries Lady Bradeen, while the telegraphist readies herself for marriage to Mr. Mudge, aware now that for her, reality "could only be ugliness and obscurity, could never be the escape, the rise" (James 499).

James's heroine inhabits a rigidly structured world, whose patterns of daily existence—work, occasional vacations, humdrum courtship and eventual marriage—are all too predictable. Her life is organized by *lines of molar or hard segmentarity*, conventional trajectories regulated by codes that impose broad social categories, fixed identities and pathways discretely divided into clear segments. But in her encounters with Everard, Deleuze and Guattari find a second kind of line, a *"line of molecular or supple segmentation* the segments of which are like quanta of deterritorialization" (MP 240; 196). This is the line of the secret (a secret that remains a pure *form*, in that James never reveals its precise nature), a line inducing imperceptible alterations in the heroine's routines, incipient metamorphoses in class relations between the telegraphist and Everard, microdisturbances in the affectively charged conversations of the protagonists. On this line "a present is defined whose form is that of something which has happened, already happened, no matter how close one is to it, since the ungraspable matter of this something is entirely molecularized, at speeds that exceed the ordinary thresholds of perception" (MP 240; 196). Yet there is a third line as well, a *line of flight* glimpsed briefly when the narrator remarks at a certain point: "She ended up knowing so much that she could interpret nothing. *There were no more obscurities for her that would make her see more clearly, there remained only a harsh light.*"[4] Such a line obliterates even the form of the secret, for it is an abstract line of mutation and potential transformation. In James's story, however, the line of flight goes nowhere, and in the end the heroine returns to her rigid lines of molar segmentarity.

In "The Crack-Up," Deleuze and Guattari find especially clear descriptions of the line of molecular segmentation and the line of flight. Fitzgerald devotes these somewhat melancholy autobiographical musings to an analysis of the changes that come upon one unawares, through emotional crises. At the age of thirty-nine, says Fitzgerald, "I suddenly realized that I had prematurely cracked" (Fitzgerald 274) and "that for two years my life had been a drawing on resources that I did not possess, but I had been mortgaging myself physically and spiritually to the hilt" (Fitzgerald 276). He had "cracked like an old plate" (Fitzgerald 276), but imperceptibly, leaving him with the implicit question, "what happened?" Here, Deleuze and Guattari recognize the molecular lines of cracks that fissure one's routines, the kind of breakage that "happens almost without your knowing it" but which "is realized suddenly indeed" (Fitzgerald 273). Such fissures disintegrate old certainties and identities ("So there was not an 'I' any more—not a basis on which I could organize my self-respect"

[Fitzgerald 283]), leaving one without discernible coordinates for future action (Fitzgerald speaks of "a feeling that I was standing at twilight on a deserted range, with an empty rifle in my hands and the targets down" [Fitzgerald 282]). Yet Fitzgerald comes to realize that "the ones who had survived" such crack-ups "had made some sort of clean break" (Fitzgerald 286). They had discovered a line of flight, which entails a decisive rupture with previous patterns and codes. "A clean break is something you cannot come back from; that is irretrievable because it makes the past cease to exist" (Fitzgerald 286). In Deleuze and Guattari's reading, then, "The Crack-Up" distinguishes two sorts of crack-ups, two kinds of inner breaks, the molecular break of imperceptible fissures and the clean break of a qualitative rupture. The first disrupts molar lines, the second opens a line of flight. Each has its promise and each its danger—in Fitzgerald's case, the molecular line inducing emptiness, and the line of flight leading not to new life, but to a bitter doctrine of radical selfishness and the promise of minimal social respectability with which he ends the essay: "I will try to be a correct animal, though, and if you throw me a bone with enough meat on it I may even lick your hand" (Fitzgerald 289).

In Deleuze and Guattari's third case study of lines, Pierrette Fleutiaux's "The Story of the Abyss and the Spyglass," the molar and molecular are quite prominent, whereas the line of flight scarcely appears at all, though when it does, it offers the possibility of genuine transformation. The story's strange universe is one of "short-viewers" and "long-viewers" who from a wooden platform gaze through telescopes across a great abyss to observe "infractions" (Fleutiaux 14), "pockets of irregularities, orders poorly obeyed, delays" (Fleutiaux 15), "rebellions" and other unspecified "Troubles" (Fleutiaux 24) on the other side. What the short-viewers see are "kinds of giant cells, in the form of a classroom, barrack, low-income housing project, or even countryside viewed from an airplane" (Fleutiaux 28). The short-viewers discern only the contours of these cells, which have the shape of "chains, rows, columns, dominoes—the number of figures is finally rather limited" (Fleutiaux 29). When infractions and rebellions are detected, the great Ray Telescope (*Lunette à Rayon*) appears, a laser gun that cuts into the giant cells and restores them to their regular contours. The story's narrator is a long-viewer (there is only one long-viewer per platform), whose sensitive instrument detects "an infinite quantity of contours, undetermined," a "continual segmentation, an endless mobility, a tangle of contours that never stop moving" (Fleutiaux 34). The long-view telescope allows for highly subtle discriminations of infractions, but these are seldom heeded by the short-viewers; the long-viewer also sees that the Ray Telescope's inscribed regularities are actually ragged gashes and serrated tears in the tissue of the cells. The long-viewer's microperceptions, then, have only a retrospective significance when confirmed by the short-viewers' observations, and the molar contours imposed by the laser Ray are revealed to be irregular and violent wounds. Throughout the story, the narrator feels alienated from the short-viewers and yearns for camaraderie, yet a transformation is possible only when a great storm from beyond the abyss lays waste to the entire platform and the narrator abandons the long-view telescope. Then, the narrator ventures over the bridge that spans the abyss and on the other side finds an identical platform of short-viewers and a long-viewer counterpart, with whom the narrator gazes back across the abyss, which now seems not a giant gulf, but "an infinitely flat surface on which I might finally begin to walk, begin to live, with my counterpart, my double, whole at last" (Fleutiaux 50).

In the *nouvelles* of James, Fitzgerald and Fleutiaux, three lines are at work, the molar or hard line of segmentarity, the molecular or supple line of segmentation and the line of flight. In each text, the molar lines are imperceptibly disturbed by molecular perturbations, such that one must ask, "what happened?" What led the telegraphist to her strangely libidinized complicity with Captain Everard? How did Fitzgerald suddenly discover he had become cracked like an old plate? What brought the long-viewer to such an anguished separation from both short-viewers and the vocation of surveillance? In each, an unknowable divagation takes place, the *form* of the secret, and in each, a line of flight opens momentarily as well, an instant of harsh light beyond interpretation, a clean break, a bridge across the great abyss. In James, the line of flight leads only to reinstated molar lines of work and domesticity, and in Fitzgerald, to a cynical void, but in Fleutiaux it opens up a possibility of new life.

We are made of lines, and hence there can be no segregation of lines of writing and lines of life. Though Deleuze and Guattari treat the three *nouvelles* of Plateau Eight as texts *about* lines, they might just as well have demonstrated the interpenetration of life and work as they do in *Kafka*, where they interrelate letters, stories and novels with the multifarious machinery of disciplinary families, factories and bureaucracies. Lines "may be equally those of a life, of a work of literature or art, of a society, according to the system of coordinates that is retained" (MP 249; 203–4). Deleuze and Guattari identify three lines, each with its particular character and danger, each immanent within the others and equally present across the domains of the personal, social and political, the human and the nonhuman. Each line has its importance, but if priority is granted any one line, it must be to the line of flight. As Deleuze explains in *Dialogues*, we may speak equally of three lines, two lines or one. There are three lines, molar, molecular and line of flight. Or there are two lines, the molecular being simply "the oscillation between the two extremes" (D 165; 137). "Or there is only one line, the primary line of flight, the line of the border or the frontier, which is relativized in the second line, which allows itself to be stopped or cut in the third" (D 165; 137). The line of creation is the line of flight, and to the extent that writers create, they engage this line. "To write is to trace lines of flight" (D 54; 43), vital lines of "experimentation-life" (D 59; 47).

VISIONS AND AUDITIONS

In *Kafka*, Deleuze and Guattari develop the concept of minor literature, and in *Superpositions* Deleuze uses the concept to comment on Bene's theater, but already in *Dialogues* it is evident that for Deleuze minor literature is less a specific subdivision of literature than a name for literature when it functions as it should. Deleuze speaks primarily of "writing" rather than "minor writing" in *Dialogues*, and though Deleuze and Guattari discuss the minor usage of language in *A Thousand Plateaus*, their focus in Plateau Eight is on lines and writing *tout court*. It comes as no surprise, then, that when Deleuze addresses the topic of "Literature and Life" in the opening essay of *Critique et clinique*, the "literature" he describes is essentially "minor literature," though framed in categories that differ somewhat from those laid out in *Kafka*. Rather than starting from the notions of high coefficients of linguistic deterritorialization, the immediately political nature of writing and collective assemblages of enunciation, Deleuze here characterizes literature in terms of becomings, the invention of a people to come and stuttering in one's own language. These, of course, are all familiar themes, bound up intimately with the exposition of the concept of minor literature in *Kafka*. Yet there is a fourth aspect of literature Deleuze identifies in "Literature and Life," one that is relatively new—the invention of visions and auditions. The topic is prominent in the preface to *Critique et clinique*, and it surfaces in several brief passages throughout the volume. It seems to be one of the last problems Deleuze had begun exploring before his death.

Critique et clinique is organized around certain problems, says Deleuze, the problem of writing (inventing a foreign language within one's language, making language delirious by carrying it off its customary tracks [*sillons coutumiers*]), but also "the problem of *seeing* [*voir*] and hearing [*entendre*]: in effect, when another language [*langue*] is created within language [*langue*], it is language [*langage*] as a whole which tends toward an 'asyntactic,' 'agrammatical' limit, or which communicates with its own outside" (CC 9; lv). The outside that is proper to language is like the linguistic surface of *The Logic of Sense*, the surface between words and things, the *limit* of language that puts language in contact with the nonlinguistic. If language is seen as a sphere, the sphere's outer surface is the sphere's outside, but it is also that which touches on the nonlinguistic (that which is outside the sphere) and allows the linguistic and the nonlinguistic to communicate with one another (the sphere's surface as membrane, or permeable limit common to inside and outside). Like *sens*, sense/meaning, which is expressed in words but which expresses an attribute of bodies, visions and auditions are expressed in language, but they are themselves nonlinguistic. Language's limit is "made" (CC 9; lv) of nonlinguistic visions and auditions, yet language alone renders them possible. Visions and auditions are like Stoic *lekta*, surface effects that haunt the bodies of words like fogs or auras emanating from their superficies: "There is also a painting and a music proper to writing, like the effect of colors and sonorities that rise up above words" (CC 9; lv). It is through words, across them, traversing them (*à travers les mots*), between words (*entre les mots*), that visions and auditions occur. Beckett speaks of "boring holes" in language to see or hear "what lurks behind." "Of every writer it must be said: he/she's a seer, a hearer, 'ill seen ill said' [the title of a prose volume of Beckett's], he/she's a colorist, a musician" (CC 9; lv).

Visions and auditions take place when a foreign language is created within one's own language, but Deleuze makes clear that fashioning an "other" language is not precisely the same as producing visions and auditions. In "Literature and Life," he speaks of three "aspects" (CC 16; 5) of literature: a "decomposition or destruction of the mother tongue [*langue maternelle*]", "the invention of a new language [*langue*] within language [*langue*], through the creation of syntax"; and the creation of "Visions and Auditions, which no longer belong to any language [*qui ne sont plus d'aucune langue*]" (CC 16; 5). The creation of a new language, it seems, never occurs without there being at the same time a general "teetering" of language, a pushing of language to its limit, toward "an outside [*un dehors*] or a reverse side [*un envers*, as in the reverse side of a reversible jacket]" (CC 16; 5) of language. Yet the new language and the teetering of language are not identical. The one is linguistic, the other involves language's nonlinguistic limit or surface. Further, auditions and visions

> are not phantasies [*fantasmes*], but veritable Ideas that the writer sees and hears in the interstices of language [*langage*], in the gaps of language. They are not interruptions of the process, but halts that form a part of it, like an eternity that can only be revealed in becoming, a landscape that only appears in movement. They are not outside language, they are language's outside. The writer as seer and hearer, the goal of literature: it is the passage of life within language [*langage*] that constitutes Ideas. (CC 16; 5)

Visions and auditions, then, are language's outside, in the interstices and gaps of language, but in what sense they are "Ideas that the writer sees and hears" and entities constituted by "the passage of life in language" requires some extended explication.

Intuitively, auditions might seem more closely related to language than are visions, in that language has a material sonic component, whereas its visual dimension would seem to be merely metaphorical, or at least mediated by complex neuro-physiological processes. But as we saw earlier in examining Kafka's style, Deleuze and Guattari treat the sonic deformations of a minor usage of language as an experimentation involving both the actual sounds of language (Kafka's German) and the sounds represented in language (Gregor's insect buzzing, his sister's violin music in "The Metamorphosis"). And in *Critique et clinique*, it is evident that auditions are not simply the traditional musical effects of alliteration, assonance, rhyme, meter, rhythm, and so on. In "He Stuttered," as we noted earlier, Deleuze says that an "affective, intensive usage of language" may act directly on phonemic and syntactic elements and induce a linguistic stuttering (such as Luca's "Passionné nez passionnem je/ je t'ai je t'aime je"), but it may also leave intact the form of expression "if a corresponding *form of content*, an atmospheric quality, a milieu that serves as a conductor of words [*un milieu conducteur de paroles*]," gathers up "the tremble, the murmur, the stutter, the tremolo, the vibrato," and makes "the indicated affect reverberate over the words [*sur les mots*]" (CC 136; 108). In Melville's *Pierre, or the Ambiguities*, "the din of the forest and the caverns, the silence of the house, the presence of the guitar testify to the murmur of Isabelle and her sweet 'foreign intonations'"; in "The Metamorphosis," Gregor's twittering is confirmed "through the trembling of his feet and the oscillations of his body"; and in Masoch, "the stammering of his characters" is doubled in "the heavy suspense of a boudoir, the din of the village or the vibrations of the steppe" (CC 136; 108).[5] Words sing, "but at the limit of the path [*chemin*] they trace in dividing themselves and composing themselves. The words make silence. The violin of the sister relays the twittering of Gregor, and the guitar reflects the murmur of Isabelle; a melody of a songbird about to die rises above the stuttering of Billy Budd, the sweet 'barbarian.' *When language [langue] is so strained that it starts to stutter, or to murmur, stammer . . . , all of language [langage] reaches the limit* which marks its outside and makes it confront silence" (CC 142; 113). Auditions arise in a stuttering style that renders the conventional elements of language strange, but they embrace actual linguistic sounds and represented sounds alike in atmospheres and milieus that "relay" and "reflect" sounds, make them "testify to," "confirm," "double" one another. And ultimately, auditions create a paradoxical silent music. When language is pushed to "its limit, its outside, its silence" (CC 142; 113), there is "a painting or a music, but a music of words, a painting with words, a silence in the words, as if the words now disgorged their content, grandiose vision or sublime audition" (CC 141; 113).

Clearly, Deleuze's allusion to "a silence in the words" cautions against a ready equation of auditions and actual sound effects in words; and in fact, it suggests that if anything, the sonic dimension of language complicates rather than clarifies the question of what is meant by auditions and visions. More helpful, it turns out, are Deleuze's remarks about visions, especially those offered in his brilliant essay on T. E. Lawrence's *Seven Pillars of Wisdom*, "The Shame and the Glory: T. E. Lawrence." Deleuze opens by paralleling Goethe's theory of colors and "the desert and its perception, or the perception of the Arabs in the desert" (CC 144; 115).[6] In his *Farbenlehre* (*Theory of Colors*, 1810), Goethe argues that light in itself is invisible and that the visible is only produced through an interplay of light and shadow, of the transparent and the opaque (the clear and the obscure—*chiaroscuro*). Colors are shadows, varying degrees of opacity whereby invisible light becomes visible. Thus, there is in color a fundamental physiological relation between the eye and the matter of the world, in that "color is that through which the visible *begins*, *archê* of the visible: it is affect" (Escoubas 233). Colors are "degrees of shadow *in* light, according to a relation of *more* and of *less*" (Escoubas 234). In white, there is the least amount of shadow; in black, the greatest. Yet if a world of pure light is invisible—like the sun, dazzling and blinding—"a world in black and white is still too blinding. Or too invisible. 'Seeing,' affect only begins *after*, when the first and the last degrees of opacity begin to decline, when white darkens [*s'obscurcit*] into yellow and black lightens [*s'éclaircit*] into blue" (Escoubas 234–35). In the genesis of the visible, the first form of visibility is that of the indistinct halo or atmosphere, which is also the most ephemeral of forms, an instantaneous glance, an *Augenblick* ("instant," "moment," from the roots *Auge*, eye, and *Blick*, glance). Hence, "the Goethean visible is *speed* [*vitesse*]," (Escoubas 235), "a world in *movement*" (Escoubas 238). As the world becomes increasingly distinct, contours of objects emerge, shapes, edges, borders, surfaces that add shadow to light, "thicken" light into colors. Thus, Goethe's color theory "is a theory of the contour, a theory of the *figure*" (Escoubas 237), color and contour together becoming visible as white passes into yellow, black into blue, with yellow and blue reaching their maximum intensification in a single color, a "culmination of all colors: red, which in its purest tint is called 'purple'" (Escoubas 240).

From Goethe's color theory, then, one can extract a three-tiered genesis of the visible, a passage from an invisible, blinding pure light; through an indistinct halo or atmosphere of black and white; to the colors and contours of distinct figures, white darkening into yellow, black into blue, yellow and blue reaching their maximum intensity in purple. In Lawrence's accounts of the Arab perception of the desert, Deleuze finds three parallel dimensions—a world of pure, invisible light; a world of mirages, hazes, gases and glowing solar vapors, contrasts of black and white ("They were a people of primary colours, or rather of black and white" [T. E. Lawrence, 37]); and a world of endless fields of yellow and blue, sand and sky and of burning colors and contours, like the hallucinatory, sublime Rumm valley, with its fiery play of crimsons and purples, domes, crags and zigzag crevices. In a literal sense, then, Lawrence's landscapes record the genesis of seeing, the stages of emergence of the visible as invisible light passes through solar fogs into colored contours. But invisible light is like the Arab God, the Idea, "the pure transparent—invisible, colorless, unformed, untouchable" (CC 144; 115), and Deleuze argues that for Lawrence the Idea is one with light. Light is "the opening that makes space [*l'ouverture qui fait l'espace*]" (CC 144; 115), the process of an expanding, unfolding, invisible force that issues forth in the fundamental visibilities of space. Like light, "the Idea extends itself across space, it is like the Open [*l'Ouvert*]" (CC 144; 115). Ideas are "forces that exert themselves in space following directions of movements: entities, hypostases, not transcendences" (CC 144; 115). Ideas are like Goethe's light, phenomena of instantaneous movement and speed, forces that have real, material existence—entities, hypostases—even if they remain invisible and manifest themselves to sight only through the "thickening" admixture of varying degrees of shadow. And these Ideas have directly political consequences: "the revolt, the rebellion is light, because it is space (it is a question of spreading out in space, of opening the most space possible) and because it is Idea (the essential is preaching [that is, the prophetic enunciation of the abstract concept of the rebellion])" (CC 144; 115). The Arabs are "incorrigibly children of the idea" who "could be swung on an idea as on a cord" (T. E. Lawrence 42), and their nomadic spread is like the expansion of light, the movement of the Idea as material force issuing forth into, and simultaneously determining, a space.

Lawrence "is one of the greatest landscape painters [*paysagistes*] in literature" (CC 162; 116), but not because he creates Goethean panoramas of light, haze and varied colors. The finest writers, says Deleuze, "have singular conditions of perception that allow them to draw on or shape aesthetic percepts as veritable visions" (CC 146; 116). Such writers may detail an outer landscape, whose features correspond to actual places or concrete, objective forms, but a visionary landscape entails as well what may be loosely termed a "subjective" element. Deleuze finds in Melville an inner ocean that "is projected into the ocean of the outside, but in order to transmute perception and 'abstract' from it a Vision" (CC 146; 117). Likewise, in Lawrence there is "an inner desert that pushes him into the deserts of Arabia, among the Arabs, and which coincides on many points with their perceptions and conceptions, but which retains the indomitable difference that introduces these perceptions and conceptions into an entirely different and secret Figure" (CC 146; 117). An inner image is projected on an outer world—an inner ocean on an outer ocean, an inner desert on an outer desert—such that the outer world, ocean or desert, is transmuted, made visionary.

This projection of an inner image on an outer world Deleuze finds at work especially in Lawrence's reputed grandiosity and mythomania. Lawrence's self-image and the image he constructs of his Arab comrades possess a kind of mythic quality, arising not from narcissistic impulses, but from "a deep desire, a tendency to project into things, into reality, into the future and even into the sky, an image of oneself and of others sufficiently intense that *it lives its own life*" (CC 147; 118). Deleuze clarifies this process through reference to a passage from Genet's *Prisoner of Love* (1986), in which Genet speaks of a desire, "more or less conscious in every man, to produce an image of himself and propagate it beyond death" (Genet 261). Individuals and groups create a profusion of self-images, adopt postures and poses, develop characteristic expressions, gestures, comportments and rhythms and then project them into the world. "From Greece to the [Black] Panthers, history has been made out of man's need to detach and project fabulous images, to send them as delegates into the future, to act in the very long term, after death" (Genet 262). A mythomaniac is simply someone "who can't project his image of himself properly," who does not know how to make the image "live a life of its own" (Genet 262). The great figures of history succeeded in "projecting an image around themselves and into the future," and whether the image conforms to what they were really like or not, the essential fact is "they managed to wrest a powerful image from that reality" (Genet 262). What Deleuze finds here is the "fabulatory function [*fonction fabulatrice*]" (CC 147; 118) of the invention of a people-to-come, the creation of a collective identity for the revolutionary group-in-formation. In this sense, "the subjective disposition, that is, the force that projects images [*la force de projection d'images*], is inseparably political, erotic, artistic" (CC 148; 118). Though "subjective," and "inner," then, the images projected on the real are nonpersonal and to the extent that they are successfully projected, autonomous.

Lawrence creates images that he projects into the world, but he also fashions abstract ideas that in Deleuze's analysis operate as material "entities" within that world. Lawrence says at several points that he shares the Arab passion for abstractions and ideas, and Deleuze follows in detail Lawrence's use of one such abstraction—shame. But for Lawrence, abstract ideas, says Deleuze, "are not dead things, they are entities that inspire powerful spatial dynamisms [*puissants dynamismes spatiaux*], and that intimately mingle in the desert with projected images—things, bodies or beings" (CC 149; 119). Lawrence has the gift of making abstractions into entities that "live passionately in the desert, alongside people and things" (CC 149; 119). He creates a world of abstract entities, and "this world of entities which pass into the desert, which *double the images*, mingle with the images and give them a visionary dimension" (CC 150; 120). At the same time, these abstract entities cause disturbances in Lawrence's style, inducing its halting rhythms, odd inversions and occasional archaisms, its "granular" character, as E. M. Forster calls it, making it "sound like a foreign language, less Arabic than a phantom German" (CC 149; 119).[7] Abstract ideas, however, are ultimately "not what one might think: they are emotions, affects" (CC 155; 124). They are "*Puissances*" (CC 156; 124), Powers or Potencies. Like Goethe's light, they are invisible forces of movement. One hears the "shock" of such abstract entities in Lawrence's style (CC 156; 124), as if these affective forces were bouncing against the words, making the words stagger, halt, accelerate, scatter. And the abstract entities "provoke at the limit of language the apparition of great visual and sonorous Images" (CC 156; 124). It is as if these abstract entities, these affective Powers, "peopled an inner desert [*un desert intime*] that applies itself to an external desert, and projects there fabulous images all across the bodies—men, beasts and rocks" (CC 156; 124).

Although Lawrence's obsessive, affective handling of abstractions, his "phantom German" style, his mythicizing narrations and his evocative, hallucinatory landscapes are idiosyncratic to his enterprise, they make particularly clear the components that go into the creation of

Visions. In *Seven Pillars of Wisdom* we have images of solar haze and mirages, of broad expanses of sand and sky, of landscapes as "in child-hood's dream, . . . so vast and silent" (T. E. Lawrence 352), variegated in color and contour. We also have the self-images and group images of a collective enterprise, the enlarged, heroic stances and gestures of the Arab rebellion. And we have the granular, erratic syncopations of Lawrence's style. Across all these play affective intensities, movements of force. In Lawrence, such forces are Ideas, but Ideas in the sense of Goethe's light—abstract material *entities*. The landscapes Lawrence pro-vides are descriptions of actual places, but projected on them are trans-forming images that come from Lawrence's inner desert. Likewise, the narrative of parleys, troop movements, skirmishes and raids records historical events, but projected on these events are images of a future collective identity. What makes *visionary* the projected images of land-scapes and groups is the doubling of images with "abstract entities"— that is, the infusion of images with invisible, affective forces. Such forces disturb language and make it "other," but at the limit of words they instigate a projection of images, and those images they permeate and animate, as invisible light permeating a world of colors.

VISIONS, TRAJECTORIES, AND BECOMINGS

Visions are inner images projected on an outer world, yet though Deleuze attributes them to a "subjective disposition," they are not "sub-jective" in the sense either of belonging to a discrete self (subject vs object) or of exhibiting some form of personal bias or predilection (sub-jective vs objective). Visions "are not phantasies, but veritable Ideas" (CC 16; 5). Not only may the images of visions be collective (indeed, Deleuze argues they always are), but they also are wrested from the real and have a life of their own. How may images be both "inner" and impersonal/autonomous, both wrested from the real and projected onto the real? Deleuze provides some indications of an answer in the essay "What Children Say," where he elaborates on the distinction between subject-centered, psychoanalytic phantasies and impersonal, asubjective visions.

In Freud's famous case of Little Hans, a five-year-old boy's phobia of horses is interpreted as a fear of castration by his father.[8] All the details of Little Hans's life—his anxiety about horses biting him or

falling in the street, his fears of animals at the zoo, his desire to visit the
girl in the facing apartment, to meet the "young lady of refinement" at
a restaurant, to imitate the "street-boys" and climb on a cart at the
warehouse, and so on—all are read relentlessly as elements of his castration complex. But Deleuze argues that desire directly invests the
world, that horses, giraffes, streets, children, buildings and rooms are
not symbols of daddy and mommy, but components of a milieu made
up of the "qualities, substances, powers [*puissances*] and events" (CC 81;
61) that Hans actively and affectively inhabits. One may draw a map of
Hans's milieu, of its various places (the family rooms, the apartment
building, the warehouse across the street, the zoo, the Gmunden
restaurant), individuals (the little girl, young lady, street-boys), animals
(horses, zoo animals), objects (carts, furniture-vans, buses), qualities
(smells of the horses, cries of the drivers), events (a horse tries to bite, a
horse falls down). One may then chart on this map the trajectories of
Hans's movements—actual, anticipated, dreamed, imagined, dreaded—
and trace the affective circuits of his world. On this map of desire, the
pathways of Little Hans combine his own qualities, substances, powers
and events with those of the milieu. "The map expresses the identity of
one's journey [*le parcours*] and what one journeys through [*le parcouru*]. It
blends with its object, when the object itself is movement" (CC 81; 61).[9]

To emphasize the affective nature of this milieu, one might create
a second map, not of trajectories, or movements in extension, but of
intensities, or movements in "intension," for "there are also maps of
intensity, of density, which concern that which fills space, that which
subtends the trajectory [*le trajet*]" (CC 84; 64). This second map would
chart affects, such as those that belong to horses in Hans's world: "to
have a big widdler, to carry heavy loads, to have blinkers, to bite, to fall,
to be whipped, to make a row with its feet" (CC 84; 64). A map of intensities plots a distribution of affects, and these affects are *puissances*, powers of affecting and being affected—that is, *becomings*. The affects of
horses on Hans's intensive map trace a becoming-horse of Hans, and
the map of intensive becomings "subtends"—underlies, extends
beneath—the extensive map of trajectories. "Becoming is that which
subtends the trajectory, as intensive forces subtend motor forces. The
becoming-horse of Hans relates to a trajectory, from the house to the
warehouse" (CC 85; 65).

The relationship between trajectories and becomings is not that of the real and the imaginary, of an individual's external movements and his/her internal psychological states. The two maps of trajectories and becomings are inseparable, and their mutual penetration undoes the traditional distinction of the real and the imaginary: "a becoming is no more imaginary than a voyage is real. It is becoming that makes of the slightest trajectory, or even a fixed immobility, a voyage; and it is the trajectory that makes of the imaginary a becoming" (CC 85; 65). On a double map of trajectories and subtending becomings, the real and the imaginary must be conceived of as "two juxtaposable or superimposable parts of a single trajectory, two faces that ceaselessly interchange with one another, a mobile mirror" (CC 83; 63). If one is to speak of the imaginary at all, one should think of it as

> a virtual image that intermingles with the real object, and vice versa, in order to constitute a crystal of the unconscious. It is not enough that the real object, the real landscape evokes similar or neighboring images; it must disengage *its own* virtual image, at the same time that this virtual image, as imaginary landscape, enters into the real following a circuit in which each of the two terms pursues the other, interchanges with the other. 'Vision' is made of this doubling or dividing in two [*doublement ou dédoublement*], this coalescence. It is in the crystals of the unconscious that the trajectories of the libido are made visible. (CC 83; 63)

Here we return to visions, landscapes and images, but now framed in terms of the virtual and the real, rather than the inner and the outer. What we referred to in Lawrence as an "inner image projected on an outer world" is here a virtual image that "enters into the real" (that is, into "the actual," in Deleuze's more customary terminology, in that the virtual and the actual are both "real"). The virtual image and real/actual image together form a "crystal of the unconscious." The figure of the crystal Deleuze develops at length in *Cinema 2. The Time Image*, describing the "crystal-image" as a particular type of cinematic time-image in which the virtual and the actual are seen simultaneously in the same image. As we recall from our discussion of Proust, Bergson argues that the past exists as a single virtual domain, extending from the most distant events into every present moment. Each present moment coexists with a portion of this virtual past, a kind of virtual "double" of the pres-

ent that is the present moment's "own" virtual moment. In certain cinematic images, claims Deleuze, one sees a present moment and its own
virtual past in a single image. The image is like a mirror, which makes
an actual object visible in a virtual reflection, but it is a multifaceted
mirror, a crystal that refracts and creates proliferating virtual images
(just as Bergson's virtual past extends from every present moment into
the entire field of the past). The crystal *doubles* the actual, as a reflection
doubles an actual object, it *divides* (*dédouble*) or splits the actual and virtual, ensuring their mutual distinction, and it makes them *coalesce* in a
single, multifaceted image, or crystal-image.

Each present moment has its own virtual moment, but in ordinary
experience that virtual moment is unnoticed, invisible. Likewise, each
landscape has its own unseen, virtual landscape within it. To make that
landscape visible, one must disengage it, extract it from the actual and
then put it in relation to the actual "following a circuit in which each
of the two terms pursues the other, interchanges with the other." When
the virtual and the actual landscapes coalesce, such that each doubles
the other and splinters from the other, a "crystal of the unconscious" is
formed, and in that crystal "trajectories of the libido are made visible."
But if the virtual landscape is simply extracted from the actual, and
hence is something that exists "out there," what has this virtual landscape to do with desire, or "trajectories of the libido," and what does it
mean to put a virtual landscape in relation to the actual, such that they
form a "crystal of the unconscious"? Deleuze provides an example that
helps elucidate these points. He mentions an artistic project under-
taken by a group of architects, artists, sculptors, writers, historians and
scientists to commemorate the 700th anniversary of the Helvetic
Confederation with the creation of an environmental artwork along a
two kilometer path from Morschach to Brunnen, near Geneva. The
project, as detailed in *Voie suisse: l'itinéraire genevois. De Morschach à
Brunnen* (Swiss Way, Genevan Itinerary. From Morschach to Brunnen),
was to take an existing path along Lake Geneva, and through various
interventions—plantings, architectural constructions, sonic installa-
tions, sculptures and so forth—convert it into a work of art, such that
it would become clear "what it signifies today to 'make a path' [*faire un
chemin*]" (*Voie suisse* 22). One of the artists, Carmen Perrin, chose to cut
away the foliage covering several boulders alongside a stretch of the
path, thereby extracting the boulders from the landscape and making

visible the glacial forces that over centuries had brought them to their present position. Perrin "disengaged" what was already there, but in such a way that geological lines of force became visible, and though the rocks were not moved or altered, only selected stones were uncovered in an erratic configuration, such that a rhythmic counterpoint was established between the boulders, the path and other features of the landscape. The "path," in the larger sense of "traversed milieu or environment," then, comes to include several trajectories—the walkway itself, the virtual flows of glacial forces, the lines interconnecting the boulders, the shifting vectors of resonance between the rocks and their surroundings engaged as the walkway is traveled—and these trajectories, though externally visible, are internal to the work of art. In this sense, "the external path is a creation that does not preexist the work [of art], and depends on the work's internal relations" (CC 87–88; 67). The trajectories of Perrin's path are virtual elements extracted from the real, but they are internal elements of the artwork imposed on the real. It is "as if virtual paths were intertwined with the real path, which receives from them new tracings, new trajectories" (CC 88; 67). In this regard, says Deleuze, Perrin's path is exemplary of every work of art. "A map of virtualities, traced by art, is superimposed on the real map, whose routes [*parcours*] it transforms" (CC 88; 67).

Art's "map of virtualities," however, is not simply a formal structure. That map of virtualities is also a double map of extensive trajectories and intensive becomings, like the double map of Little Hans's libidinal milieu, with its various pathways between the apartment building, the street, the warehouse and the zoo, and its various affects involved in a process of becoming-horse. Perrin extracts virtual trajectories from the Genevan landscape, and she fashions those trajectories into an internally coherent configuration that is imposed on the site, but the virtual trajectories also inhabit, and are inhabited by, Perrin. Though we can only surmise what affective trajectories and becomings make up Perrin's libidinal map, we must assume that the virtual trajectories of the Genevan landscape extend, combine and intersect with the artist's other pathways, and that the artistic process of creation is continuous with all the other activities that make up her life and world.

Let us now consider Lawrence once again. For years Lawrence inhabits the desert, traversing its expanses, passing through its valleys. As he indicates in his evocative first chapter, the trajectories he and his comrades trace are affective and erotic: "We lived always in the stretch or sag of nerves, either on the crest or in the trough of waves of feeling. . . . The men were young and sturdy; and hot flesh and blood unconsciously claimed a right in them and tormented their bellies with strange longings. Our privations and dangers fanned this virile heat, in a climate as racking as can be conceived" (T. E. Lawrence 28–29). In this "naked desert, under the indifferent heaven" (T. E. Lawrence 28), Lawrence charts a double map of trajectories and becomings, on which he, his companions and his milieu combine and coalesce as so many interpenetrating "qualities, substances, *puissances* and events" (CC 81; 61). Traced there are trajectories of a becoming-Arab of Lawrence, a becoming-heroic Rebellion of his Arab followers, a becoming-camel of both, and a general becoming-imperceptible before an overwhelming environment, as the men are "fermented" by the sun, "dizzied by the beating wind," "stained by dew, and shamed into pettiness by the innumerable silences of the stars" (T. E. Lawrence 28). The actual paths forged by Lawrence and his comrades demarcate processes of metamorphosis; they are virtual lines of force that have been actualized in the real. The landscapes Lawrence describes are imbued with the dynamic forces of light and heat and with the affects of various bodies—human, animal, vegetable, mineral. Immanent within each landscape is a virtual landscape, its *own* virtual double, which Lawrence extracts from the actual panorama. In that expanse, Lawrence and his milieu adhere as loci of nonpersonal, nonindividuated forces, and through his writing a landscape-image is formed, a landscape-crystal in which the virtual and the actual are made to double, divide and coalesce, at once interpenetrating, passing into and out of one another, separating and cohering. This landscape-crystal belongs no more to Lawrence than to the Arabian desert, no more to an internal than an external reality. It is an autonomous image that lives its own life, and though one may speak loosely of an inner desert projected on an outer world, the image-crystal is both *extracted* from the actual landscape and *detached* from any personal, psychological world in the process of its projection.

That process of projection is the process of artistic creation. Lawrence actually inhabits the Arabian desert, but the landscapes he describes only come into existence through the writing of *Seven Pillars of Wisdom*. The specific configuration of a given landscape's trajectories and becomings is internal to the work of art. The configuration is extracted from and projected back into the real, where it induces transformations and transmutations, but the final landscape is "a creation that does not preexist the work and depends on the work's inner relations" (CC 88; 67). Through words, Lawrence invents a landscape, and at the limits of language it rises like a nonlinguistic image floating above the words. Within that landscape-image invisible forces become visible, forces of light passing through solar fogs into colors and contours. Like Cézanne's paintings of Mont St. Victoire, with its tectonic thrusts and surges, or van Gogh's late landscapes of swirling skies, pulsating fields and bending roadways, Lawrence's landscape-images render invisible forces visible. But those forces are not simply forces of light, for the landscape images communicate with the fabulative images of a people-to-come. Through the process of artistic creation, the immense vistas become saturated by the heroic impulses of the collective rebellion, just as the rebels acquire an aura of grandeur from the landscapes they traverse. In Lawrence's landscape visions, the movement of light and the movement of the rebellion—"the Movement" as it is called—are as one.[10]

CODA: BECKETT'S TELEVISION PLAYS

Visions and auditions are the nonlinguistic outside *of* language, sights and sounds produced through words but existing above words, between them, "as if words now disgorged their contents" (CC 141; 113). They are "veritable Ideas that the writer sees and hears" (CC 16; 5), but ideas in the sense of Lawrence's abstractions, "emotions, affects" (CC 155; 124), "powerful spatial dynamisms" (CC 149; 119), invisible material forces, "entities, hypostases" (CC 144; 115). It is the "passage of life within words" (CC 16; 5) that constitutes these Ideas. In "Literature and Life," Deleuze speaks of literature in terms of becomings, the invention of a people and stuttering, and each of these concepts Deleuze ties to visions and auditions. Literary characters are determined by the becomings that traverse them, and all their individual traits "elevate them to a vision that carries them into an indefinite as a becoming that is too powerful for them: Ahab and the vision of Moby Dick" (CC 13; 3). Visions and auditions are always collective, like Lawrence's fabulative images of the Arab rebellion. Hence, "These visions, these auditions, are not a private affair, but form the figures of a ceaselessly reinvented History and geography. It is delirium that invents them, as *process* carrying the words from one end of the universe to the other. They are events on the frontier of language" (CC 9; lv). And of course visions and auditions only arise when language begins to stammer and teeter on the edge of its own silence.

In "The Exhausted" ("L'Épuisé")(E), Deleuze's 1992 study of Beckett's television plays (included in the English translation but not the French edition of *Critique et clinique*), Deleuze offers two very clear examples of such linguistic stuttering, one in which "short segments are ceaselessly added to the interior of the phrase in an effort to break the surface of words open totally" ("folly seeing all this—/ this—/ what is the word—/ this this—/ this this here—/ all this this here—/ seeing—/ folly seeing all this this here—" ["What Is the Word," in *As the Story Was Told*, p. 132; CC 105; 174]), the other in which "the phrase is riddled with dots or dashes [*traits*] that ceaselessly reduce the surface of words" ("Less best. No. Naught best. Best worse. No. Not best worse. Naught not best worse. Less best worse. No. Least. Least best worse" ["Worstword Ho," in *Nohow On*, p. 118; CC 106; 174]). Yet Deleuze's main aim is to show how Beckett in his television plays overcomes the limitations of words by nonlinguistic means, through the exhaustion of space and above all through the creation of visual and sonic images. Here, in these remarks on Beckett's television images and their relationship to language, Deleuze makes several points that will help round out our understanding of visions and auditions.

Over the years, remarks Deleuze, "Beckett was less and less able to put up with words" (E 103; CC 172), though this was not a newfound intolerance. Indeed, Deleuze sees Beckett's entire *oeuvre* as dominated by a struggle with language, first enunciated in critical remarks from the 1930s. In a key 1937 letter, to which Deleuze makes frequent reference, Beckett expresses his impatience with "official English," stating that "more and more my own language appears to me like a veil that must be torn apart in order to get at the things (or the Nothingness) behind it" (Disjecta 171).[11] Language cannot be eliminated "all at once," he says, but it should be torn apart and riddled with holes. "To bore one hole after another in it, until what lurks behind it—be it something or nothing—begins to seep through; I cannot imagine a higher goal for a writer today." Beckett laments that literature adheres to practices "long ago abandoned by music and painting," and then asks, "Is there any reason why that terrible materiality of the word surface should not be capable of being dissolved, like for example the sound surface, torn by enormous pauses, of Beethoven's seventh Symphony, so that through whole pages we can perceive nothing but a path of sounds suspended in giddy heights, linking unfathomable abysses of silence?" (Disjecta 172). Beethoven creates music that emphasizes the silence *between* sounds, and by implication literature should likewise reveal the "something or nothing" *between* words. Beckett in fact says as much in the 1932 fragment *Dream of Fair to Middling Women* (another seminal text to which Deleuze often alludes), in which the character Belacqua voices his desire to write a book such that "the experience of my reader shall be between the phrases, in the silence, communicated by the intervals, not the terms, of the statement" (Disjecta 49). This literary project puts Belacqua in mind of "the dehiscing, the dynamic décousu of a Rembrandt, the implication lurking behind the pictorial pretext threatening to invade pigment and oscuro." In Rembrandt he discerns "a disfaction, a désuni, an Ungebund, a flottement, a tremblement, a tremor, a tremolo, a disaggregating, a disintegrating, an efflorescence, a breaking down and multiplication of tissue, the corrosive ground-swell of Art," and in Beethoven he notes a similar "punctuation of dehiscence, flottements, the coherence gone to pieces" such that the compositions are "eaten away with terrible silences" (Disjecta 49).

In these early critical texts, a parallel is established between painting, music and literature as so many efforts to penetrate a surface to a "something or nothing" beneath. In Rembrandt the various pictorial figures and objects separate from one another, become disunited and make visible the empty space between them, just as in Beethoven the phrases disaggregate and make audible the silences between sounds. Yet empty space, it seems, is not simply the space between, but the entire expanse beneath the surface of the painting, the background depths from which the painting arises ("the corrosive ground-swell of Art"), just as the "unfathomable abysses of silence" form the background dimension beneath the surface of the music. Hence, to tear apart the veil of language, to bore holes in words, to dissolve the word surface, is in an analogous fashion to reveal whatever background nonlinguistic element may lurk behind words, whatever counterpart to the visible void or sonic silence might function as language's underlying depths.

It might seem that Beckett's aesthetic project is essentially negative, that what lurks behind the art work's surface is much more a "nothing" than a "something," but Deleuze reads Beckett otherwise. Deleuze comments that when one bores holes "in the surface of the painted canvas, as does Rembrandt, Cézanne, or Van Velde, in the surface of sound, as does Beethoven or Schubert," it is in order that "the void or the visible in itself, silence or the audible in itself, may surge forth" (E 103; CC 173). What these painters and composers do is to create a "pure intensity that pierces the surface" (E 104; CC 173), a pure visual or sonic image that reveals *the visible in itself, the audible in itself*—that is, the invisible or inaudible forces that play through the visible or the audible. In Deleuze's reading, painting's void and music's silence are not empty but full, and what Beckett's favored painters and composers bring to the fore is the virtual, the plenum of forces on the plane of consistency.[12]

The problem for writers is that language's surface is more difficult to tear apart than are the surfaces of visibilities or sounds. "It is not simply that words are liars; they are so laden with calculations and significations, and also with intentions and personal memories, with old habits that cement them together, that scarcely has their surface been broached when it closes over again. The surface sticks. It imprisons us and suffocates us" (E 103; CC 173). In his study of the painter Francis Bacon, Deleuze observes that Bacon's aim is to wrest the visual figure from the clichés of narration and representation and thereby make sensible a "matter of fact,"[13] and in Beckett's writing Deleuze sees an equivalent goal. When painters or composers manage to undo the narratives and codes that organize and regularize sights or sounds, they are then able to create pure images, indefinite entities that are neither general nor particular. "Music manages to transform the death of this young girl into *a young girl dies*; music brings about this extreme determination of the indefinite as pure intensity that pierces the surface" (E 103–4; CC 173). No longer "the young girl" as universal, nor Jane Marie Jones, a specifically identified subject, she is the locus of a process of becoming, "a young girl." Music and painting have a facility for creating such indefinite images that pierce the surface, but not so words, "with their adhesions that maintain them in the general or in the particular. They lack that 'punctuation of dehiscence,' that 'disconnection' that comes from a groundswell proper to art" (E 104; CC 173).

Deleuze frames his analysis of Beckett's television plays in terms of exhausting the possible. (In the French text of *Quad*, the first of the four television plays Deleuze examines, Beckett insistently repeats the phrase "all possible combinations thus exhausted" [E 10-13] when detailing the movements of the characters, the lighting, percussion sounds and costumes.) To *realize* the possible is to pursue "certain goals, projects and preferences: I put on my shoes in order to go out and slippers in order to stay in" (E 58; CC 152). But the pursuit of goals, projects and preferences has no end, for whatever choices one makes, there are always others that remain possible. To *exhaust* the possible requires an abandonment of preferences, aims and plans, a disconnection of elements from the endless sequence of wants and desires, such that a closed set of limited terms may undergo a thorough and exhaustive permutation of combinations. Murphy's calculation of the five biscuits' "total permutability, edible in a hundred and twenty ways" (*Murphy* 96-97), Watt's list of "twelve possibilities" regarding Mr. Knott and his eating habits (*Watt* 89-90), Molloy's description of the "sucking-stones" and all their possible placements in his pockets and mouth (*Molloy* 69-74) are well-known instances from Beckett's fiction of this exhaustion of the possible, and in *Quad* a similar operation takes place, as four indistinguishable actors traverse all possible paths connecting the four corners of a square in all combinations of performers (solos, duos, trios, quartet), lighting, percussion and costumes. What is crucial in all these instances is that the elements to be combined be stripped of all preference, all purpose and all signification, such that they form a closed set of terms whose permutations are finite. To disconnect these elements is to cut them off from the normal function of language, for "language enunciates the possible, but in preparing it for a realization" (E 58; CC 153). Language articulates all the codes, conventions, narratives and representations of human wants and needs, whose continuations, connections and combinations are open and inexhaustible. The purpose of exhausting the possible is finally that of undoing language, of dissolving the glue of calculations, significations, intentions, personal memories and old habits that cement words together.

Deleuze identifies three means whereby Beckett undoes ordinary language and exhausts the possible. The first is through the creation of a metalanguage, "a very special language such that the relations between objects are identical to those between words" (E 66; CC 156). This metalanguage Deleuze calls *language I* (*langue I*), a language that is "atomic, disjunctive, cut up, chopped, in which enumeration replaces propositions, and combinatory relations replace syntactic relations: a language of nouns" (E 66; CC 156). Such a language is that of Watt's and Molloy's lists of permutations, a collection of words severed from their usual networks of linguistic connotations, asignifying save in their one-to-one correspondence to the objects undergoing permutation. But if one exhausts the possible *with* words through *language I*, there is also a need to exhaust words themselves, and "hence the necessity of another metalanguage, of a *language II*, which is no longer one of nouns, but one of voices" (E 66; CC 156). If the words of *language I* are disconnected particles, the voices of *language II* are "waves or flows that pilot and distribute the linguistic corpuscles" (E 66; CC 156). The object of *language II* is to dry up the flows, to put an end to the surrounding din of incessant voices, each of which is an Other articulating a possible world, narrating an endless stream of stories with all their significations, preferences and goals. The problem, however, is that even when voices cease, they soon start again, and when one speaks *of* those voices, one risks continuing their stories. Thus the need of a *language III*, "which no longer relates language to enumerable or combinable objects, nor to emitting voices, but to immanent limits that are ceaselessly displaced, hiatuses, holes or rips" (E 69; CC 158). *Language III* involves "something that comes from outside or elsewhere" (E 70; CC 158), and that something is an "Image, visual or sonorous" (E 70; CC 158).

The image of *language III*, however, is an image in a very specific sense. It is a pure image, a sight or sound that "surges forth in all its singularity, without retaining anything of the personal, or of the rational, acceding to the indefinite as to a celestial state" (E 71; CC 158). Like a Baconian "matter of fact," a *language III* image is disconnected from the narratives and codes of normal language and conventional representation. It is defined by "its 'internal tension,' or by the force that it mobilizes in order to create the void or bore holes, to loosen the grasp of words, dry up the oozing of voices, in order to disengage itself from memory and reason, a small alogical, amnesic, almost aphasic image, now standing in the void, now shivering in the open" (E 72; CC 159). Such images possess a "mad energy . . . ready to explode," but they are "like ultimate particles, they never last long" (E 76; CC 160). Their energy is "dissipative," for they "capture all the possible in order to make it explode" (E 77; CC 161), dissipating themselves as they put an end to the world of inexhaustible possibilities, that world of language, "weighed down with calculations, memories and stories" (E 73; CC 159).

Pure images form the outside of language, but that outside includes as well "the 'vastitude' of space" (E 74; CC 160), for which reason *language III* consists of both images and *un espace quelconque*, an any-space-whatever, "deconsecrated and put to another use [*désaffecté*], unalloted [*inaffecté*], although it is geometrically completely determined (a square, with such and such sides and diagonals, a circle with such and such zones, a cylinder 'sixty meters round and sixteen high')" (E 74; CC 160). In such a disconnected, "indefinite" any-space-whatever, all the potentialities of space may be exhausted, all the permutations of movement between the specified points of a closed area, and within an any-space-whatever, visual and sonic images may arise, explosive events tearing apart the surface of words and dissipating into the background expanse beneath.

Deleuze thus identifies four means of exhausting the possible: "forming exhaustive series of things" (*language I*), "drying up flows of voices" (*language II*), "extenuating the potentialities of space" (*language III*), and "dissipating the power [*puissance*] of the image" (also *language III*) (E 78; CC 161). The first two means (*language I* and *language II*) dominate in Beckett's novels, dramas and radio plays, but the latter two, the twin elements of *language III*, only come to the fore in the television plays. *Quad* (1980) extenuates the potentialities of space through the creation of an any-space-whatever, the actors traversing the sides and diagonals of a featureless square in all possible combinations of trajectories and assemblages (solos, duos, trios, quartet). *Ghost Trio* (1975) also depotentializes space, the set consisting of a nondescript room with a door on the right, a window straight ahead and a pallet on the left. The door opens onto a blank corridor, the window onto a uniform rainy night, and the pallet has no distinguishing features. A voice sounds from a tape recorder, yet it articulates no stories, plans or preferences, instead merely naming the places and actions as they appear on the screen ("At the far end a window. [*Pause.*] On the right the indispensable door. [*Pause.*] On the left, against the wall, some kind of pallet" [*Dramatic Works* 408]). But *Ghost Trio* also "goes from space to the image" (E 93; CC 168), the play's final section including a close-up of the actor's face in the mirror above the pallet, a floating, decontextualized smile of an indefinite yet determinate visage-image that appears just as the incessantly repeated sound-images of Beethoven's Ghost Trio come to a close. . . . *but the clouds* . . . (1976) also takes place in an any-space-whatever, in this case a nondescript circular area, its western, northern and eastern coordinates characterized by the off-camera voice as respectively roads, sanctum and closet. The voice describes the man's repeated movements from point to point, but it also talks about the pure image that appears on the screen from time to time, a close-up of a woman's face "reduced as far as possible to eyes and mouth" (*Dramatic Works* 417), a Cheshire cat smile of yet another indefinite visage-image. *Nacht und Träume* (1982), finally, unfolds in the any-space-whatever of a "a dark empty room," a "dreamer" seated at a table, facing right, "clearly visible only head and hands," while "his dreamt self" (*Dramatic Works* 465), a mirror double facing left, periodically appears four feet above the dreamer, a pair of woman's hands on occasion descending from the shadows to wipe his brow, offer a cup, gently rest on his head and eventually join with his hands. A voice accompanies the dream image, but it is primarily a sound-image, the voice initially humming the tune of Schubert's "Nacht und Träume," words entering the play only when the voice repeats the melody and sings the *Lied* with lyrics.

Quad dispenses with words entirely, *Nacht und Träume* introduces words solely as song lyrics; and *Ghost Trio* and . . . *but the clouds* . . . offer words as doubles of an any-space-whatever and the pure images that arise within that space. Visions and auditions are the outside *of* language, nonlinguistic visual and sonic images that language alone makes possible, and Beckett's television plays provide a kind of pedagogy of visions and auditions, a dramatization of the complex and elusive relationship of images to words. The visual and sonic images of the television plays are distinct from words—indeed, in *Quad* words are shone to be entirely dispensable—but in *Nacht und Träume* and . . . *but the clouds* . . . words are put in relation to images, in one case through song, in the other, through poetry. In *Nacht und Träume*, the lyrics of Schubert's *Lied* are heard as components of the sonic image of the song and accompaniments of the visual image of the dreamer being caressed by the female hands. The words remain distinct from sounds and sights, but their co-presence with the sonic and visual images suggests, at least for a moment, that words and images emanate one from another, words producing images, images summoning up words. In . . . *but the clouds* . . . , words are used primarily to describe the visual space and the unfolding action, but with the appearance of the visual image of the woman's eyes and mouth, words take on a new relationship with the image. The woman's lips move as she inaudibly utters words that the off-camera male voice enunciates. The words are lines from Yeats's "The Tower," fragments at first (" . . . clouds . . . but the clouds . . . of the sky . . . "), but in the final appearance of the woman's face, they form two complete lines (" . . . but the clouds of the sky . . . when the horizon fades . . . or a bird's sleepy cry . . . among the deepening shades . . . " [Dramatic Works 421–22]). The autonomous visual image of the woman's face is synchronized with the poetic voice, while the words enunciate their own images, the visual image of clouds fading into the horizon and the sonic image of a bird's cry sinking into silence. Not only are those poetic images elements produced by words and autonomous in their own right (like the visual image of the woman's face), but they suggest as well the fleeting and ephemeral nature of images and their relationship to the visible in itself and the audible in itself, to the void and the abyss of silence within which images explode and then dissipate. At least for a few moments in *Nacht und Träume* and *. . . but the clouds . . .* , "the voice manages to conquer its repugnancies, its adherences, its ill will, and, carried along by the music, it becomes speech [*parole*], capable of making in its turn a verbal image, as in a *Lied*, or capable itself of making the music and the color of an image, as in a poem" (E 73; CC 159).

Beckett bores holes in language throughout his writings, but in his television plays he finds words more and more difficult to tolerate. To exhaust the possible requires the invention of a metalanguage of disconnected words, but also the cessation of voices and the creation of an image within an any-space-whatever. Beckett works by subtraction, by paring away the significations of words, the stories of voices, the individualizing features of space, the universal or particular aspects of images, and in the television plays it seems the tendency is toward an elimination of words altogether. But in *Nacht und Träume* and *. . . but the clouds . . .* , even as the autonomous, indefinite image arises, a few spare words appear and through song or poetry assume a relationship with the image. Beckett's subtractions might seem nihilistic, but for Deleuze these ascetic practices aim less at nothingness than at purification, at the creation through elimination of a pure any-space-whatever, a pure image, a pure poetry that can produce its own visions and auditions.

What is crucial is the impersonality of the space, the image, the words, an impersonality that makes possible the production of asubjective, anorganic, asignifying intensities. There is in Deleuze's thought, as in Beckett's work, an ascetic strain, but always in the service of intensities, an effort, as Deleuze is wont to say, to get drunk on pure water. "We attempt to extract from alcohol the life it contains, without drinking: the great scene of drunkenness on pure water in Henry Miller. To do away with alcohol, with drugs and madness, this is becoming, the becoming-sober for a richer and richer life" (D 67; 53). In Deleuze's reading, Beckett's ascetic subtractions sever words, voices, spaces and images from their subjective and conventional associations, but not from the real. Instead, they allow words, voices, spaces and images, as they are reduced to their minimal conditions and purified of all external associations, to become part of a single intensive plane of consistency.

Visions and auditions are nonlinguistic visual and sonic images that language alone makes possible. They form the outside *of* language, the surface membrane *between*. They are images, indefinite yet determinate mobilizations of force that explode and dissipate as they appear. They may be treated loosely as inner images projected on an outer world, but finally they are neither inner nor outer. They are crystals of the unconscious, virtual images extracted from the actual and then put back in relation with it, in such a fashion that virtual and actual simultaneously double each other, divide from one another and coalesce. Autonomous and impersonal, visions and auditions live their own lives, but they only come into existence through artistic creation. Extracted from the actual, their internal coherence arises from the artwork's own trajectories and becomings, which themselves extend through the artist and into the world he or she inhabits. The paths of these extensive trajectories and intensive becomings form a double map of an affective milieu, made up of qualities, substances, powers and events. They are so many lines, sometimes rigidifying as molar lines of segmentation, sometimes fragmenting as molecular lines of destabilization but ultimately opening toward an Outside as lines of flight. What one sees and hears in visions and auditions are lines of flight produced as language teeters in disequilibrium.

What does this mean in commonsense terms? Deleuze starts, it seems, with the observation that in some works of literature the visual and aural images represented through language appear to have a kind of solidity, vividness and autonomy, as if words had somehow disgorged their contents and emitted palpable nonlinguistic sights and sounds. One might see this simply as an illusion made possible by the complex relationship between language and sense experience, the life of the senses being in one regard separate from language (the taste of the plum is not the word "plum") yet in another intimately tied to language (the sensual experience of plums permeates my linguistic usage of the word "plum," and the semantic networks of "plum" shape my experience of plums—as instances of the categories of foods, sweets, treats, rewards, subjects of nursery rhymes, etc.). But for Deleuze, these arrestingly solid and palpable visual and aural images are not mere illusions, for they have a real existence, like Stoic *lekta*, on the mutual surface between words and things. They come into being when commonsense distinctions between inside/outside, subject/object, words/things, and so forth, collapse—and here our commonsense explanation must also collapse. All we can say at this point is that visions and auditions render visible and audible the invisible and inaudible circuits of forces that are immanent within the real. Such circuits of forces, by their very nature, can be characterized only in terms of velocities and affects, trajectories and becomings. They form a plane of consistency, in which there is no means of differentiating a sound or sight from a word. Here, there are only lines, and painters, musicians and writers all experiment on the same lines, each finding a different means of manifesting those lines—in actual visual constructions, in sound objects or in words. In visions and auditions, writers make sensible the limits of language, the nonlinguistic painting and music that language alone can produce.

Conclusion

Language for Deleuze is a mode of action, and it is within a broad domain of practices and power relations that writers at once follow and generate lines of flight. Linguistic constants and invariants are not primary in a language, but secondary productions of structures of power. Immanent lines of continuous variation pass through the phonemic, syntactic and semantic elements of language, the regularities of correct pronunciation, standard syntax, denotative meaning, and so on, representing a restricted and controlled usage of variables. Minor writers activate those lines of continuous variation, pursue their trajectories and instigate their further variation. The words writers manipulate form part of a regime of signs, a configuration of assemblages that interrelate heterogeneous entities in complex patterns of action and movement. A regime of signs brings into relation a discursive, collective assemblage of enunciation and a nondiscursive assemblage of social technological machines, the discursive assemblage intervening in the nondiscursive, words performing incorporeal transformations of things through speech-actions. Words are thus entwined with things, and both are shaped through interconnected yet separate processes of production.

Literary works do not mean so much as they function. When properly constructed, they are machines that make something happen. The writers Deleuze admires, those who practice a minor usage of language, experiment on the real, thereby at once fashioning a critique of power and opening a passage toward new possibilities for living. Kafka's depiction of the Law operates directly on the representations structuring power relations within the Austro-Hungarian Empire, extracting vectors of the diabolical powers of the future, connecting them in paradoxical networks and dispersing them in unpredictable directions. Kafka's literary machine of *The Trial* functions as a component of larger social and material machines, collective assemblages of enunciation and assemblages of social technological machines operating both within and without the novel. No firm distinction exists between work and world, for which reason Kafka's experimentation on language is immediately political and social. There is likewise no meaningful division between art and life, Kafka's diaries and letters functioning together with the short stories and novels as parts of the same writing machine.

Kafka's writing machine is constructed like a burrow, an open network of tunnels and topological passages between heterogeneous spaces that spreads indefinitely in all directions. In this sense, the literary machine is always unfinished. It is a process in perpetual motion, less a completed burrow than a ceaseless burrowing. Yet Deleuze also allows for the possibility of a certain wholeness of the literary machine. Proust's *Recherche* is a massive sign machine, and it has a kind of unity. Although its components are conjoined through "transversals," which, like the topological nodes and intersections of Kafka's burrow, interconnect incommensurable and noncommunicating parts and intensify their differences rather than suppressing them, it also has the added component of a whole that induces a unity-effect. The "whole" is an extra part, like a seed crystal which, once introduced into a metastable solution, instigates a cascade of crystallizations within the solution. The whole as added part produces a "chaosmos," a chaos-become-cosmos that issues from a dynamic self-differentiating difference.

The chaosmos of the *Recherche* is a chaosmos of signs, and in Marcel's apprenticeship in signs Deleuze finds indications of the relation between interpretation and artistic creation. The sign as dynamic self-differentiating difference is in one regard like a fertilized ovum, which splits and divides into more and more cells as it grows to become a fully formed organism. The process of division and multiplication is an unfolding, or explication, of the dynamic difference initially present in the single-celled ovum, but that difference is also enfolded, or implicated, in each of the cells of the fully formed organism. In this sense, the whole of the organism is enfolded in each of its cells. Each cell then is a sign, an enfolded, implicated difference that is unfolded, explicated when interpreted. But the cosmos of signs has no privileged points of origin, and any sign may function as a fertilized ovum from which an organism may grow. The cosmos of signs in this regard is like a city, which may be viewed from many perspectives. Each point within the city is a possible vantage for a vision of the whole. If the figures of ovum and city are combined, we may say that each vantage point is a potential ovum that may differentiate itself at any moment into a fully formed organism-city.

The interpretation of signs begins with an unsettling disequilibrium, a jolt produced by the hieroglyph of a sign that enfolds a hidden difference and hints at a world beyond itself. Marcel's madeleine impinges on him and compels him to unfold the world of Combray enfolded in its taste and smell. But the essence of Combray is neither the madeleine itself nor the past moments of the real Combray. It is an essence, a self-differentiating difference that unfolds itself in the signs of the madeleine and the real Combray. When Marcel grasps that essence, it is as if he had leaped from his room and risen to a lookout tower from which he could view the cosmos-city below. That cosmos in one sense is already created, and Marcel is simply reconstituting the past world enfolded in the madeleine, but in another sense the leap to the lookout tower initiates a process of creation, as if the vantage point from which he views the city *itself produced* the city, as if the lookout tower were an ovum at that moment unfolding itself into an organism-city. In this regard, the interpretation of signs is one with the production of signs. To explicate or unfold the differences hidden in signs is to attain to a vantage from which a cosmos is forever in the process of beginning to unfold. Marcel learns that the essence of signs is in art, but the only genuine means of grasping essences is in producing them, that is, in creating works of art. And Marcel's apprenticeship in signs is at the same time the writing of the *Recherche*. But in no way is the interpretation or production of signs a mere subjective expression of the self or a simple objective recording of reality. The leap to the lookout tower discloses an apersonal view of a cosmos-city in which the viewer, as it were, is one of the objects seen in the city. And though the cosmos-city is a real, constituted entity that in one sense has already produced the sign that initiated the leap to the lookout tower, in another sense the leap itself brings the cosmos-city into existence.

For Deleuze, writers are always engaging the actual world in its becoming, but at the same time they are creating a world within the world, or rather they are cocreating with the world. Interpretation is not a matter of the reception of signs, finally, but of the production of signs. Nietzsche's interpretation and evaluation of the signs of culture is a diagnostic reading of civilization's symptoms of disease and health, but that diagnosis itself is an intervention. To interpret is to engage and shape forces, and to evaluate is to produce values. Only in the creative appropriation of forces and donation of values do genuine interpretation and evaluation take place. Writers experiment on the real, their interpretations and evaluations of the world at the same time instigating an alteration in the world. Proust's account of the apprenticeship in signs that eventuates in the *Recherche*, like Kafka's *Trial* or Bene's *Richard III*, is at once a critical reading of the world and a creative unfolding of a world, a chaosmos issuing from a germinative difference.

The writer's interventions in the world, however, cannot be separated from interventions in language. The great works of art are written in a kind of foreign language, according to Proust, and in Deleuze's view that foreign tongue is a stuttering within language, a minor usage of the variables of language that sets them in continuous variation and thereby makes the language itself halt and stammer. Such a minor usage of language involves a formal experimentation with linguistic sounds, syntax and semantics, but it extends as well to elements that are generally considered to be extralinguistic. As a form of action, language is inextricably intertwined with its contexts of performance. Each semantic unit is an actualization of a virtual continuum of speech-acts that execute incorporeal transformations of bodies, and every usage of language takes place within larger structures of actions and forces. For this reason, the theater may be seen as the paradigmatic form of literary creation, and Bene's minor usage of speech, sound, gesture, costume, props, sets and lighting may be regarded as the logical culmination of minor writing, his theater extending minor writing's linguistic experimentation further and further into the supposedly extralinguistic contexts of its performance.

The writers Deleuze admires attempt to push language beyond itself, to induce a becoming within language that presses language to its limits. Carroll explores the surface between words and things through the paradoxes of the incorporeal event, while Artaud makes that surface dissolve, word-shards penetrating the body and lacerating the flesh,

sonic blocks ecstatically melding with a body without organs. Artaud
creates *cris-souffles* that mutate words into corporeal screams and animal
howls, and in a similar fashion Céline, cummings, Luca and Beckett
push language toward the limits of the inarticulate, Céline with his proliferation of exclamatory interjections, cummings with his amalgama-
tions of incompatible syntactic structures, Luca with his stuttered
reiterations of a multiply fragmenting sentence, Beckett with his obsessive repetitions, accretions, deletions and permutations of terms. Even
in writers like Melville and Kafka, whose prose leaves intact the forms of
standard usage, an atmospheric strangeness characterizes the style as
reverberations, buzzings and twitterings pass through and above the
words. Melville and Kafka create "auditions," hallucinatory sonic elements at the edge of language, just as T. E. Lawrence creates "visions" at
the periphery of the seeable and the sayable. Visions and auditions form
the outside of language, the membrane between sight, sound and
speech, and in producing visions and auditions within language, writers
fashion a painting and a music proper to language. Beckett attempts to
bore holes in language, to efface words and reveal the "nothing or something" below, and Deleuze insists that below is definitely a "something"—the something of visions and auditions, pure visual and sonic
images that haunt and inhabit words. In his television plays, Beckett
exhausts language and voices in an effort to create pure images, in some
cases at the limits of language (. . . *but the clouds . . .*), in others at a point
beyond words altogether (*Quad*). Like Bene's dramas, Beckett's television
plays ultimately move into areas outside language entirely, but what is
staged in these works is the passage of language beyond itself, and this
passage is the becoming-other of language characteristic of all minor
writing, whether it be that of Carroll's nonsense, Artaud's *cris-souffles*, the
linguistic mutations of Céline, cummings, Luca and Beckett or the
visions and auditions of Melville, Kafka and T. E. Lawrence.

From first to last, literature for Deleuze is a matter of health. Writers
are Nietzschean physicians of culture whose critique at once destroys and
creates. Sade and Masoch, Carroll and Artaud, are great diagnosticians of
signs and symptoms, but they also articulate new possibilities for life that
extend beyond the limits of a given perversion, neurosis or psychosis.
Proust is a profound interpreter of signs, but he also produces the signs
of the *Recherche*, a great time machine whose transversals across an open
whole restore to time its regenerative vocation. Kafka, too, builds an elab-

orate writing machine, whose parts include diaries, letters, short stories and novels, and whose connections traverse personal, familial, social and political spheres. He details the pathologies of the diabolical powers to come, the power relations of fascist, communist and capitalist bureaucracies immanent within the Austro-Hungarian Empire, but he also invents lines of flight, perverse uses of the law that make its cogs slide and slip. He develops a minor usage of a major language, thereby engaging a deterritorialized collective enunciation that prepares the way for the creation of a people to come. Bene in his minor theater likewise critiques power, stripping Shakespeare of the accoutrements of the State and its official History, but in the becoming-woman of Richard he stages the utopian, "impossible" possibility of a transformed island on which Richard/Caliban and Lady Jane/Miranda may invent new modes of living. Lawrence diagnoses the multiple ways in which the British betray the Arabs, the Arabs the British, and he both British and Arabs, but in his visions he discloses the opening of space, the movement of forces and the fabulative image of a future people as vast as the landscapes they inhabit. And Beckett critiques through subtraction, eliminating narratives, conventions and significations, but only in order that, for a brief instant, a pure image may explode and dissipate into an indefinite space.

"Literature is a health" (CC 9; lv). When it falls into the clinical state, "words no longer open out on anything, one neither hears nor sees anything through them, except a night that has lost its history, its colors and its songs" (CC 9; lv). When it is healthy, words are carried "from one end of the universe to the other" (CC 9; lv). Paths are opened, the zigzag lines of an anorganic life are invented. "Every work is a voyage, a journey [*trajet*], but one which only traverses this or that external path by virtue of the internal paths and trajectories [*trajectoires*] that compose it, that constitute its landscape or its concert" (CC 10; lvi). Writing is a becoming-other, an opening of language to forces of variation within and to lines of flight without. The trajectories of anorganic life are passages-between—between words, between states, between things and between words, states and things. To write is to flee, to make flee, to be delirious, to leave the track, to betray, to become, to conjoin flows, to form assemblages, to deterritorialize. But more than anything, to write is to trace a line of flight and thereby engage the line of an anorganic life, a line-between toward health and new possibilities for living.

Notes

CHAPTER ONE

1. Both *critique* and *clinique* pose problems for the translator. *La critique* may mean "criticism" (as in "literary criticism" "to engage in criticism of a work of art, a policy, an action") and "critique" (as in "to conduct a critique," or Kant's *Critique of Pure Reason*). *Le critique* designates "the critic, " and as an adjective *critique* may be rendered as "critical," "crucial," "decisive." *La clinique* may refer to a medical clinic, but it is also the name for the medical practice of making a diagnosis by direct observation, as well as the teaching method in which physicians instruct students while making their hospital rounds. *Clinique* may also function as an adjective, as in *médecine clinique*, "clinical medicine."

2. See my *Deleuze and Guattari* for general introductions to *Nietzsche and Philosophy* (15–34), *Presentation of Sacher-Masoch* (45–54), and *The Logic of Sense* (67–80).

3. Throughout *Nietzsche and Philosophy* Deleuze tends to distinguish between *puissance*, "power" in the sense of ability, capability, potency, strength, and *pouvoir*, "power" in the sense of political power, authority, domination, generally treating *puissance* as positive and *pouvoir* as negative (though this differentiation is not maintained at all times). The standard French translation of Nietzsche's *Wille zur Macht*, it should be noted, is "volonté de puissance."

4. In *The Gay Science*, Nietzsche writes, "I am still waiting for a philosophical *physician* in the exceptional sense of that word—one who has to pursue the problem of the total health of a people, time, race or of humanity—to muster the courage to push my suspicion to its limits and to risk the proposition: what was at stake in all philosophizing hitherto was not at all 'truth' but something else—let us say, health, future, growth, power, life" (p. 35).

5. See *Thus Spoke Zarathustra*, Fourth Part, "The Awakening" : "He carries our burden, he took upon himself the form of a servant, he is patient of heart and never says No; and whoever loves his God, chastises him./ But the ass brayed: Yea-Yuh" (*Portable Nietzsche*, p. 424).

6. In *Nietzsche* (N), Deleuze's brief study guide that appeared in the series "Philosophes," he says of the aphorism and poem that "the aphorism is at once the art of interpreting and the thing to interpret; the poem, at once the art of evaluating and the thing to evaluate. The interpreter is the physiologist or physician, the one who considers phenomena as symptoms and speaks through aphorisms. The evaluator is the artist, who considers and creates 'per-

spectives,' which speaks through the poem. The philosopher of the future is artist and physician—in a word, legislator" (N 17).

7. Deleuze and Guattari briefly address this question in QP 63–65; 65–67 when they differentiate conceptual personae (*personnages conceptuels*) and aesthetic figures. I am not convinced that the distinction is as clear-cut as they claim. I discuss this issue in the closing chapter of *Deleuze on Music, Painting, and the Arts*.

8. Deleuze, like many commentators before him, gives Sacher-Masoch's year of birth as 1835, although others provide dates as early as 1830. Bernard Michel, in his 1989 biography of Sacher-Masoch, addresses this and a number of other questions in the life of Masoch, establishing conclusively that Masoch was born in 1836. Michel praises Deleuze for separating Masoch from Sade and for drawing attention to Masoch's achievements as a novelist. However, he does challenge Deleuze's reading of Masoch's *Venus in Furs*, arguing that Deleuze's incomplete knowledge of the considerable corpus of Masoch's writings (much of which is available only in German) prevents him from understanding the role of *Venus in Furs* in the sequence of novels Masoch planned under the title *The Legacy of Cain*. He also questions Deleuze's tripartite categorization of Masochian women, as well as the existence of any influence of Bachofen on Masoch. See especially Michel, pp. 164–73.

9. In his 1988 discussion of plans for a literary study titled *Critique et clinique*, Deleuze says that "this does not mean that great authors, great artists are sick—not even sublimely so—nor that one finds in them the mark of a neurosis or a psychosis as a secret in their work, as the key to their work. They are not patients; on the contrary, they are physicians of a rather special sort. . . . As Nietzsche said, the artist and the philosopher are physicians of civilization" (PP 195; 142–43). Although Nietzsche called for a "philosophical *physician*" who addresses "the problem of the total health of a people, time, race or of humanity" in *The Gay Science* (p. 35), the term "physician of civilization" does not occur in the works Nietzsche published under his own supervision. In a letter to Rohde, March 22, 1873, Nietzsche referred to a projected book on Greek philosophy as *Der Philosoph als Artzt der Kultur* (*The Philosopher as Cultural Physician*), and under this title the editors of the 1901–1913 *Nietzsches Werke* published a brief selection from Nietzsche's 1873 notebooks. Nietzsche's most complete discussion of the notion of "cultural physician" may be found in paragraphs 77 and 78 of the 1873 notebook entries published in *Nietzsches Werke* under the title *Gedanken zu der Betrachtung: Die Philosophie in Bedrängniss* (*Thoughts on the Meditation: Philosophy in Hard Times*). See *Philosophy and Truth: Selections from Nietzsche's Notebooks of the early 1870's*, translated and edited by Daniel Breazeale, "The Philosopher as Cultural Physician" (pp. 69–76), "Philosophy in Hard Times" (pp. 119–21), and Breazeale's "Note on the Texts, Translation, and Annotation" (pp. lv–lxv).

10. In *Dialogues* (D 143; 152), Deleuze cites René Cruchet`s *De la méthode en médecine* as the source for his discussion of symptomatology. Cruchet identifies four aspects of medicine: symptomatology, the study of signs; etiology, the study of causes; prognostics, the study of probable outcomes; and therapeutics, the study of treatments and cures. *La clinique*, the direct observation of signs, he insists, is the foundation upon which all other aspects of medicine are built. The characteristic of an illness he describes as the "*grouping of a certain number of signs, which, always appearing the same in a given order, permit the determination of that illness*" (Cruchet p. 61).

11. Freud's *Phantasie* has caused major problems for translators in French and English. As Laplanche and Pontalis observe in *The Language of Psycho-Analysis*, the French "fantaisie" carries "connotations of whimsy, eccentricity, triviality, etc." (p. 314) that are inimical to Freud's conception of *Phantasie*. As a result, many French psychoanalysts have resorted to the word *fantasme* (or *phantasme*) to render *Phantasie*. A similar problem exists in English, and most English psychoanalysts have proposed to distinguish between "fantasy" in the ordinary sense of the word and "phantasy" in its technical, psychoanalytic meaning. I have chosen to render Deleuze's *le phantasme* as "phantasy." For an enlightening discussion of the complexities of

this term, see Laplanche and Pontalis, "Phantasy (or Fantasy)," in *Language*, pp. 314–19.

12. "Creative Writers and Daydreaming" (1908), *Standard Edition*, IX, pp. 141–53. "The creative writer does the same as the child at play. He creates a world of fantasy which he takes very seriously—that is, which he invests with large amounts of emotion—while separating it sharply from reality" (p. 144).

13. Deleuze states that "medicine distinguishes syndromes and symptoms: symptoms are specific signs of an illness, but syndromes are meeting-places or crossing-points which bring together very different causal lines and variable contexts" (SM 11). Cruchet, we should note, simply characterizes a syndrome as a "concurrence of signs" (Cruchet, p. 99). In Cruchet's terminology, all diseases are syndromes, and hence in symptomatology, the primary distinction is between true syndromes and false syndromes.

14. Lacan and other French psychoanalysts have discussed at length the distinction between Freudian *Verleugnung* (translated both as disavowal and denial in English, and as *déni* and *dénégation* in French), *Verneinung* (negation, denial, *négation*, *dénégation* in various translations), and *Verwerfung* (foreclosure, repudiation, *foreclusion*). See Lacan, *Ecrits*, "Introduction au commentaire de Jean Hippolyte sur la 'Verneinung' de Freud," "Réponse au commentaire de Jean Hyppolite sur la 'Verneinung' de Freud" (pp. 369–99), and "Appendice I: Commentaire parlé sur la *Verneinung* de Freud, par Jean Hyppolite" (pp. 879–87).

15. For a succinct introduction to the concept of the phantasy, see Laplanche and Pontalis, *The Language of Psycho-Analysis*, pp. 314–19. Central to Deleuze's treatment of the phantasy is Susan Isaacs's classic study, "The Nature and Function of Phantasy" (1948) and Laplanche and Pontalis's influential "Fantasme originaire, fantasmes des origines, origine du fantasme" (1964). In his work after *Anti-Oedipus*, we should note, Deleuze explicitly rejects the psychoanalytic concept of the phantasy. In *Dialogues*, for example, he remarks that "one cannot emphasize enough the damage the phantasy has done to writing (it has even invaded the cinema), in nourishing the signifier and the interpretation of one by the other, the one with the other" (D 59; 47).

16. Deleuze says at another point, "it seems that, for Masoch as for Sade, language assumes its full value in acting directly on the senses [*sur la sensualité*]" (SM 17; 17). How language acts directly on the senses Deleuze does not explain. The direct effect of paint on the senses is one of Deleuze's central concerns in his study of Francis Bacon. I discuss this question in chapter 5 of *Deleuze on Music, Painting, and the Arts*.

17. For a particularly lucid reading of *The Logic of Sense*, see Lecercle, *Philosophy through the Looking-Glass*, pp. 86–117.

18. Deleuze's primary source for his remarks on incorporeals is Bréhier's *La théorie des incorporels dans l'ancien stoïcisme*. Due to the fragmentary nature of the evidence from antiquity, much of Stoic thought on this topic remains controversial.

19. Deleuze's schematic opposition of Chronos and Aion somewhat simplifies the thorny issues inherent in this area of Stoic thought. For his remarks on the Stoic theory of time, Deleuze relies principally on Bréhier, *La théorie des incorporels dans l'ancien stoïcisme* (pp. 54–59) and Goldschmidt, *Le système stoïcien et l'idée de temps*. Sextus Empiricus (Adv. Math. X, 218; Arnim II, 331) says that the Stoics recognized four incorporeals, the *lekton*, the void (*kesos*), place (*topos*) and time (*chronos*), although he does seem to differentiate between time as that which passes and the present (which would have actual being, if one could ever seize hold of it). Only in the late phases of Stoicism with Marcus Aurelias is the concept of *aion* employed in a systematic fashion in discussions of time. For a succinct treatment of the complexities of this question, see Rist, "Three Stoic Views of Time," *Stoic Philosophy* (pp. 273–88).

20. "Three things, according to the Stoics, are connected with one another: (1) the significans, or sign; (2) the significate; and (3) that which exists. The significans is the sound, for example, the sound 'Dion.' That which exists is the externally existing object, which in the

same example would be Dion himself. These two—the sound and that which exists—are described as 'the actual entity indicated or revealed by the sound and which we apprehend as subsisting together with [i.e., in] our thought" [Sextus Empiricus, *Adv. Math.* VIII, 12]. It is what the Barbarians do not understand when they hear Greek words spoken. The Stoic technical name for it is *lekton*, which may be translated literally as 'that which is meant'" (Mates, *Stoic Logic*, p. 11). Deleuze sees a parallel to the Stoic *lekton* in the Scholastic concept of the *complexe significabile*, which Hubert Elie traces in detail in the works of Gregory of Rimini and André de Neufchâteau. Elie also relates the Scholastic *complexe significabile* to the theory of *objectives* put forward by Meinong in the late-nineteenth and early-twentieth centuries. Elie's primary source for his remarks on Meinong is Findlay's *Meinong's Theory of Objects and Values*. Deleuze relies mainly on Elie for his comments on the Scholastics and Meinong in *The Logic of Sense*.

21. This is what I take to be the basic point of Deleuze's extended footnote on novelists and neurotics (LS 278; 359): "What then is the difference between such a lived novel [*roman vécu*], neurotic and 'familial,' and the novel as work of art? The symptom is always taken up in a novel, but the novel sometimes determines the *realization* [*effectuation*] of the symptom, yet sometimes on the contrary it disengages from the symptom *the event* which it counter-realizes [*contre-effectue*] in the fictional characters (what is important is not the fictive nature of the characters, but that which the fiction explicates, that is, the nature of the pure event and the mechanism of counter-realization [*contre-effectuation*]). For example, Sade and Masoch make a novel-work of art out of that which sadists or masochists merely turn into a neurotic and 'familial' novel, even if they write it." The notion of *contre-effectuation* Deleuze develops in the Twenty-First Series of *The Logic of Sense* (LS 174–79; 148–53), contrasting the apersonal unfolding of the event (*contre-effectuation*) and the concrete actualizations of bodies as they assume individuated forms (*effectuation*). The concept of an "explication" or "unfolding" of differences in a work of literature will be one of the central concerns of the next chapter on Proust.

22. In his preface to Louis Wolfson's 1970 book, *Le schizo et les langues* (reprinted in revised form as "Louis Wolfson, ou le procédé" [Louis Wolfson, or the Procedure] in *Critique et clinique*), Deleuze compares Wolfson's linguistic experiments to those of the novelist Raymond Roussel. Deleuze remarks, however, that "Wolfson's book is not a literary work, and it does not claim to be a poem. What makes the procedure of Roussel a work of art is that the gap between the original phrase and its conversion is filled by proliferating, marvelous stories, which always push the point of departure further and further away and ultimately end up hiding it entirely" (CC 21; 10). Wolfson's procedure, by contrast, lacks autonomy; it generates a single story with an always evident, obsessive point of departure.

23. In "Lewis Carroll," a brief reprise of the arguments of *The Logic of Sense* first published in *Critique et clinique* (1993), Deleuze indicates that even in Carroll's work the opposition of surfaces and depths tends to disappear: "Carroll's third great novel, *Sylvie and Bruno*, brings still further progress. One could say that the former depths are themselves flattened out and made into a surface alongside the other surface. Thus two surfaces coexist, on which two contiguous stories are written, one major and the other minor; the one in a major key, the other in a minor key" (CC 35; 22). In *The Logic of Sense*, however, Deleuze makes no such claim for *Sylvie and Bruno*, maintaining throughout that Carroll's entire *oeuvre* is structured by the opposition of surfaces and depths.

CHAPTER TWO

1. Of Swann's first reaction to the Vinteuil sonata, Proust writes: "An impression of this order, vanishing in an instant is, so to speak, *sine materia*. Doubtless the notes which we hear at such moments tend, according to their pitch and volume, to spread out before our eyes over surfaces of varying dimensions, to trace arabesques, to give us the sensation of breadth or tenuity, stability or caprice. But the notes themselves have vanished before these sensations

have developed sufficiently to escape submersion under those which the succeeding or even simultaneous notes have already begun to awaken in us" (Proust I 228).

2. Deleuze discusses Bergson's virtual past at some length in chapter 3 of *Bergsonism* (see especially B 45–57; 51–61).

3. *Republic*, VII, 523a–524b. On contradictory sensations, see also *Philebus* 24d and *Parmenides* 154–55. Deleuze discusses these passages in "Plato and the Simulacrum" (appendix to *The Logic of Sense*, LS 292–307; 253–66), and in *Difference and Repetition*, DR 180–86; 138–43.

4. Gilbert Simondon uses the crystal as a paradigm for the process of individuation in his *L'individu et sa genèse physico-biologique*. Simondon stresses that individuation precedes the existence of the individual, the process of the formation of the crystal proceeding always along the surface of the entity in formation, the formed entity coming into existence only after the process of individuation has ended. Deleuze makes frequent reference to Simondon; see especially LS 125–26; 103–4, DR 316–17; 246–47, MP 508–10; 408–10, and FB 86.

5. "... but as for Balbec, no sooner had I set foot in it than it was as though I had broken open a name which ought to have been kept hermetically closed, and into which, seizing at once the opportunity that I had imprudently given them, expelling all the images that had lived in it until then, a tramway, a café, people crossing the square, the branch of the savings bank, irresistibly propelled by some external pressure, by a pneumatic force, had come surging into the interior of those two syllables which, closing over them, now let them frame the porch of the Persian church and would henceforth never cease to contain them" (Proust I 710).

6. Marcel recalls at one point a journey by train, during which he saw a beautiful pink sky framed in the window. As the train turned, the sky disappeared, but he found it again framed in a window on the opposite side, this time red, "so that I spent my time running from one window to the other to reassemble, to collect on a single canvas the intermittent, antipodean fragments of my fine, scarlet, ever-changing morning, and to obtain a comprehensive view and a continuous picture of it" (Proust I 704–5). Deleuze comments that "this text indeed invokes a continuity and a totality; but the essential point is to know where these are elaborated—neither in the point of view nor in the thing seen, but in the transversal, from one window to the other" (PS 153; 153).

CHAPTER THREE

1. With the concept of "desiring production," Deleuze and Guattari combine the Freudian and Marxian motifs of desire and production, but in such a way as to alter both. Their stress on production subsumes the traditional notions of the production, exchange, distribution and consumption of goods within a universal process of activity and energy circulation. Their insistence on the ubiquity of desire depends on a characterization of desire not as lack but as affect or intensity, a mutual affecting of elements whereby flows of libidinized matter, energy and information pass among, through and between one another. For helpful discussions of desiring production, see especially Massumi, Goodchild, *Deleuze and Guattari: An Introduction to the Politics of Desire*, and Holland, *Deleuze and Guattari's Anti-Oedipus: Introduction to Schizoanalysis*.

2. The connection between the unity of the body without organs and the unity of Proust's *Recherche* is explicitly drawn in *Anti-Oedipus*: "Thus Proust said that the whole is produced, that it is itself produced as a part alongside the parts, that it neither unifies nor totalizes, but that it applies itself to them only in establishing aberrant communications between non-communicating vessels, transverse unities between elements that preserve their entire difference in their proper dimensions" (AO 51; 43).

3. The term "miraculating" Deleuze and Guattari take from Daniel Paul Schreber, who in

his *Memoirs of My Nervous Illness* describes various ways in which his body was "miraculated" by the rays of God, such that, for example, he "lived for a long time without a stomach, without intestines, almost without lungs, with a torn oesophagus, without a bladder, and with shattered ribs" (cited in AO 14; 8).

4. "The body without organs is an egg: it is traversed by axes and thresholds, by latitudes, longitudes, geodesic lines, it is traversed by *gradients* that mark the becomings and passages, the destinations of that which develops there. . . . Nothing but bands of intensity, of potentials, of thresholds and of gradients" (AO 26; 19). The language of this passage is taken from embryological descriptions of the splitting of an embryo along geodesic lines determined by energy differentials on its surface. Deleuze frequently cites Dalcq's *L'oeuf et son dynamisme organisateur* as a source for these concepts.

5. In *Francis Bacon* Deleuze likewise defines a "provisional organ" as a passage from one level of intensity to another (FB 35). The equivalence of nomadic subjects and provisional organs should caution against any identification of the nomadic subject with a traditional psyche or consciousness.

6. As the translators of *Anti-Oedipus* note, *prélèvement* has no real equivalent in English: "The French word has a number of meanings, including: a skimming or a draining off; a removal of a certain quantity as a sample or for purposes of testing; a setting apart of a portion or share of the whole; a deduction from a sum of money on deposit" (*Anti-Oedipus*, p. 36). They translate *coupures-prélèvements* at one point as "breaks that are a slicing off" (p. 39), thereby recalling Deleuze and Guattari's initial characterization of the cut of desiring machines as functioning "like a ham-slicing machine [*comme machine à couper le jambon*]" (AO 43–44; 36).

7. The psychoanalytic term "partial object," or "part-object," (German: *Partialobjekt*; French: *objet partiel*) was first introduced by Melanie Klein. In *The Language of Psycho-Analysis*, Laplanche and Pontalis define the partial object as a "type of object towards which the component instincts are directed without this implying that a person as a whole is taken as love-object. In the main part-objects are parts of the body, real or phantasied (breast, faeces, penis), and their symbolic equivalents. Even a person can identify himself or be identified with a part-object" (p. 301). Deleuze and Guattari insist that partial objects "in no way refer to an organism that would function phantasmatically as a lost unity or totality to come." If partial objects pertain to an "erogenous body," such a body is "not a shattered organism, but an emission of pre-individual and pre-personal singularities, a pure dispersed and anarchic multiplicity, without unity or totality, and whose elements are welded, glued together by the real distinction or the very absence of a link" (AO 387; 324).

8. "Partial objects and the body without organs are the two material elements of schizophrenic desiring machines" (AO 390; 327). "Here, then, are the desiring machines—with their three pieces: working pieces, the immobile motor, the adjacent piece—their three energies: Libido, Numen and Voluptas—their three syntheses: the connective syntheses of partial objects and flows, the disjunctive syntheses of singularities and chains, the conjunctive syntheses of intensities and becomings" (AO 404; 338).

9. Deleuze and Guattari state further that "the body without organs is immanent substance, in the Spinozist sense of the word; and the partial-objects are like its ultimate attributes, which belong to it precisely insofar as they are really distinct and cannot on this account exclude or oppose one another" (AO 390; 327). In *Spinoza: Practical Philosophy*, Deleuze states, "Really (formally) distinct attributes thus are affirmed [*se disent*] of an absolutely single substance, which possesses them all and enjoys *a fortiori* the properties of causality by itself, of infinity and of necessary existence. Infinite essences, which are distinguished formally in the attributes which they express, are merged ontologically in the substance to which the attributes refer them (I, 10, sc. 1). The real-formal distinction of attributes is not opposed to the

absolute ontological unity of substance; on the contrary, the distinction constitutes that unity" (S 148; 109). See Hardt, pp. 56–85, for a detailed discussion of Deleuze's treatment of substance, attributes and the real distinction in Spinoza.

10. In *Difference and Repetition*, Deleuze presents three "passive syntheses" of time. Some sense of what Deleuze means by "passive synthesis" can be gained from this passage concerning the first temporal synthesis: "This synthesis must, at any rate, be named: passive synthesis. Although it is constitutive, it is in no way active. It is not performed by the mind, but it takes place *in* the mind that contemplates it, preceding all memory and all reflection. Time is subjective, but it is the subjectivity of a passive subject" (DR 97; 71).

11. For a general introduction to *The Large Glass*, see Golding. For an exhaustive study of the technological and scientific allusions in *The Large Glass*, see Henderson. Duchamp's notes to *The Large Glass* are available in *Salt Seller: The Writings of Marcel Duchamp*, as well as Arturo Schwarz's edited and translated edition of *Notes and Projects for The Large Glass*. Duchamp's first commentary on *The Bride*, a box containing fifteen documents, is commonly referred to as *The Box of 1915*. The ninety-four documents Duchamp assembled in *The Green Box* in 1934 provide the most substantive comments on *The Bride*. In 1967 Duchamp published a third collection of documents, entitled *À l'Infinitif* (also known as *The White Box*), containing notes originally excluded from *The Green Box*, forty-one of which were gathered in a blue folder entitled *Couleur*, and thirty-eight in a green folder entitled *Perspective*.

12. The operation of Duchamp's machine is much more complicated than can be detailed here. See Schwarz's "The Mechanics of the Large Glass," pp. 11–13, in *Notes and Projects for The Large Glass*, for a succinct description of the work's functioning. For additional details, see the diagram of *The Large Glass* on pp. 20–21 of *Salt Seller* and Henderson's schematic of the Bride on Plate 82 of *Duchamp in Context*.

13. In Chapter Three of *Deleuze on Music, Painting, and the Arts*, I discuss Deleuze's treatment of the extremes of purposive inefficiency and purposeless efficiency in natural systems. In the Appendix to the expanded edition of *Anti-Oedipus*, Deleuxe and Guattari offer reproductions of two Rube Goldberg cartoons as illustrations of desiring-production, each showing a machine with a clear purpose (reminding a man to mail a letter in the case of "You Sap, Mail That Letter," and helping a man lose weight in the case of "Simple Reducing Machine"), but each ludicrously complicated and improbable in its componenets and its functioning. Early in *Anti-Oedipus* (AO 8–9; 3) Deleuse and Guattari characterize the interconnection of desiring-machines by referring to a section from Beckett's *Molloy* (*Three Novels* 69–74), in which the narrator exhaustively describes the movement of sixteen "sucking stones" distributed in two greatcoat pockets and two trouser pockets, the stones passing from one pocket to another via the mouth that sucks the stones. The stones, pockets, transferring hands and sucking mouth form a circuit of clearly delineated components whose interrelations are demarcated by a discrete and regular series of operations, yet thay comprise a machine that seems devoid of any purpose other than its own functioning.

14. Speaking in general of Carrouges's celibate machines, Deleuze and Guattari say, "first the celibate machine testifies to an older paranoiac machine, with its tortures, its shadows, its old Law [of all the machines Carrouges treats, this description only suits Kafka's machine well]. However, it is not itself a paranoiac machine. Everything in it is different, its gears [*rouages*, Kafka], carriage [*chariot*, Duchamp], scissors [Duchamp], needles [Kafka and Duchamp], magnets [Duchamp], rays [Kafka: as Carrouges emphasizes, the four brass rods supporting the Designer "almost flashed out rays in the sunlight" (Complete Stories 143); also an allusion to Schreber's obsession with the miraculating rays of God]. Even in its torturing or in the death it delivers, it manifest something new, a solar power [again, descriptive primarily of Kafka's machine]" (AO 24–25; 18).

15. Gregor's sister "accepted Gregor; she, like him, wanted schizo incest, incest with strong

connections, incest with the sister that opposes Oedipal incest, incest that witnesses to a non-human sexuality like that of becoming-animal" (K 27; 15).

16. Elizabeth Boa asserts that Deleuze and Guattari "excise many of the conflictual features of Kafka's work, and, a brief discussion of Austro-Hungarian masochism apart, leave desire as an ahistorical force impacting on the historical field of capitalist society in a complacently sexist celebration of the bachelor-hero" (28). In their remarks on the *célibataire* as exemplary practitioner of desire (K 128–30; 70–71), Deleuze and Guattari make use of an early draft of a story about a *Junggeselle* in Kafka's *Diaries* (1910, pp. 22–29), but Kafka's *Junggeselle* hardly seems heroic, and Deleuze and Guattari's *célibataire* is no conventional bachelor-hero. In fact, Boa's detailed readings of the gender, class and ethnic conflicts in Kafka accord well with Deleuze and Guattari's sense of the historical actualizations of desire in Kafka. Deleuze and Guattari would simply claim that a virtual dimension of deterritorialized desire is also immanent within the real, and that such desire is *célibataire* in the specialized sense they give the term (and which is perhaps less evident in its English translation).

17. Carrouges states that "the essential definition of a machine" is "to produce or transmit movement" (Carrouges, p. 152).

18. They exclude the Diaries from their enumeration because "the Diaries traverse everything: the Diaries are the rhizome itself. They are not an element in the sense of an aspect of his works, but the element (in the sense of milieu) that Kafka declares he does not want to leave, like a fish. It's because this element communicates with the entire outside, and distributes the desire of the letters, the desire of the short stories, the desire of the novels" (K 76; 96).

19. Much of Deleuze and Guattari's analysis is based on Elias Canetti's *Kafka's Other Trial: The Letters to Felice*, though they distance themselves from Canetti's emphasis on "Kafka's shame for his body, his humiliation, his distress, and his need for protection" (K 55; 94).

20. Deleuze and Guattari cite as a source an unpublished study of vampires and Kafka by Claire Parnet. Boa examines vampire imagery in "A Country Doctor" and *The Trial* (pp. 153–54, 198–200) and notes that Walter Sokel, Ritchie Robertson and Detlev Kremer have also discussed the vampire motif in Kafka.

21. The motifs of letters and "devilish innocence," as Deleuze and Guattari point out, appear in an interesting configuration in "The Judgment." The father initially doubts the existence of Georg's Russian friend, with whom Georg has been in correspondence. Later, however, the father reveals that he himself has been exchanging letters with the Russian friend—"the flow of letters has changed direction, has turned against . . . ." (K 60; 33). At the story's climax the father says "in a louder voice: 'So now you know what else there was in the world besides yourself, till now you've known only about yourself! An innocent child [*Ein unschuldiges Kind*], yes, that you were, truly, but still more truly have you been a devilish human being! [*aber noch eigentlicher warst du ein teuflischer Mensch!*]—And therefore take note: I sentence you [*Ich verurteile dich*] now to death by drowning!'" (Complete Stories 87).

22. Deleuze and Guattari argue against Max Brod's placement of the chapter "The End" at the conclusion of *The Trial*. They argue that this chapter, which recounts the death of Joseph K., is a dream sequence, and that the novel has no genuine conclusion. See K 80–81; 44.

23. Reuleaux's classic definition appears in his *Theoretische Kinematik: Grundzüge einer Theorie des Maschinenwesens* [*The Kinematics of Machinery: Outlines of a Theory of Machines*, 1876] : "A machine is a combination of resistant bodies so arranged that by their means the mechanical forces of nature can be compelled to do work accompanied by certain determinate motions" (p. 35). In a footnote to this definition, Reuleaux provides a fascinating extended summary and critique of efforts by his predecessors to define the machine (pp. 583–89).

24. In "On Four Poetic Formulas That Might Summarize the Kantian Philosophy" (CC 40–49; 27–35), Deleuze draws parallels between the Law in Kafka and Kant's pure and empty form of the law in the *Critique of Practical Reason*. He also ties the law in Kafka and Kant to the

masochistic contract in chapter 7 of *Masochism*, especially SM 72–73; 72–73.

25. In *Anti-Oedipus*, Deleuze and Guattari comment: "As Reich says, the astonishing thing is not that people steal, that others go on strike, but rather that starving people don't steal all the time and that the exploited aren't always out on strike: why have people for centuries put up with exploitation, humiliation, enslavement, to the point of *wanting* it not only for others, but for themselves?" (AO 37; 29). In *Kafka*, Deleuze and Guattari observe that Kafka makes a similar remark to Brod: "Kafka will himself say that he is astonished at the docility of injured workers: 'Instead of storming the institute and smashing it to little pieces, they come and beg' [Brod p. 82]" (K 147; 82).

26. Deleuze and Guattari take this phrase from an oblique parenthetical remark of Kafka's in a postcard to Max Brod, October 25, 1923: "(There is a certain point in my saying this, because at the time we had truly innocent innocence—perhaps that's not worth regretting—and the evil powers, whether on good or bad assignments, were only lightly fingering the entrances through which they were going to penetrate someday, an event to which they were already looking forward with unbearable rejoicing.)" (*Letters to Friends*, p. 387). The original text reads as follows: "(Es hat einen gewissen Sinn, das zu sagen, weil wir damals jene, der Sehnsucht vielleicht gar nicht werte, aber wirklich unschuldige Unschuld hatten und die bösen Mächte, in gutem oder schlimmem Auftrag, erst die Eingänge leicht betasteten, durch die sie einmal einzubrechen sich schon unerträglich freuten.)" (Briefe, p. 452). Deleuze and Guattari rely on the version of the passage included in the French translation of Wagenbach (*Franz Kafka*), which renders the sense of the German in a somewhat different way than does the English version: "(Ce n'est pas sans raison que je le dis puisque, à cette époque, nous avions cette candeur vraiment digne de ce nom, quoique peut-être indigne de cette nostalgie, et les puissances diaboliques, quel que fût leur message, ne faisaient qu'effleurer les portes par où ils se réjouissaient déjà terriblement de s'introduire un jour)." (p. 156).

27. Throughout most of *Kafka*, Deleuze and Guattari use the term "abstract machine" to refer to machines such as the penal colony torture apparatus, "still too transcendent, too isolated and reified, too abstract" (K 72; 39–40). In the final chapter, however, they suggest another way of understanding the term: "In another sense of 'abstract' (nonfigurative, nonsignifying, nonsegmentary), it is the abstract machine that passes from the side of the unlimited field of immanence and mingles now with it in the process or the movement of desire: the concrete assemblages are no longer that which gives a real existence to the abstract machine, in depriving it of its transcendent pretense, it's rather the reverse, it's the abstract machine that measures the mode of existence and reality of the assemblages according to the capacity they demonstrate in undoing their own segments, in pushing their points of deterritorialization, in following the line of flight, in filling up the field of immanence. The abstract machine is the unlimited social field, but it is also the body of desire, and it is also Kafka's continuous oeuvre, on which intensities are produced and where all the connections and polyvocities are inscribed" (K 154–55; 86–87). It is in this second sense that Deleuze and Guattari use the term in *A Thousand Plateaus* (see especially MP 175–84; 140–48).

CHAPTER FOUR

1. Robertson, p. 24. Robertson notes that Deleuze and Guattari are among the few commentators to have stressed the importance of this diary entry, though he differs from them in his interpretation of the passage. Robertson's reading of the entry is quite illuminating, as is his entire discussion of Kafka's encounters with Yiddish literature (see especially pp. 12–28).

2. Wagenbach takes the notion of a "paper German" [*papierenes Deutsch*] from Fritz Mauthner, who in his 1918 recollections of Prague remarks, "The German, in Bohemia, in the midst of a rural Czech population, speaks a paper German . . . he lacks the plenitude of native expression, the richness of dialectical forms. The language is poor. And with the loss of the

plenitude of the dialect, its melody is also lost" (cited in Wagenbach p. 77). Wagenbach also cites Rudolf Vasata, who in 1946 made a similar observation when commenting on Kafka's style: "a dead language like medieval Latin, free from the living terms of language, pure in the sense of sterile . . . it became the vehicle of Kafka; correct and sober but expressive and flexible" (Wagenbach, p. 80).

3. Deleuze and Guattari take the phrase "incorporeal transformation" from the Stoic theory of incorporeals, which Deleuze treats at length in *The Logic of Sense*, especially in the Twenty-Third Series, LS 190–97; 162–68. See also my *Deleuze and Guattari* (67–73) for a discussion of Deleuze and incorporeals in *The Logic of Sense*.

4. The term *agencement*, translated variously as "assemblage," "arrangement," or "organization," can denote both a particular arrangement of entities and the act of assembling or combining elements in a given configuration. Particularly useful are Deleuze's remarks about language and assemblages in *Dialogues*: "The minimal real unit is not the word, the idea, the concept or the signifier, but the *assemblage*. It is always an assemblage that produces statements [*énoncés*]. Statements do not have as their cause a subject that would act as a subject of enunciation [*sujet d'énonciation*], any more than they are related to subjects as subjects of statements [*sujets d'énoncés*]. The statement is the product of an assemblage—always collective—which brings into play within us and outside us populations, multiplicities, territories, becomings, affects, events" (D 65; 51).

5. See, for instance, Robertson: "It is, however, hard to believe that Kafka wanted in any sense to subvert the German language. He was a linguistic purist who, before allowing any of his writings to be published, took pains to adjust their spelling, vocabulary, and punctuation to the High German standard" (Robertson, p. 27). See also Corngold, pp. 89–90.

6. Blaise Cendrars's novel *Moravagine* in fact ends with such a word, the Martian "Ké-ré-keu-ko-kex": "Knowing my curiosity about celestial matters, Moravagine created for my use a dictionary of the two hundred thousand principal meanings of the only word in the Martian language; this word was an onomatopoeia: the crunching of a ground-glass stopper" (Cendrars, p. 417).

7. Deleuze and Guattari do not explicitly limit their remarks on individualism and major literature to the culture of Western capitalism, but their broad historical analyses in *Anti-Oedipus* and *A Thousand Plateaus* make clear that the specific characteristics of a major usage of language could well vary significantly in different contexts, such as that of the Chinese imperial bureaucracy or the Medieval monastic order.

CHAPTER FIVE

1. Deleuze formulates the same distinction in *Dialogues*: "Literature? But now Kafka puts literature in immediate relation with a minority machine, a new collective assemblage of enunciation for German (an assemblage of minorities in the Austrian Empire was already, in another fashion, the idea of Masoch). Now Kleist puts literature in immediate relation with a war machine" (D 146; 123).

2. Actually, in *A Thousand Plateaus* Deleuze and Guattari cite "an unpublished study of Kleist by Mathieu Carrière" (MP 329; 542). Carrière's text was first published in German in 1981 as *Für eine Literatur des Krieges, Kleist*. It appeared in a French translation by Martin Ziegler in 1985 as *Pour une littérature de guerre, Kleist* (note the allusion in Carrière's title to Deleuze and Guattari's *Kafka: Pour une littérature mineure*). Carrière's thorough incorporation of Deleuze and Guattari's terminology within his discourse, and Deleuze and Guattari's frequent allusions to specific arguments in Carrière's text, suggest that the three were in close contact in the mid 1970s. My references throughout are to the French edition.

3. For details about Kleist's life and literary activities, see Maass.

4. Bene refers to his 1994 *Hamlet Suite* as the "fifth edition" of *Hamlet*. However, a review of

Bene's 1988 *Hommelette for Hamlet* (which Bene labels the "fourth edition") refers to this production as "his seventh 'Hamlet'" ("Carmelo Bene: Scenografia 'Hommelette for Hamlet'" 7). This review includes photographs of the stunning sets for the production, designed by the painter Gino Marotta, which consist of famous statues (such as Bernini's St. Teresa) in a funerary sculpture garden. The statue-figures, which appear to be made of stone, prove to be actors in frozen tableaux-vivants that come to life later in the play.

5. Little on Bene has appeared in English, save for a few descriptions of his productions and two perceptive studies of *Superpositions* by Kowsar and Fortier. A "Critical Anthology" of commentaries on Bene in Italian is included in his *Opere*, pp. 1381-1549. For Bene's views on the theater and his own dramas, Deleuze uses as his primary source a dossier of interviews and other materials assembled for the Festival d'automne and later published as "L'énergie sans cesse renouvelée de l'utopie." I rely mainly on the same dossier for my own summaries of Bene's theoretical positions. I am deeply grateful to Florin Berindeanu for his assistance with Bene's Italian texts.

6. Bene, however, also remarks: "And what can assure us in fact that the actor does not know everything? The actor, not Richard, or both of them?" (SP 31).

7. In his stage production of *Our Lady of the Turks*, Bene placed a glass wall with windows between the actors and the audience. As a result, the audience could only hear the actors when they deigned to open the windows. "Because of this aquarium space, there was a total impossibility of communication: it was a fact, and I thus succeeded in realizing the impossible" (L'énergie, p. 70). Bene also remarks, "when I say: the theater *is* non-representable, I say *is*. Thus the theater is. It *is*. But it is *non-representable*. I didn't say that the theater is not representable, which would be something else: the theater *is* non-representable" (L'énergie, p. 77).

8. Bene takes his title from the ironic closing lines of Jules Laforgue's "Hamlet, or the Consequences of Filial Piety." In Laforgue's tale, when Hamlet meets Laertes at Ophelia's grave, Laertes stabs and kills Hamlet. Kate, an actress from the traveling troupe at Elsinore, mourns Hamlet's death and then returns to her lover, Bibi (her nickname for "Billy" Shakespeare). Bibi beats her for having tried to leave him, at which point the narrator concludes the tale: "And everything returns to order. One Hamlet less [*Un Hamlet de moins*]; it's not the end of the human race, as they say" (p. 69).

9. In *Superpositions*, Deleuze cites no source for his discussion of difformity in medieval physics, but in *A Thousand Plateaus* Deleuze and Guattari refer to Pierre Duhem's monumental *Le Système du monde* in their treatment of the related concepts of "latitude" and "longitude." (See especially Duhem v. 7, pp. 462-653.) For Nicolas Oresme's remarks on uniformity and difformity, see *Nicole Oresme and the Medieval Geometry of Qualities and Motions: A Treatise on the Uniformity and Difformity of Intensities Known as Tractatus de configurationibus qualitatum et motuum*, edited, with introduction, translation and commentary by Marshall Clagett.

10. Deleuze implies that the play's primary action is that of the construction of Richard's prosthetic body, and he remarks at one point that in Bene's theater, "the play concludes with the constitution of the character, it has no other object than the process of that constitution, and it does not extend beyond it" (SP 91; 206). Of the second half, Deleuze simply says "it would be necessary to analyze all the rest of the play, and the admirable constitution of the ending: where one sees clearly that it was not a question for Richard of conquering a State apparatus but of constructing a war machine, inseparably political *and* erotic" (SP 119; 217).

CHAPTER SIX

1. For a discussion of the concept of the refrain, see chapters 1 and 3 of my *Deleuze on Music, Painting, and the Arts*.

2. Deleuze often refers to the line of flight as the "abstract line" (e.g., D 89; 74), but all lines are abstract to some extent, as is evident in the vocabulary with which Deleuze and Guattari

describe the processes whereby regimes of signs are generated and transformed (MP 182; 146). *Tracings (calques)* delineate the most regular of assemblages; *maps (cartes)* the transformations of one set of assemblages into another; *diagrams* the vectors of a virtual, deterritorialized non-formed matter and *programs* the processes whereby virtual trajectories become actualized in concrete assemblages. But whether tracings, maps or diagrams, the configurations of lines are not identical with the elements from which they are abstracted (the map is not the territory, as the saying goes), and in a sense they are all "programs," or dynamic processes of action.

3. Deleuze had briefly drawn the same distinction in a slightly different formulation in *The Logic of Sense* (LS 79; 63), the *conte* posing the question, *"qu'est-ce qui va se passer?"*, the *nouvelle*, *"qu'est-ce qui vient de se passer?"*. The term *nouvelle* was first introduced into French to translate the Italian *novela* and used to designate a brief story with few characters. Although a distinction is sometimes made between *contes* as traditional tales and *nouvelles* as newly invented stories, the two terms at present are roughly synonymous, both meaning "stories," "short stories." Since a *nouvelle* is by no means a "novella," or short novel, I have chosen simply to use the French terms *conte* and *nouvelle* rather than English approximations of these categories.

4. As Massumi notes in his translation of *Mille plateaux*, this key sentence from the French version of James's tale reverses the meaning of the original. James's words are "She knew at last so much that she had quite lost her earlier sense of merely guessing. There were no different shades of distinctness—it all bounced out" (p. 472). Far from indicating an inability to interpret any longer, the sentence marks the apex of the heroine's interpretive self-certainty. The French version does, however, reflect the reader's eventual understanding of the heroine's interpretive powers, in that by the end of the story it is evident that the telegraphist has misconstrued virtually every important piece of information concerning Everard and Lady Breeden. On this point, see Norrman, "The Intercepted Telegram Plot in Henry James's 'In the Cage.'"

5. In "Re-presentation of Sacher-Masoch," a brief refashioning of his earlier study of Masoch, Deleuze says that Masoch "makes language [*langue*] stutter, and thus pushes language [*langage*] to its point of suspension, song, cry or silence, song of the woods, cry of the village, silence of the steppe" (CC 74; 55). He cites Pascal Quignard's *L'être du balbutiement, essai sur Sacher-Masoch* as a study in Masoch's stuttering style, but nowhere does Quignard deal directly with Masoch's German text, nor does he discuss specifically linguistic elements of style, noting simply that Masoch's first wife, Wanda, spoke of a certain "trembling" in her husband's writing. As with Deleuze's treatment of Kafka and Kleist, one looks in vain for specific examples of stuttering of a directly linguistic kind.

6. Deleuze makes frequent reference to Goethe's theory of color and his critique of Newtonian optics. Deleuze bases his reading of Goethe's *Farbenlehre* primarily on Eliane Escoubas's incisive essay "L'oeil (du) teinturier."

7. In a letter to Lawrence, E. M. Forster offers the following observation: "Dividing literature into fluid and granular, you come into the latter class. It's not merely your subject matter that makes me say this. You do present (though you don't see) life as a succession of items which are organically connected but yet have some sort of intervals between them, i.e., you give a series of pictures. I see people on camels, motionless, I look again and they are in a new position which I can connect with its predecessor, but is similarly immobile. There never can have been a Movement with so little motion in it!" (Letters to T. E. Lawrence, p. 58).

8. Freud, "Analysis of a Phobia in a Five-Year-Old Boy (1909)," *Standard Edition*, Vol. X, 1–149. Deleuze also discusses this case in *Dialogues*, D 97–100; 79–82. See also MP 313–17; 256–59, and "L'interprétation des énoncés," by Deleuze, Guattari, Claire Parnet and André Scala, in Deleuze and Guattari's *Politique et psychanalyse* [PO] (1977), in which the authors juxtapose in parallel columns what Little Hans actually says and what Freud understands Hans to be saying.

9. Throughout "What Children Say," Deleuze employs a number of terms for travel and movement that pose problems for translation. Besides *voyage*, "journey, trip, voyage," Deleuze uses the word *parcours*, which may denote a trip, run or journey, but also a distance traveled, and hence the path of a journey. He also uses the word *trajet*, which like *parcours*, may denote both an action of travelling and the course traveled. Despite the fact that Deleuze also employs the word *trajectoire*, "trajectory," in this essay, I have followed the practice of Deleuze's English translators and rendered *trajet* as "trajectory" in an effort to maintain the dynamic sense of the term. (*Trajet* can be used to describe the path of a projectile, which provides further justification for translating it as "trajectory.") Finally, Deleuze uses the generic *chemin*, "way, path, track," which in certain contexts may serve as a synonym of *parcours* and *trajet*.

10. Deleuze makes a similar point concerning the inextricability of the political and the aesthetic in Whitman's visions and auditions. Whitman "without doubt created one of the most coloristic of literatures that could ever have existed" (CC 79; 59), and that colorism is inseparable from his political vision of camaraderie and the journey on the Open Road. The society of comrades is Whitman's "revolutionary American dream," and the spontaneous fragments of his works "constitute the element through which, or in the intervals of which, one accedes to the great and carefully pondered visions and auditions of Nature and of History" (CC 80; 60).

11. These observations come from the typescript of a letter written in German to Axel Kaun. I cite the English translation by Martin Esslin provided in the notes to *Disjecta*. The editor of *Disjecta* says that this letter Beckett "now dismisses as 'German bilge'" (p. 170); nonetheless, Deleuze and several other commentators regard the document as a particularly lucid expression of the tenets of Beckett's art.

12. In *Beckett and Poststructuralism*, Anthony Uhlmann speaks at length of Deleuze's affinities with Beckett. He notes intially that "strictly speaking, their projects should be considered irreconcilable. After all, Beckett is, in caricature, associated with negation, the expression of nothing, failure, the misery of being; all of these are (no doubt justifiably) critical commonplaces in the field of Beckett studies. On the other hand Deleuze is, like Spinoza, seen as a philosopher of affirmation, of joy, of positive Being which requires no negation" (Uhlmann, p. 9). Uhlmann asserts, however, that "Some of the key ideas which Beckett uses in working towards negation seem closely aligned with key ideas Deleuze uses in moving towards affirmation. In short, these ideas, which are all interrelated, are: immanence (the univocity of Being, with Being identified with Chaos); a kind of 'anti-Platonism'; and an emphasis on movement (as change, becoming)" (Uhlmann, p. 12).

13. I discuss this question in chapter 5 of *Deleuze on Music, Painting, and the Arts*.

Works Cited

Alliez, Eric. *La Signature du monde, ou qu'est-ce que la philosophie de Deleuze et Guattari*. Paris: Cerf, 1993.

Ansell Pearson, Keith. *The Difference and Repetition of Gilles Deleuze*. London: Routledge, 1999.

Arnim, Hans Friedrich August von. *Stoicorum Veterum Fragmenta*. 4 vols. 1924; Stuttgart: Teubner, 1964.

Beckett, Samuel. *As the Story Was Told*. London: Calder, 1990.

Beckett, Samuel. *The Complete Dramatic Works*. London: Faber and Faber, 1986.

Beckett, Samuel. *Disjecta: Miscellaneous Writings and a Dramatic Fragment*. Ed. Ruby Cohn. New York: Grove Press, 1984.

Beckett, Samuel. *Murphy*. 1938; New York: Grove Press, 1958.

Beckett, Samuel. *Nohow On*. London: Calder, 1989.

Beckett, Samuel. *Three Novels by Samuel Beckett: Molloy, Malone Dies, The Unnamable*. New York: Grove Press, 1965.

Beckett, Samuel. *Watt*. New York: Grove Press, 1953.

Bene, Carmelo. "L'énergie sans cesse renouvelée de l'utopie." *Travail Théâtral* 27 (1977): 61–89.

Bene, Carmelo. *Opere*. Milan: Bompiani, 1995.

Bensmaïa, Réda. "The Kafka Effect." Trans. Terry Cochran. In Gilles Deleuze and Félix Guattari, *Kafka: Toward a Minor Literature*, ix–xxi. Minneapolis: University of Minnesota Press, 1986.

Bensmaïa, Réda. "On the Concept of Minor Literature. From Kafka to Kateb Yacine." In *Gilles Deleuze and the Theater of Philosophy*, ed. Constantin V. Boundas and Dorothea Olkowski. New York: Routledge, 1994, pp. 213–28.

Bensmaïa, Réda. "Traduire ou 'blanchir' la langue: Amour Bilingue d'Abdelkebir Khatibi." *Hors Cadre* 3 (spring 1985): 187–206.

Bensmaïa, Réda, "Les transformateurs-deleuze ou le cinéma comme automate spirituel." *Quaderni di Cinema / Studio* 7–8 (July-December 1992): 103–16.

Boa, Elizabeth. *Kafka: Gender, Class, and Race in the Letters and Fictions*. Oxford: Clarendon, 1996.

Bogue, Ronald. *Deleuze and Guattari*. London: Routledge, 1989.

Bogue, Ronald. *Deleuze on Cinema*. New York: Routledge, 2003.

Bogue, Ronald. *Deleuze on Music, Painting, and the Arts*. New York: Routledge, 2003.

Boundas, Constantin V. "Deleuze-Bergson: An Ontology of the Virtual." In *Deleuze: A Critical Reader*, ed. Paul Patton. London: Blackwell, 1996, pp. 81–106.

Braidotti, Rosi. *Nomadic Subjects*. New York: Columbia University Press, 1994.

Bréhier, Emile. *La théorie des incorporels dans l'ancien stoïcisme*. 4th ed. 1928; Paris: Vrin, 1970.

Brod, Max. *Franz Kafka: A Biography*. Trans. G. Humphreys Roberts and Richard Winston. New York: Schocken, 1963.

Buchanan, Ian. *Deleuzism: A Metacommentary*. Durham, NC: Duke University Press, 2000.

Buchanan, Ian, and Claire Colebrook, eds. *Deleuze and Feminist Theory*. Edinburgh: Edinburgh University Press, 2000.

Buydens, Mireille. *Sahara: l'esthétique de Gilles Deleuze*. Paris: Vrin, 1990.

Canetti, Elias. *Kafka's Other Trial: The Letters to Felice*. Trans. Christopher Middleton. New York: Schocken, 1974.

Carrière, Mathieu. *Pour une littérature de guerre, Kleist*. Trans. Martin Ziegler. Arles: Actes Sud, 1985.

Carroll, Lewis. *Alice's Adventures in Wonderland and Through the Looking-Glass*. New York: Signet, 1960.

Carrouges, Michel. *Les Machines célibataires*. Rev. and aug. 1954; Paris: Chêne, 1976.

Céline, Louis-Ferdinand. *Guignol's Band*. Trans. Bernard Frechtman and Jack T. Nile. New York: New Directions, 1954.

Cendrars, Blaise. *Moravagine*. Paris: Denoël, 1962.

Colebrook, Claire. *Gilles Deleuze*. London: Routledge, 2001.

Colombat, André. *Deleuze et la littérature*. New York: Peter Lang, 1990.

Corngold, Stanley. "Kafka and the Dialect of Minor Literature." *College Literature* 21 (February 1994): 89–101.

Cruchet, René. *De la méthode en médecine*. 2nd ed. Paris: PUF, 1951.

Dalcq, Albert. *L'oeuf et son dynamisme organisateur*. Paris: Albin Michel, 1941.

Duchamp, Marcel. *Notes and Projects for The Large Glass*. Ed. and trans. Arturo Schwarz. New York: Henry N. Abrams, 1969.

Duchamp, Marcel. *Salt Seller: The Writings of Marcel Duchamp (Marchand du sel)*. Ed. Michel Sanouillet and Elmer Peterson. New York: Oxford University Press, 1973.

Duhem, Pierre. *Le Système du monde: Histoire des doctrines cosmologiques de Platon à Copernic*. Vol. VII. Paris: Hermann, 1954.

Elie, Hubert. *Le complexe significabile*. Paris: Vrin, 1936.

Escoubas, Eliane. "L'oeil (du) teinturier." *Critique* 418 (March 1982): 231–42.

Findlay, J. N. *Meinong's Theory of Objects and Values*. Oxford: Clarendon, 1933.

Fitzgerald, F. Scott. *The Bodley Head Scott Fitzgerald*. Vol. 1. London: The Bodley Head, 1958.

Fleutiaux, Pierrette. *Histoire du gouffre et de la lunette*. Paris: Julliard, 1976.

Fortier, Mark. "Shakespeare as 'Minor Theater': Deleuze and Guattari and the Aims of Adaptation." *Mosaic* 29 (March 1996): 1–18.

Foucault, Michel. *Discipline and Punish: The Birth of the Prison*. Trans. Alan Sheridan. New York: Pantheon, 1977.

Foucault, Michel. *The History of Sexuality: Vol. I: An Introduction*. Trans. Robert Hurley. New York: Pantheon, 1978.

Freud, Sigmund. "Analysis of a Phobia in a Five-Year-Old Boy (1909)." *Standard Edition of the Complete Psychological Works of Sigmund Freud*. Vol. X, pp. 1–149. Trans. James Strachey. London: Hogarth Press, 1955.

Freud, Sigmund. "Creative Writers and Daydreaming," *Standard Edition of the Complete Psychological Works of Sigmund Freud*. Vol. IX, pp. 141–53. Trans. James Strachey. London: Hogarth Press, 1955.

Genet, Jean. *Prisoner of Love*. Trans. Barbara Bray. Hanover, NH: Wesleyan University Press, 1992.

Golding, John. *Marcel Duchamp: The Bride Stripped Bare by her Bachelors, Even*. New York: Viking, 1972.

Goldschmidt, Victor. *Le système stoïcien et l'idée de temps*. 4th ed. 1953; Paris: Vrin, 1977.

Goodchild, Philip. *Deleuze and Guattari: An Introduction to the Politics of Desire*. Thousand Oaks, CA: Sage, 1996.

Goodchild, Philip. *Gilles Deleuze and the Question of Philosophy*. Madison, N.J.: Fairleigh Dickinson University Press, 1996.

Grosz, Elizabeth. *Volatile Bodies: Towards a Corporeal Feminism*. Bloomington: Indiana University Press, 1994.

Hardt, Michael. *Gilles Deleuze: An Apprenticeship in Philosophy*. Minneapolis: University of Minnesota Press, 1993.

Henderson, Linda Dalrymple. *Duchamp in Context: Science and Technology in The Large Glass and Related Works*. Princeton, NJ: Princeton University Press, 1998.

Holland, Eugene W. *Deleuze and Guattari's Anti-Oedipus: Introduction to Schizoanalysis*. London: Routledge, 1999.

Holland, Eugene W. "Deterritorializing 'Deterritorialization'—From the *Anti-Oedipus* to *A Thousand Plateaus*." *SubStance* 66 (1991): 55–65.

Holland, Eugene W. "Schizoanalysis and Baudelaire: Some Illustrations of Decoding at Work." In *Deleuze: A Critical Reader*, ed. Paul Patton. London: Blackwell, 1996, pp. 240–56.

Isaacs, Susan. "The Nature and Function of Phantasy." In *Developments in Psycho-Analysis*. Ed. Joan Riviere. London: Hogarth Press, 1952.

James, Henry. *The Novels and Tales of Henry James. New York Edition*. Vol. XI. New York: Charles Scribner's Sons, 1908.

Janouch, Gustav. *Conversations with Kafka*. Trans. Goronwy Rees. London: Quartet Books, 1985.

Kafka, Franz. *The Complete Stories*. Ed. Nahum N. Glatzer. New York: Schocken, 1971.

Kafka, Franz. *Dearest Father Stories and Other Writings*. Trans. Ernest Kaiser and Eithne Wilkins. New York: Schocken, 1954.

Kafka, Franz. *The Diaries of Franz Kafka*. 2 vols. Ed. Max Brod, trans. Joseph Kresh. New York: Schocken, 1948–49.

Kafka, Franz. *Letters to Friends, Family and Editors*. Trans. Richard and Clara Winston. New York: Schocken, 1977.

Kafka, Franz. *The Trial*. Trans. Willa Muir and Edwin Muir. New York: Modern Library, 1956.

Kennedy, Barbara M. *Deleuze and Cinema: The Aesthetics of Sensation*. Edinburgh: Edinburgh University Press, 2000.

Klee, Paul. *Paul Klee: On Modern Art*. Trans. Paul Findlay. London: Faber and Faber, 1948.

Kleist, Heinrich von. *An Abyss Deep Enough: Letters of Heinrich von Kleist with a Selection of Essays and Anecdotes*. Ed. and trans. Philip B. Miller. New York: E. P. Dutton, 1982.

Kleist, Heinrich von. *Penthesilea*. Trans. Humphrey Trevelyan. In *The Classic Theatre, Vol. II: Five German Plays*. Garden City, NY: Doubleday Anchor, 1959, pp. 313–419.

Kowsar, Mohammad. "Deleuze on Theatre: A Case Study of Carmelo Bene's *Richard III*." *Theatre Journal* 38 (1986): 19–33.

Lacan, Jacques. *Ecrits*. Paris: Seuil, 1966.

Laforgue, Jules. "Hamlet, ou les suites de la piété filiale." In *Oeuvres complètes*. Vol. 3, pp. 11–69. 1922; rpt. Geneva: Slatkine, 1979.

Lambert, Gregg. *The Non-Philosophy of Gilles Deleuze*. London: Continuum Books, 2002.

Laplanche, Jean, and J.-B. Pontalis. "Fantasme originaire, fantasmes des origines, origine du fantasme." *Les Temps modernes* 215 (April 1964): 1833–68. [English translation: "Fantasy and the Origins of Sexuality." *The International Journal of Psycho-Analysis* 49 (1968): 1, 1–18.]

Laplanche, Jean, and J.-B. Pontalis. *The Language of Psycho-Analysis*. Trans. Donald Nicholson-Smith. New York: Norton, 1973.

Lawrence, A. W., ed. *Letters to T. E. Lawrence*. London: Jonathan Cape, 1962.

Lawrence, D. H. *Studies in Classic American Literature*. 1923; Harmondsworth: Penguin, 1971.

Lawrence, T. E. *Seven Pillars of Wisdom: A Triumph*. 1926; New York: Dell, 1962.

Lecercle, Jean-Jacques. *Philosophy through the Looking-Glass: Language, Nonsense, Desire*. La Salle, Ill.: Open Court, 1985.

WORKS CITED

Maass, Joachim. *Kleist: A Biography.* Trans. Ralph Manheim. New York: Farrar, Straus and Giroux, 1983.

Massumi, Brian. *A User's Guide to Capitalism and Schizophrenia: Deviations from Deleuze and Guattari.* Cambridge, MA: MIT Press, 1992.

Mates, Benson. *Stoic Logic.* Berkeley: University of California Press, 1961.

May, Todd. *Reconsidering Difference: Nancy, Derrida, Levinas, and Deleuze.* University Park: Pennsylvania State University Press, 1997.

Michel, Bernard. *Sacher-Masoch: 1836–1895.* Paris: Robert Laffont, 1989.

Mumford, Lewis. *The Myth of the Machine. Technics and Human Development.* New York: Harcourt, Brace and World, 1967.

Nietzsche, Friedrich. *The Gay Science,* 1887; trans. Walter Kaufmann. New York: Vintage, 1974.

Nietzsche, Friedrich. *Philosophy and Truth: Selections from Nietzsche's Notebooks of the Early 1870's.* Trans. and ed. Daniel Breazeale. Atlantic Heights, NJ: Humanities Press, 1979.

Nietzsche, Friedrich. *The Portable Nietzsche,* Ed. and trans. Walter Kaufmann. Harmandsworth: Penguin, 1976.

Norrman, Ralf. "The Intercepted Telegram Plot in Henry James's 'In the Cage.'" *Notes and Queries* 24 [new series] (October 1971): 425–27.

Olkowski, Dorothea. *Gilles Deleuze and the Ruin of Representation.* Berkeley: University of California Press, 1999.

Oresme, Nicole. *Nicole Oresme and the Medieval Geometry of Qualities and Motions: A Treatise on the Uniformity and Difformity of Intensities Known as Tractatus de configurationibus qualitatum et motuum.* Ed., intro., trans., and commentary by Marshall Clagett. Madison: University of Wisconsin Press, 1968.

Patton, Paul. *Deleuze and the Political: Thinking the Political.* London: Routledge, 2000.

Plato. *Republic.* Trans. Paul Shorey. In *Collected Dialogues,* ed. Edith Hamilton and Huntington Cairns. Princeton, NJ: Princeton University Press, 1961.

Proust, Marcel. *Remembrance of Things Past.* 3 vols. Trans. C. K. Scott Moncrieff and Terence Kilmartin. New York: Vintage, 1982.

Quignard, Pascal. *L'être du balbutiement, essai sur Sacher-Masoch.* Paris: Mercure de France, 1969.

Rajchman, John. *The Deleuze Connections.* Cambridge, MA: MIT Press, 2000.

Reuleaux, Franz. *The Kinematics of Machinery: Outlines of a Theory of Machines.* Trans. Alexander B. W. Kennedy. 1876; New York: Dover, 1963.

Rist, J. M. *Stoic Philosophy.* Cambridge: Cambridge University Press, 1969.

Robertson, Ritchie. *Kafka: Judaism, Politics, and Literature.* Oxford: Clarendon, 1985.

Rodowick, D. N. *Gilles Deleuze's Time Machine.* Durham, NC: Duke University Press, 1997.

"Scenografia 'Hommelette for Hamlet.'" *Domus* 695 (June 1988): 7–8.

Shakespeare, William. *The Complete Works.* Ed. Alfred Harbage. Baltimore: Penguin, 1969.

Simondon, Gilbert. *L'individu et sa genèse physico-biologique.* Paris: PUF, 1964.

Smith, Daniel W. "'A Life of Pure Immanence': Deleuze's 'Critique et Clinique' Project." In Deleuze, *Essays Critical and Clinical.* Trans. Daniel W. Smith and Michael A. Greco. Minneapolis: University of Minnesota Press, 1997.

Smith, Daniel W. "Deleuze's Theory of Sensation: Overcoming the Kantian Duality." In *Deleuze: A Critical Reader,* ed. Paul Patton. London: Blackwell, 1996, pp. 29–56.

Stivale, Charles J. *The Two-Fold Thought of Deleuze and Guattari: Intersections and Animations.* New York: Guilford, 1998.

Uhlmann, Anthony. *Beckett and Poststructuralism.* Cambridge: Cambridge University Press, 1999.

Voie suisse: l'itinéraire genevois. De Morschach à Brunnen. Geneva: Republic and Canton of Geneva, 1991.

Wagenbach, Klaus. *Franz Kafka: Années de jeunesse (1883–1912).* Trans. Elisabeth Gaspar. 1958; Paris: Mercure de France, 1967.

Zourabichvili, François. *Deleuze: Une philosophie de l'événement.* Paris: PUF, 1994.

Index